THE LAST COMANCHE CHIEF

THE LAST COMANCHE CHIEF

THE LIFE AND TIMES OF
QUANAH PARKER

BILL NEELEY

This edition published in 2007 by
Castle Books ®

A division of Book Sales, Inc.
276 Fifth Ave., Suite 206
New York, NY 10001

This edition published by arrangement with and permission of
John Wiley & Sons, Inc.
111 River Street
Hoboken, New Jersey 07030

Originally published by John Wiley and Sons, Inc., Hoboken, New Jersey
Published simultaneously in Canada

Library of Congress Cataloging-in-Publication Data:

Neeley, Bill.
 The last Comanche chief: the life and times of Quanah Parker / Bill
 Neeley
     p.   cm.
Includes bibliographical references and index.
1.   Parker, Quanah, 1845?-1911. 2. Comanche Indians-Biography.
3. Comanche Indians-Kings and rulers. 4. Comanche Indians-History. I. Title.
E99.C85P385 1995
976'.004974-dc20
[B]

94-38101

ISBN-13: 978-0-7858-2259-2
ISBN-10: 0-7858-2259-3

Printed in the United States of America

For Poppy Hulsey

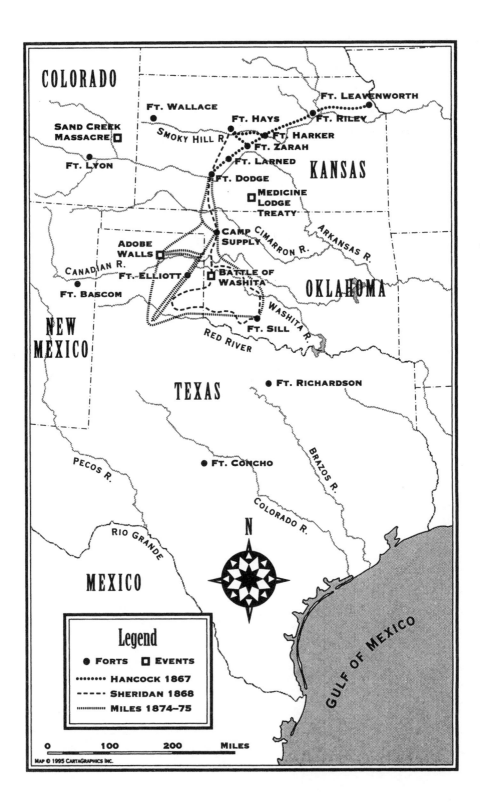

COLORADO

FT. WALLACE

SAND CREEK
MASSACRE

FT. LYON

SMOKY HILL R.

FT. HAYS

FT. HARKER

FT. ZARAH

FT. LARNED

FT. DODGE

MEDICINE
LODGE
TREATY

FT. LEAVENWORTH

FT. RILEY

KANSAS

CAMP
SUPPLY

Cimarron R.

Arkansas R.

ADOBE
WALLS

CANADIAN R.

FT. ELLIOTT

FT. BASCOM

BATTLE OF
WASHITA

OKLAHOMA

WASHITA R.

NEW
MEXICO

FT. SILL

RED RIVER

TEXAS

FT. RICHARDSON

PECOS R.

FT. CONCHO

BRAZOS R.

COLORADO R.

RIO GRANDE

N

MEXICO

GULF OF MEXICO

Legend

● FORTS   ☐ EVENTS

••••••• HANCOCK 1867

----- SHERIDAN 1868

▫▫▫▫▫ MILES 1874-75

0   100   200   MILES

MAP © 1995 CARTAGRAPHICS INC.

CONTENTS

FOREWORD

by James M. Cox, grandson of Quanah Parker and former chairman of the Comanche Tribe

Many views have been written about my grandfather, Quanah Parker, the last chief of the Comanches, who guided the Comanche people at a most perilous time in the history of the tribe. Like him, I was also a chief of my people, having been elected chairman of the Comanche Tribe in 1976. One of the Comanche's greatest needs, I realized, was a tribal complex composed of offices, meeting rooms, coffee shop, and gymnasium, to bring the tribe together to plan for the preservation of our culture. It was my destiny to build the Comanche Tribal Complex during my tenure as chairman.

My mother, Nau-Noc-Ca Parker Cox, was the firstborn child of Quanah and Weckeah Parker. It is to her credit that I speak the Comanche language. I must add that my father, E. E. Cox, taught me English. Having lost his eyesight, he taught me to spell and read before I started school, so I would be able to read the newspapers to him.

Bill Neeley has gathered a vast amount of research on Quanah and his people, which allowed him to view Quanah from many angles. Neeley concluded that Quanah was a great war chief who made the change to become an effective civil chief because Quanah was a man of great intellect and personal integrity. Quanah observed how the non-Indian transacted business and became a successful rancher and cattleman. Through it all, he did not lose his Indian identity.

Through Bill Neeley's book runs a theme of preserving Quanah and his people. To show appreciation for a positive written document, I gave Mr. Neeley a Comanche name of "Chatuh-bohtuh"—meaning "good writer."

It is my hope that Bill Neeley's book will cause others to realize there is another side of Comanche life that is beautiful and caring.

ACKNOWLEDGMENTS

To all who have supported this study of Chief Quanah Parker and the Comanche people, I express my deepest gratitude.

Especially helpful to me in compiling this volume have been Mr. and Mrs. James M. Cox of Midwest City, Oklahoma. Mr. Cox is Quanah's grandson and a former chairman of the tribe. Many other members of the Parker family, along with other Comanches, particularly present Comanche Chairman Wallace E. Coffey, have provided me with valuable insight and information. To all of them I am grateful.

This work, which is built upon the careful analysis of many pieces of data, owes its existence largely to the archivists and librarians who directed my path along this journey through time. Claire Kuehn of the Panhandle–Plains Historical Museum in Canyon, Texas, was my principal mentor. Another of my teachers was Towana Spivey of the Fort Sill Museum at Lawton, Oklahoma. In Amarillo, Texas, I was blessed with the dutiful attention of Art Bort and the rest of the staff of the Amarillo Public Library. Professionals at the following institutions also contributed to the body of knowledge encompassed in this book: Western History Collections, University of Oklahoma; Archives and Manuscript Division, Oklahoma Historical Society; Museum of the Great Plains, Lawton, Oklahoma; Barker Texas History Center, the University of Texas at Austin; Southwest Collection, Texas Tech University; Archives Division, Texas State Library; Cornette Library, West Texas A&M University; Wichita Falls Times and Record

News; Quanah Tribune-Chief; and the Library of Congress and the National Archives.

Thanks also to Shirley Yarnall for helping to bring this book to its final form.

For all those, Indian and non-Indian, who taught me important parts of the story through personal interviews, I am truly indebted. At this writing, more than one has since slipped into the spirit world, but their words live on in print and in our hearts.

Certainly, this book would never have become a reality without the presence of a Higher Power. Father Bill Brashears and my fellow parishioners in Amarillo prayed, along with members of my family, to Him who makes all things possible. My final thank you, therefore, is to all who prayed.

1

THE BIRTH OF A NATIVE AMERICAN: THE ATTACK ON PARKER'S FORT

At the eventful period of the discovery of America, the whole continent was inhabited by numerous tribes of red men who were destitute of the arts and sciences that distinguish the present age, and were also exempt from most of the vices that now corrode and canker what is popularly called civilized life.
— Colonel Edward Stiff, 1839[1]

Sometime around 1850, in a Comanche tepee, Quanah Parker, the last chief of the Comanches, was born. He was the son of Peta Nocona, chief of the Quahada band of the Comanches, and Cynthia Ann Parker, a white girl whom the Quahada warriors had captured in 1836. Parker was a name Quanah would not know, acknowledge, or assume for many years, years that would see him grow from great war chief Quanah to Quanah Parker, the man who understood the necessity of Indians' adapting to the white man's culture and who came to play a prominent role in the politics of the emerging United States of America. Quanah the chief would lead his warriors against the U.S. Army and the Texas Rangers, and then in the late nineteenth century become a rancher and cattleman, a capitalist in the tradition of the Gilded Age. The birth of this child to an Indian father from a doomed culture and a white mother from the encroaching one is peculiarly symbolic of the times that led up to the birth of the new nation.

The Comanche raid that led to Cynthia Ann Parker's capture took place on a quiet morning in late May of 1836. The Parkers, farmers and preachers of the hard-shell Baptist faith, had established a settlement along the banks of the Navasota River in what was later to be known as Limestone County, Texas. In 1836, the area was part of Comanchería, a vast territory claimed by the several bands of "The People" (the Comanches) and their allies. Elder John Parker, along with his wife and sons, daughters, in-laws, grandchildren, and friends, had made a tactical error in locating their "Parker's Fort" farther west and north into Comanchería than any American immigrants had ever settled. They might have taken a lesson from the Spanish who had preceded them. In their centuries-long effort to populate Texas, the Spanish had in 1774 established a village called Pueblo de Bucareli along the banks of the Trinity at the crossing of the San Antonio road. It prospered until the Comanches swept down in 1778. The settlers armed themselves and managed to kill three of the Indians, but the warriors returned and stole over two hundred horses. Now the terrorized inhabitants dared leave the village only to hunt, and even then they had to do so in large parties. They could not plant their crops and had to guard their remaining stock night and day. Soon Bucareli was a ghost town, as these settlers moved back to safer territory.

Two generations later, the Parkers chose a spot north and west of the old site of Bucareli, even deeper into Comanchería. They had no fear of Indians; they had fought Indians from Georgia to Tennessee to Illinois. Also, the Parkers had a mission: to bring their Baptist doctrine to the wilderness. "The elect," said Elder Daniel Parker, son of patriarch Elder John, "are a wrathful people because they are the natural enemies of the non-elect."[2]

So the Parkers, confident in their ability to subdue Indians in Texas as they had in previous locations, set to work in late spring of Texas's first year as a republic to raise crops, enjoy their families, and propagate the gospel according to the Articles of Faith in the Pilgrim Church. Article 8 states that ". . . it is the duty of the Church of God to distinguish herself from all false sects." Fellowship or Christian union with anyone who disagreed with the Pilgrim Doctrine was forbidden. The church's attitude toward natural man, as stated in Article 10, was, "We believe that the Church or kingdom of God set up in the world is a spiritual kingdom—that MEN IN A STATE OF NATURE cannot see it . . ."[3]

This doctrine accorded with that of Manifest Destiny, the belief that the territorial expansion of the United States was divinely destined. To the men in Parker's Fort and in the surrounding tree-ringed fields, the red man was a savage, a heathen. Each Sunday, the Parkers engaged in the exercise of making ". . . the home of the savage . . . vocal with hymns of praise."[4] God's power, they believed, would sustain the energy of his children and direct them through the Holy Scriptures in the way they were to live. Among the millions of Americans along the edge of the frontier who were slowly inching west past burning stumps and the echoing ring of the ax, the Parkers believed it was their Manifest Destiny to possess the land. Newspapers from the eastern seaboard to Chicago agreed, urging the restless, growing population to settle the wilderness. In 1845, John O'Sullivan wrote in the *United States Magazine and Democratic Review*, "Our manifest destiny is to overspread the continent allotted by Providence for the free development of our yearly multiplying millions."[5] So pervasive was the sentiment favoring the spreading of the English language and conservative Protestant theology west of the Appalachians that even men who could not read believed in this mission.

The Comanches who appeared on the clearing in front of Parker's Fort that May morning had a mission of their own. They were living out the generations-old rite of spring in Comanchería. They were on a raid. This was as natural to them as the grass greening in the early spring and as regular as the rising of the new moon.

Comanche warriors, being men, were subject to the vanity of men in whatever society. To be respected, these men had to prove their bravery. One way was by touching an enemy, preferably before killing him, although "coup" (the touching) could be counted on dead foes as well. Stealing was another badge of honor, because to deprive one's enemy, white or red, of his animals was to render him helpless before these fabled horsemen, virtual centaurs of the Plains. These young Comanches sitting their horses in front of Parker's Fort this day in May had an opportunity to improve their status in their own villages and bring honor to the tribe.

And they were ready. They had smoked the sacred war pipe and prayed to the Great Spirit for good fortune in this raid. They had painted themselves and their horses and danced the war dance. They were armed with fourteen-foot lances and bows and arrows and were more than a match for any number of unmounted men who had to reload their rifles after each shot, a process that took sixty seconds if you were good at it. In a minute's time, twenty Comanche arrows could be flying toward a rifleman with enough force to pass completely through a buffalo bull.

Estimates of their numbers vary from five to eight hundred. There had to have been a larger purpose than the usual raid to account for these numbers. Probably this was the start of a drive to rid Comanchería of the Americans, as the Comanches had only recently succeeded in doing with the Spanish and Mexicans to protect their hunting grounds.

Within the fort, the Parkers had only a handful of men. The previous year, Silas Parker had been selected as an officer in the Texas Rangers, organized in 1835 as groups of mounted law officers to protect the settled areas of Texas while the army was otherwise occupied with the impending war with Mexico. Silas was responsible for gathering neighboring farmers to "range" the country between the Trinity and the Brazos rivers. On this spring day, however, the men of his command were widely scattered across the thinly populated land. Texas was to lose a good man in the attack the Comanches were about to mount; no Ranger ever fought with more courage against greater odds than did Silas Parker that day when his daughter Cynthia Ann and his son John were captured.

The Parkers, for all their piety, were fighters in the tradition of the frontier, warriors in their own right. Elder John Parker had fought in the Revolutionary War against Great Britain; others had been with Jackson at the Battle of New Orleans; they had fought foot Indians in the forests far to the north and east of the Navasota. Now, however, they were facing, in the words of the historian T. R. Fehrenbach, ". . . conditions, human and geographical, of which they had no knowledge or experience, and against which their tried and true techniques and organization did not serve."[6] To say nothing of the fact that they were absurdly outnumbered.

Inside the fort were Elder John Parker, Benjamin and Silas Parker, Samuel and Robert Frost, G. E. Dwight, ten women, and fifteen children. Earlier that morning, James W. Parker, L. D. Nixon, and L. M. T. Plummer had gone to their fields near the river, about a mile away.

Silas's brother Benjamin saw the Indians first. Mounted on mustangs of varying colors, their horses painted with symbols of their "medicine" (spiritual power), the Comanche warriors slowly advanced toward the stockade. Then two rode out ahead, brandishing a white flag, a sign of friendship. This was not as improbable as it might seem. Farther north, other white men were receiving cordial treatment from Comanches. Kit Carson and Will Drannan traded at Comanche villages along the upper reaches of the Arkansas River, and many of their furs were taken from animals Carson and company had trapped on land claimed by the

Comanches in the southern Rockies. It was not unusual for Comanches to treat whites with hospitality, especially when the men in question possessed those qualities respected by Comanche society: courage, generosity, horsemanship, the ability and inclination to fight, and respect for the land.

This may have crossed Benjamin's mind when he stepped out of the stockade to talk with the warriors. There he stood, and looking down on him from their mustangs were the greatest horsemen in the history of mounted warfare. Because he was brave, Benjamin Parker would make it possible for these proud warriors to count coup before and after killing him.

Unconvinced by the white flag, Mrs. Nixon, Silas Parker's niece, was running to the adjoining farm to alert the men working in the fields, and most of the women and children followed her. Rachel Plummer stayed behind, knowing her small son could not keep up with her. Silas asked her to ". . . stand here and watch the Indians' motions until I run into the house."[7] While he rushed to get his shot pouch, Mrs. Plummer saw her Uncle Benjamin approach the Indians. She wrote later:

> When Uncle Benjamin reached the body of Indians they turned to the right and surrounded him. I was now satisfied they intended killing him. I took up my little James Pratt, and thought I would try to make my escape. As I ran across the fort, I met Silas returning to the place where he left me. He asked me if they had killed Benjamin. I told him, "No, but they have surrounded him." He said, "I know they will kill him, but I will be good for one of them at least." These were the last words I heard him utter. I ran out of the fort, and passing the corner I saw the Indians drive their spears into Benjamin. The work of death had already commenced . . . I tried to make my escape, but alas, alas, it was too late, as a party of the Indians got ahead of me. Oh! how vain were my feeble efforts to try to run to save myself and little James Pratt. A large sulky looking Indian picked up a hoe and

knocked me down . . . the first I recollect, they were dragging me along by the hair. I made several unsuccessful attempts to raise to my feet before I could do it. As they took me past the fort, I heard an awful screaming near the place where they had first seized me. (I think Uncle Silas was trying to release me, and in doing this he lost his life; but not until he had killed four Indians.) I heard some shots. I then heard Uncle Silas shout a triumphant huzzah! I did, for one moment, hope the men had gathered from the neighboring farms, and might release me. . . . I was soon dragged to the main body of the Indians where they had killed Uncle Benjamin. His face was much mutilated and many arrows were sticking in his body. As the savages passed by, they thrust their spears through him.[8]

Samuel and Robert Frost were killed inside the fort while fighting to protect the remaining women and children. Granny Parker was raped, stabbed, and left for dead. Elder John Parker and Mrs. Kellogg fled the fort but were seen by the Indians about three quarters of a mile away and were driven back toward the stockade, where a shrill chorus of whoops and shrieks created a horrendous din. Elder John was caught and killed, his body badly mutilated.

Also captured, along with Rachel Plummer and Elizabeth Kellogg, were Cynthia Ann Parker, nine years old, and her brother John, three years her junior, both children of Silas Parker. And so began a saga in Texas history that was to blaze across the land, as Western man fought Native American for its possession. Through Cynthia Ann Parker the blood of the hard-shell Baptist was to mingle with that of The People.

In the final, frenzied moments before the Comanches took their captives and started the return trip to their villages on the streams of upper Comanchería, they plundered the fort. They slashed bed ticks and hurled feathers into the air, creating a dense cloud. They took most of James W. Parker's books, useful for padding shields, destroying those they didn't want. They smashed most of the bottles of medicine they found in James Parker's cabin, taking with them only a bottle of pulverized arsenic. Later, Rachel Plummer was to look on with grim satisfaction as four Indians melted the powder in saliva and painted their faces and bodies with it—and soon died.

The warriors killed a number of the settlers' cattle as they rode through the fields surrounding the fort. The slaughter, rape, and plunder were clear signals to the encroaching whites to abandon their settlements in the edge of Comanchería or suffer the consequences. If the whites had Manifest Destiny on their side, the Comanches had the power of their conviction that the Great Spirit had made the land for their use. Terror had driven the Spanish out of Bucareli two generations ago; surely that same terror would send the Americans running across the Sabine never to return.

Rachel Plummer's account provides a vivid picture of the first night on the trail:

> About midnight they stopped. They now tied a plaited thong around my arms, and drew my hands behind me. They tied them so tight that the scars can be easily seen to this day. They then tied a similar thong around my ankles, and drew my feet and hands together. They now turned me on my face and I was unable to turn over, when they commenced beating me over the head with their bows. . . . I suppose it was to add to my misery that they brought my little James Pratt so near me that I could hear him cry. . . . The rest of the prisoners were brought near me, but we were not allowed to speak one word together. My aunt called me once, and I answered her; but, indeed, I thought she would never call or I answer again, for they jumped with their feet upon us, which nearly took our lives. Often did the children cry, but were soon hushed by such blows that I had no idea they could survive. They commenced screaming and dancing around the scalps; kicking and stomping the prisoners.[9]

The next morning the Comanches headed north. They tied the prisoners every night for the first five nights, and they were given only enough food and water to sustain life. "Notwithstanding my sufferings," Mrs. Plummer wrote, "I could not but admire the country—being prairie and timber, and very rich. I saw many fine springs."[10] Rachel Plummer and the other captives were possibly the first white people to see the woodland north and west of Parker's Fort known as the Cross Timbers. "The range of timber is of an irregular width, say from 5 to 25 miles wide . . . abounding with small prairies, skirted with timber of various kinds—oak, of every description, ash, elm, hickory, walnut and mulberry."[11]

The Indians split up at Grand Prairie, where Dallas and Fort Worth were established some years later. Elizabeth Kellogg went with an allied band, Mrs. Plummer and James Pratt with one band of Comanches, and Cynthia Ann and John Parker with another.

Cynthia Ann would soon forget her Baptist faith, but surely prayer must have sustained her in the early days of her captivity, for children of nine on the frontier were mature beyond their years, and she had learned her Christian lessons from infancy. Frontier conditions taught self-reliance and courage; it took courage and work to tackle the land, to make it nourish the alien seeds. So it was a strong and courageous Cynthia Ann who went about adapting to her new environment.

This environment demanded hard work from the women. All Comanche girls were taught to cut wood and build fires, to dismantle and put up a tepee, to skin and butcher game, especially buffalo. Hides had to be tanned. Making a buffalo hide into a soft, supple robe was exhausting labor, and this the captives were forced to do, tromping a mixture of deer brains and basswood bark deep into the freshly scraped buffalo hide, often for days, until the woman in charge approved of the robe's condition. Some of the Comanche women were humane to the captives, while others were brutal. Rachel Plummer's overseer beat her frequently and forced her to work constantly.

On one occasion, Mrs. Plummer struck back. Tired of the grinding existence to which fate had subjected her, she longed for death, and she attacked her Comanche tormenter with a large buffalo bone, assuming she would be killed for doing so. But no one interfered as she beat the other woman, leaving deep cuts on her face and head. At last the white captive relented, dropped her club, and began to wash the woman's wounds.

It was a turning point; she had earned respect, both for the beating and for the show of compassion. Several of the men who had witnessed the fight congratulated Mrs. Plummer for her courage, and one of the tribal elders told her that the Great Spirit had blessed her with the strength to offer mercy, as Indians seldom did to a fallen foe. From that moment on, Rachel Plummer was treated with respect and was known as "the fighting squaw."

Because she was a child, Cynthia Ann was more fortunate. Even though she, like the others, was bound and beaten in the early days of her captivity, her sufferings were probably brief in comparison to those of the adults. Captive children and young teenagers adapted quickly to Comanche culture, picking up the language, customs, and religion with the thirsty skill of the young, while the adult captives, whose attitudes were already fixed, could never be more than slaves. These were usually women, and those who were ransomed from the Comanches by their families or compassionate citizens usually died after being rescued. Captive women were virtual prisoners, subject to overwork, constant travel astride a horse, and sexual abuse. White women were always raped and made to serve the warrior who captured them; if there was a question of ownership, the woman became the property of all.

This treatment broke a woman's health, even that of a young woman like Rachel Plummer. She died a little over one year after being ransomed from a captivity of twenty-one months. Many of the rescued women and teenaged girls returned to white society with blank, empty stares, their will broken. Even Indian women captured from other tribes were treated similarly.

But often the children thrived. John Parker, only six at the time of his capture, grew to be a Comanche warrior; Cynthia Ann became the mother of Quanah. She must have feared the Comanches at first, especially the men. They were rough and aggressive. But as Rachel Plummer's account indicates, she and the other children were seldom beaten after the first night.

Comanche girls were influenced by their grandmothers, but the daily necessities of camp life made it convenient for a daughter to help her mother, especially as she got older. Cynthia Ann, being nine years old at the time of her capture, was of an age to help with the work. She had no doubt assisted her own mother with the younger children back at Parker's Fort. After reaching the village of the band with whom she was to live, it is almost certain that she received kindly treatment from that moment on. Accounts of child captives later released by the Comanches are filled with stories of kindness and familial love extended to them by their Comanche families. For example, when Dot Babb was ransomed in his early teens, his Comanche foster mother and brother were very sad. Babb recalled, "The close companionship had cemented bonds of affection almost as sacred as family ties. Their kindnesses to me had been lavish and unvarying, and my friendship and attachment in return were deep and sincere, and I could scarcely restrain my emotions when the time came for the final goodbye."[12]

Cynthia Ann Parker was adopted by a family who grew to love her too much to sell her for ransom. Her foster family were a part of Chief Pa-ha-u-ka's band; in 1840, only four years after her capture, Colonel Len Williams, a trader named Stoal, and a Delaware guide paid them a visit. Colonel Williams had heard there was a blue-eyed child fitting Cynthia Ann's description living with this band. Williams offered to ransom her, but her Indian father declared that all the goods the colonel had were not enough to make him relinquish the girl, now thirteen years old. The colonel asked to speak to Cynthia Ann, and was given permission to do so. She walked quietly to him and sat in front of a tree. She would not speak or indicate whether she understood him as the colonel told her of her childhood friends and relatives and asked what message she wanted to send them. Stoically she kept her silence, but according to James T. DeShields's account in *Cynthia Ann Parker: The Story of Her Capture*, ". . . the anxiety of her mind was betrayed by the perceptible quiver of her lips, showing that she was not insensible to the common feelings of humanity."[13]

In the mid-1840s, four or five years after Colonel Williams's attempt, P. M. Butler and M. G. Lewis made contact with Cynthia Ann as officials representing the United States government, only to have their efforts to reclaim her for her white family rebuffed. In a letter to the Commissioner of Indian Affairs dated August 8, 1846, Butler and Lewis wrote, ". . . we succeeded in rescuing one white child and three Mexicans. We heard of but three other children of white parents, but it is said that there is a large number of Mexican children."[14] Of the whites they reported, "one is a girl about seventeen years old, and her brother, of the age of ten, known as the Parker children. . . . [they] were on the head of the Washita, where our runners saw them last. The young woman is claimed by one of the Comanches as his wife. From the influence of her alleged husband, or from her own inclination, she is un-willing to leave the people with whom she associates. . . . A large amount of goods and four or five hundred dollars were offered, but the offer was unavailing, as she would run off and hide herself to avoid those who went to ransom her."[15]

DeShields indicates that eleven years after Colonel Williams talked to Cynthia Ann in 1840, a group of white hunters visited with her at a Comanche camp on the upper Canadian. When asked by the hunters, some of whom were friends of the Parkers, if she wanted to return to her white family, the young mother pointed to her children and shook her head.

She was a Comanche now. Not in blood, but in language, religion, and custom. Her husband, the renowned Chief Peta No-cona, fought for her protection and hunted to provide her food. They had children to care for. And although she couldn't know it, her firstborn was destined for greatness.

2

COMANCHERÍA

To our shame, the Indians have appeared very early, making their raids and murders, and the [only] company . . . that has organized, has set very diverse objectives [has to fight Indians in many different locations], in a manner that has augmented more and more the boldness of the barbarians, that without injury commit all types of bad things.

— Editorial in a Monterrey, Mexico, newspaper, 1840[1]

At the time of Quanah's birth, about 1850, the territory known as Comanchería was part of the United States of America. Prior to that, much of the Comanches' territory had been claimed by the Republic of Texas, which had been established in 1836 following the fall of the Alamo to the Mexicans and the subsequent capture of the Mexican dictator, Santa Anna, by General Sam Houston and his forces. The Mexican threat to the settlers had ended for the moment; Houston's imprisonment of Santa Anna had succeeded in pressuring the "Mexican Napoleon" into signing documents that led to the independence of Texas. Mexico would never again menace the Texas territory that lay beyond the Navasota River. But the Comanches still controlled Comanchería, regardless of which flag the Texans flew over their capital. The Comanches' lands reached from the plains and mountains of what is now south-central Colorado to the Trans Pecos region of Texas, and from west of the Pecos River to the Cross Timbers of Texas on the east, and it included western Oklahoma and parts of Kansas. Since the Comanches also controlled all of the Texas Hill Country and the Nueces River area, it was indeed a large portion of the southern Plains that became known as Comanchería. The name "Comanche" itself had been Hispanicized by Spanish authorities in New Mexico from the Ute Komantcia, meaning "anyone who wants to fight me all the time."[2]

Comanchería's boundaries were never entirely clear because of the ebb and flow of war and peace between scattered bands of Comanches and other tribes. These nomadic warrior-hunters still had the unique freedom of going where the grass was greener, and dominance over land rich in water, timber, and game was worth the sacrifice of many of their young men.

The Utes had reason to call the Comanches "anyone who wants to fight me all the time"; Comanches and Utes had been warring for years over who had the right to live and hunt in South Park, a lush valley in the Rockies between the Arkansas and the South Platte Rivers. In 1852, with yet another Comanche–Ute battle impending, Kit Carson and Will Drannan, both of whom were friendly with the band of Comanches involved, were invited by Chief Kiwatchee to side with The People against the Utes. Carson said that he would like to oblige, but that he would prefer to watch from the sidelines, since he had never witnessed such a battle before. Kiwatchee agreed, proud of his opportunity to prove Comanche superiority.

Carson and Drannan had fought Utes on numerous occasions and knew full well the ferocity with which the coming battle would be waged. In his book *Thirty Years on the Plains and in the Mountains,* Drannan described what ensued:

> At the first beat of the drum warriors emitted war-whoops and quickly lined up on their side of the stream. The Utes formed a similar line on the opposite side. Drums ceased until

after each war chief had passed along in front of his men. Then the drums beat again, followed by a rain of arrows from either side . . . of all the war-whoops I ever heard they were [the most savage], and the more noise the Indians made the harder they would fight. . . . Among the Comanches was one Indian in particular that I saw victorious, but he got badly used up during the day. . . . That evening after eating I went over to his wick-i-up and found him sitting there, bloody from head to foot, with a large cut on one cheek, another on one side of the head, and numerous other wounds. . . . He had not even washed the blood from his face or hands, but was sitting there telling his squaw and children how many Utes he had killed during the day, apparently as cool and unconcerned as though nothing had happened to him. But he was not able for duty the next day, and died about ten o'clock.[3]

In spite of the loss of many of their men, the Comanches won the battle on the third day. South Park now belonged to The People. The victors held a great war dance in celebration and returned the next day to their camp along the Arkansas River.

A large part of the continuing success of the Comanches in such battles was that they were among the first tribes to acquire the horse in the early 1700s, and as a result of their superior horsemanship they rarely lost to any other tribe. The Kiowas, although outnumbered by the Comanches, were also formidable, so, out of mutual respect, these two tribes in time built a lasting alliance. The Comanches also eventually made peace with the Cheyenne after several years of hostilities. But in spite of their victory in 1852, they never achieved a lasting settlement with the Utes.

Intertribal warfare, of course, was traditional. Far more threatening to the Indian way of life in Comanchería were the inroads being made by invading whites, settlers like the Parkers, among less savory sorts of intruders. From 1821 to 1836, Texas had been a province of the state of Mexico and so was at that time to American citizens a foreign country. Mexico's generous immigration laws had attracted all types of people, the majority of them fiercely ethnocentric and exceedingly hostile to non-Anglo-Celts, Catholics, and a centralized, authoritative form of government. The Comanches, ironically, were responsible for Mexico's opening of Texas to American settlers. By thoroughly defeating the Mexicans and the Spanish before them, The People had prevented widespread Hispanic settlement of Texas. So Mexico, in an effort to encourage a buffer zone of Anglo-American colonists between the Comanches and the northern provinces of present-day Mexico, enticed Americans and small numbers of Europeans and Mexicans to settle in Texas. Hispanic civilization had virtually withdrawn from Comanchería after the massacre at San Saba Mission in 1758, during which Father Santiesteban was beheaded while kneeling at the altar in prayer.

The Celts (Irish, Welsh, Scots) and Anglos (English) who immigrated to Texas by way of Kentucky, Tennessee, Alabama, Louisiana, and other primarily southern states were not to be dissuaded from their goal of possessing the land, whatever it took. The Spanish settlers who had fled from Bucareli in 1778 never returned, but those who survived Comanche attacks like the one on Parker's Fort in 1836 drifted back to their farms and put down roots. And not only did the Anglo-Celts stay on the land, they originated a new tactic for fighting Comanches—not since before the decline of Spanish power in the latter part of the eighteenth century had an offensive war been waged against The People. Now Texas's white warriors decided to go on the warpath themselves.

Conflicts between invading whites and Indians were common, and would soon lead to all-out war between the settlers and all Indians on the Texas frontier, in spite of the fact that many whites and Indians had formed friendly relationships. Hundreds of the settlers were squatters, helping themselves to the land without title; thousands had come to Texas to escape indebtedness in what was then a very bad economic climate in the United States, and they included gamblers, rustlers, outlaws, and other predatory types. Among the rougher element in the early days of the Republic were the lead miners, who had immigrated to Texas from mines in the Ohio and Mississippi Valleys. They were a tough, bad lot and would brook no insult. Anyone who offended them had to fight a duel with Bowie knives or lose his honor. One or both combatants usually died. Small farmers, speculators, and a few propertied people made up most of the population, and all of them had to be good with knives and guns. Survival demanded it.

These rough frontier men formed quick, incisive opinions on everything and everyone. They checked a stranger's eyes; he had to pass inspection or life would be hard for him in old Texas. Also, a man needed friends or partners or family, because single men on the move were assumed to be up to mischief. Historian Lewis J. Wortham has provided a description of this group as it existed in the East Texas town of Nacogdoches:

> . . . there was an element which had infested this region ever since . . . 1806, the so-called "border ruffians" and other desperate characters, fugitives from justice, gamblers and sharpers, and idlers among the younger generation of the Mexicans. A traveler with any amount of money on his person would be likely to disappear in the territory between the Sabine and Nacogdoches in those days, and the true explanation of his disappearance would generally be that he had been waylaid, robbed and murdered by some of these outlaws.[4]

Along with this motley crew were the men who had migrated to Texas from river towns or small farms hacked out of Southern forests. The Parkers exemplified these men. English, Irish, and Scottish blood coursed through their veins in a constant reminder that they were fighters. Among other things, a man had to fight the land itself. He had to spend his energy cutting trees and clearing land. He had to break the sod with a mule and crude plow. He had to build a house. He had to fight the weather and the constantly changing political situation.

But most of all, the new immigrant to Texas had to fight the wilderness, and that meant the men of the wilderness as well. This demand was not that unfamiliar; tribal warfare was hardly a distant memory to the Scots and Irishmen. The Scottish and Irish descendants of the Celtic warriors who had once repelled Roman legions and Viking hordes were among the greatest fighting men the world has ever seen. Unlike the majority of Spanish and Mexican soldiers, the Anglo-Celtic frontiersmen of Texas, like the Mexican vaqueros, did not shrink from the Comanche terror. While Comanche warriors rode arrogantly in front of the early Texas frontiersmen, the blood of the tribal warrior beat in the breasts of those white men too, although they were at first far out-horsed by the Comanches.

In tribal fashion, the Texans united. Better horses were brought into Texas from Kentucky. Arabian and thoroughbred sires were crossed with Spanish mustangs, and the Texans slowly developed a hardy horse that thrived on grain but could maintain his strength and stamina by grazing on the trail. Because the regular army could not be sure whether Mexico would attempt to retake Texas, their services were required elsewhere, so the settlers had to rely on themselves and on the Texas Rangers. Since the strength of the Rangers lay in their horses and their horsemanship, many settlers parted with their best horses to mount the Rangers. They were fighting for survival, and old Texans believed that Mexicans and Indians should be cut down like trees of the forest if they got in the way of that survival.

The fate of the peaceful Cherokees is an example of this policy. A rumor was spread that the agricultural Indians were planning an alliance with Mexico against the Texans, and the

Cherokees were driven out of East Texas before they could harvest their crops. They tried to resist, but their fields were burned and they lost heavily in terms of men and property. Their reward for their efforts to adapt to the white man's ways was exile to Arkansas and Indian Territory. It was clearly the intention of the political leaders of Texas, with the notable exception of Sam Houston, to drive *all* Indians out of the Lone Star Republic.

The Rangers were a special breed. When they took the field, they fought like Silas Parker, who, though sure of death during the attack on Parker's Fort, fought until his strength left his body. Even so, U.S. Army officers were often grudging in their respect for the Rangers because of their disheveled appearance and their lack of uniformity. Every Ranger dressed as he pleased. According to Nelson Lee, a Texas Ranger captured by the Comanches, the Rangers' ". . . usual habiliments were buckskin moccasins and overhauls, a roundabout and red shirt, a cap manufactured by his own hands from the skin of a coon or a wildcat, three revolvers and a bowie knife in his belt, and a short rifle on his arm."[5] Like a Comanche, a Ranger fought as an individual. Orders were seldom given in military fashion; instead, men led by example, and words were few. The Rangers were mostly young and single, and the trail offered a thousand thrills. Like the Comanches, Rangers learned to attack the enemy on his own ground. And as they engaged the Comanches again and again, their tactics improved. They learned to think like Comanches. Like Comanche warriors, Rangers were always on the lookout for a fast horse with a sense of the land and the creatures of the wilderness. A good horse could take his master over great distances at top speed while avoiding prairie dog holes and other natural hazards. He was more than just a mount; he was the Ranger's companion by day and his sentry at night.

John "Jack" Hays is a prototype of the Rangers who won the respect of the Indians. Brave and steady in all situations, Hays was a great warrior who led by example. Nelson Lee describes young Captain Hays in *Three Years Among the Comanches:*

> . . . he was a slim, smooth-faced boy, not over twenty years of age, and looking younger than he was in fact. In his manners he was unassuming in the extreme, a stripling of few words, whose quiet demeanor stretched quite to the verge of modesty. Nevertheless, it was this youngster whom the tall, huge-framed, brawny-armed campaigners hailed unanimously as their chief and leader when they had assembled together in their uncouth garb on the grand plaza of Bexar. . . . young as he was, he had already exhibited abundant evidence that, though a lamb in peace, he was a lion in war. . . .[6]

For over a century, Comanche raiders had left their villages in the most remote areas of Comanchería to make raids on the New Mexican and Mexican frontiers. The isolated ranches of northern Mexico were traditional favorites of The People. Documents from various Mexican provinces of the desert north reveal the extraordinary feats of Comanche and Kiowa warriors during such raids:

6 of September—Agualeguas

> The Primary Judge of Peace to the Prefect of the District of Cadereyta Jimenez:

> Repeatedly news has come at Rancho Botellas to me from the countrymen and neighbors of a large number of barbaric Indians in this jurisdiction. There are two hundred barbarians. At three in the afternoon yesterday, they attacked this ranch, taking two families captive, leaving dead one man, capturing another man, five women and two children. These barbarians, having continued their march along the royal road [camino real] until almost to this villa, countermarched for the rancho de Cochinitos, which they attacked at dawn. The Indians killed another man, while the rest of the families escaped to a corral which had been constructed for defense. The enemies sacked the majority of the dwellings, leaving the

unhappy residents in the most abject misery. Because these barbarians are not encountered by mounted men, they unleash their savagery on the unhappy defenseless ones. Without any way to help each other in joining together in pursuing the enemy, for lack of being able to mount men (in effect, there was not a horse to be found), I am reduced to defend the population with neighbors that on foot have been able to come together.[7]

In a letter to the Subprefect of the District of Monterrey, the Primary Judge of Peace for the area surrounding Villaldama described the theft of two hundred or more horses from a ranch in the region. The judge also reported that sixty Indians had left Villaldama and headed toward Monterrey. As there were evidently enough horses in that area to mount a citizen militia, the judge of Villaldama optimistically reported that it was possible for the ranchers and vaqueros to unite and defeat the Indians.

On September 8, 1840, the Primary Judge of Peace of Agualeguas sent a letter to the Prefect of Cadereyta Jimenez containing a long list of depredations by the Comanches, Kiowas, and their allies. After telling his superior that the battle begun on the 6th was still raging, the judge gave the following account of the actions of the *bárbaros:*

> I took charge by ordering all families to gather at the ranches of Punteagudo, Nogales, Escondida and Cieneguita. At last all of the families had gathered. At that moment, I wrote to the Judge of Peace at Cerralvo, asking him to notify the people in that region of the danger and guard against a surprise attack on those ranches, as at those times their defenses are less than on full alert. And according to this, at the same hour I ordered the village to be placed in a state of defense, placing all of the inhabitants in the avenues of the town. At dawn today, I sent out scouts to explore the trails north of the village.
>
> At eight that morning a delegation from Punteagudo arrived. At daybreak the Indians had stolen a drove of mules.

Right away another band attacked the Maldonado ranch, but as the people already knew the Indians were in the country, the families had all gathered behind a wooden fort and gave such a strong resistance that the Indians retreated.

Before I arrived here a neighbor came on foot looking for a boy who that morning had been lost. . . . At dawn on the 7th forty-six mounted men left, looking for the lost boy, toward the east; another ten men also left to look for the mule lost the night before, which they found and corralled on the Zacatosa ranch. At nine that morning, while the ten men were in the corral, a woman arrived, almost naked, with a two or three year old girl, and she said: that she is from Botellos, jurisdiction of Cerralvo. That her name was Maria del Carmen Garcia. That her father Vicente Guerra and her sister were killed in the same house. The Indians took her, another sister, and her mother with them. After walking a short distance, she saw approaching her an Indian who had her child, making her believe he was going to kill her. He then came up quickly and said: Take your daughter, and he gave her the child saying there were houses near and he would come back. Soon he returned to her, saying he was not an Indian, but a Christian, blond, slim, thick beard, and he carried her until they came to the royal road where it leads from Mier to this house, assuring this woman, that the most of that party [in which the blond warrior rode] were gentlemen, but as a whole the Indians were barbarians.[8]

On October 7, 1840, the Judge of Peace at Marin wrote to his superior that on the previous day, vaqueros from Rancho del Palo Blanco not only defended their ranch, but put the Indians into full flight. As the Mexicans followed the Comanches' trail, they found many of the Indians' belongings abandoned in an attempt to increase their speed. Thus, the Mexicans achieved one of their earliest victories over the Comanches and their allies.

In 1840, within months of the Mexican triumph, the Texans learned that they, too, could whip the Comanches. Comanche power had not been tested north of Mexico since New Mexico Governor Don Juan Bautista de Anza's punitive expedition from Santa Fe in the late 1700s had resoundingly defeated the northern Comanches. Spanish cavalry had for brief periods been an effective deterrent against the early Comanche horsemen, but from the latter 1700s until Spain's expulsion from Mexico in 1821, Spain could provide little money to protect the frontier because of the drain on the royal treasury from European wars and the extravagance of the Spanish court.

While brave Spanish settlers had been denied arms by the Crown, the Anglo-Celtic warriors of early Texas were not dependent upon a distant government for guns and ammunition. Vociferously democratic, Texans considered it their right as men born and bred in America to bear arms. Once the white warriors secured good horses and learned to ride like Mexicans, the odds evened out. The long rifles of the Texans were deadly at a far greater range than flint-tipped arrows, and though the Rangers fought individually, they had the advantage of a sense of going into battle as a clan or unit rather than depending on one's individual medicine as the Indians did.

Open hostilities between Anglo-Texans and The People did not begin in earnest until attacks like the one on Parker's Fort in 1836 occurred. If the Texans were angry about Comanche raiders stealing horses or killing cattle on the scattered farms and ranches along the frontier, the capture of their women and children was the last straw, demanding something more than haphazard retaliation by the Rangers. In an attempt to impress upon the Comanches that Texans had sovereign rights over all "vacant" lands and that settlers were no longer to be raided and kidnapped by Comanche warriors, President Mirabeau Lamar of the Republic of Texas called for a council with Penateka Comanche chiefs, whose bands roamed the Texas Hill country northwest of San Antonio.

The Texan leaders knew that several white prisoners were then being held in Comanche villages along such streams as the Llano and Colorado, and they wanted them back. In March of 1840, Chief Muguara (sometimes spelled Maguara or Muk-wa-rah), the Spirit Talker, rode into San Antonio at the head of sixty-five Indians, including chiefs, women, and children. With them was a white captive, Matilda Lockhart, sixteen years of age. If the three commissioners representing the whites in the council about to be held in the courthouse, or Council House as it was called, expected the Comanches to bring in all their captives at once, they did not understand Indian trading sense. Ransom for the captives would be greater in the long run if each transaction was handled separately over an extended period of time. Such had been the Comanches' experience with ransoming Mexican captives. But the men Muguara was dealing with now were hard-nosed warriors in their own right.

The appearance of the Lockhart girl enraged the Texans. Mrs. Samuel Maverick, who helped bathe and dress her, gave this description of the captive:

> Her head, arms, and face were full of bruises and sores, and her nose actually burnt off to the bone, all the fleshy end gone, and a great scab formed on the end of the bone. Both nostrils were wide open and denuded of flesh. She told a piteous tale of how dreadfully the Indians had beaten her . . . and how they would wake her from sleep by sticking a chunk of fire to her flesh, especially to her nose. . . . her body had many scars from the fire. Ah, it was sickening to behold, and made one's blood boil for vengeance.[9]

The Lockhart girl, having learned the Comanche language in her two years with them, revealed their plan to bring in the captives one by one in an effort to exact a higher ransom.

In the Council House, Chief Muguara, brightly attired and painted for council, demanded high prices for the remaining captives. He wanted ammunition, vermillion, and blankets. While the discussion was under way, Texas soldiers surrounded the small, one-story limestone building. Indian boys were playing outside, and curious whites were looking on from the street.

When asked by the Texas commissioners why the other prisoners had not been brought in to San Antonio, Muguara, bald and aged, replied that they were with other bands and could be ransomed later. Then, arrogantly, in the tradition created by generations of Comanche military superiority over their Hispanic foes, the old chief said, "How do you like that answer?"

Pale with anger, the commissioners ordered the soldiers into the room. Chief Muguara was told that all the Indians would be held in jail until the other white captives were brought in. As soon as he conveyed this last message, the interpreter ran from the room.

War whoops rang out. The Texans opened fire and rifle fire and smoke filled the room, already a bedlam of Comanche shrieks and the shouts of the soldiers. One chief killed a soldier who was blocking his exit, but in a short time all the chiefs, including Muguara, were dead, along with the Bexar sheriff and an army officer, and Comanche boys in the street killed a judge who was visiting San Antonio. In the end, all the Indian men were killed, along with some women and children. The survivors were imprisoned.

A Comanche woman, widow of one of the chiefs, was given a horse and told to ride out to the bands and tell them they had twelve days to bring the other white captives in or the Indian prisoners would be killed. Twelve days passed, but no white captives appeared. Instead, it was discovered from a white boy who had been adopted by the Indians and later returned to his family, thirteen white captives were burned over a fire or killed in other lingering ways. The white children and young women were pegged out naked beside a campfire. "They were skinned, sliced, and horribly mutilated, and finally burned alive by vengeful women determined to wring the last shriek and convulsion from their agonized bodies."[10]

For months no road leading to San Antonio was safe to travel. The mutual lack of understanding between Western-thinking whites and the men of the wilderness was never more clearly focused than on that tragic day when the Council House erupted into battle. Council was sacred to a Comanche. To talk in time of peace, especially after smoking the pipe, meant to tell the truth, and if the truth offended, to agree to war, but to fight in council was to go against the Spirit World. Muguara had told the truth, and he had done so with the arrogance the Comanches had long successfully exhibited to Spaniards and Mexicans. Rather than capitulating, however, the Texans had fought, thereby assuring the death of the captives they had hoped through the Council to save.

The loss of their chiefs was a blow to the Penatekas. Devoid of leadership and spiritual direction, the enraged warriors swarmed in the hills northwest of San Antonio, confused and uncertain. In their grief, many of them cut their sacred hair. The ritual destruction of the dead chiefs' horses took two days to complete. Within weeks the Penatekas had disappeared from central Texas to join The People on the bison ranges to the northwest.

The massacre at the Council House poisoned relations between the two peoples for many years. Revenge came with the rising of the full moon of August 1840, when a large band of up to a thousand warriors under Chief Buffalo Hump killed a number of slaves and white citizens en route to the town of Victoria. After terrorizing the citizens, most of whom had taken cover in their houses, the war party secured several hundred horses from outlying farms and ranches, and captured Mrs. Crosby, granddaughter of Daniel Boone, and her baby at Nine Mile Point.

From there, on August 8, the Comanches left their camp on Placido Creek and headed east across the coastal prairie toward the seaside village of Linnville. On the way they killed a man named O'Neal and two black men laboring for Major H. O. Watts. Mistaking the Indians for friendly Mexicans with horses for sale, the citizens of Linnville realized the fearful truth just in time for most of them to escape in boats riding in shallow water about a hundred yards from shore. Major Watts was killed in the water while attempting to escape, and his young bride was captured along with a black woman and her child.

With the town deserted, the Comanches were unmolested as they loaded up goods from the well-stocked warehouses. It took several hundred Indians the entire day to pack the horses for their return to the hill country west of Austin and to points hundreds of miles to the north, for this was a unified war party, made up of reinforcements from the northern Comanches in retribution for the Council House Massacre. It is likely that Peta Nocona, Quanah's father, participated in the raid. While the people of Linnville sat safely in their boats, they had to endure the sight of their homes and all the warehouses but one pillaged and burned. During the night, the jubilant Indians began the return trip to the hill country, following a route that passed up the west side of Garcita Creek about fifteen miles east of Victoria.

While the sack of Linnville was taking place, the Texans were preparing to ambush the Indians at Plum Creek, a tributary of the Guadalupe River below the present town of New Braunfels. At nineteen, John Henry Brown was one of the youngest participants in the ensuing battle. In his words:

> After rest and breakfast, and strengthened by a few recruits, we moved on and camped that night at the old San Antonio crossing of the San Marcos. The 11th was intensely hot, and our ride was chiefly over burnt prairie, the flying ashes being

blinding to the eyes. Waiting some hours at noon watching
for the approach of the enemy after night we arrived at
Goode's cabin, on the Gonzales and Austin road, a little east
of Plum Creek. Here Felix Huston, General of militia, with
his aide, James Izard, arrived from Austin about the same
time. We moved two or three miles and camped on Plum
Creek, above the Indian trail. . . . Our united force was then
one hundred men. We camped at midnight and sent pickets
to watch the trail. Men and horses were greatly jaded, but the
horses had to eat while the men slept.[11]

At daylight, the lookouts rushed into camp and reported that
the Indians were about three miles below. Soon, every man was
mounted, with General Felix Huston in command. Upon hearing
that a force of eighty-seven volunteers led by Colonel Burleson
were galloping toward his command, Huston halted to wait for
the reinforcements. Altogether, the Texans would have only two
hundred men against a force five times that size.

As Huston's men waited for Colonel Burleson and his men
to arrive, they were able to observe the oncoming Comanches
from behind a stand of timber, ". . . singing and gyrating in diverse
grotesque ways, evidencing their great triumph, and utterly oblivi-
ous to danger. Up to this time they had lost but one warrior, at
the Casa Blanca; they had killed twenty persons . . . they had as
prisoners Mrs. Watts, Mrs. Crosby and child, and the Negro woman
and child; they had about 2,000 captured horses and mules, and
an immense booty in goods of various kinds."[12]

As soon as Burleson arrived, the Texans advanced at a trot,
quickly increasing to a gallop. About two hundred yards from the
Indians, the whites dismounted on the open plain. As Brown
described it:

Bands of warriors then began encircling us, firing and using
their shields with great effect. From the timber a steady fire
was kept up, by muskets and some long rifles, while about

thirty of our men, still mounted, were dashing to and fro among the mounted Indians, illustrating a series of personal heroisms worthy of all praise . . . at last, perhaps half an hour after dismounting, an Indian chief, wearing a tremendous headdress, who had been exceedingly daring, approached so near that several shots struck him, and he fell forward on the pommel of his saddle, but was caught by a comrade on either side and borne away, evidently dead or dying, for as soon as he was led among his people in the oaks they set up a peculiar howl, when Capt. Caldwell sang out, "Now General, is your time to charge them! They are whipped!" The charge was ordered and gallantly made. Very soon the Indians broke into parties and ran, but ran fighting all the time. At the boggy branch [creek] quite a number were killed in clusters for ten or twelve miles.[13]

The running fight continued, with the Indians' stolen horses and mules scattering in all directions. Mrs. Watts and the black woman were wounded, but were rescued. The black woman's child escaped unhurt. Mrs. Crosby was lanced through the heart as she tried to escape into a thicket. Brown estimated the Indian casualties at eighty-six killed in action, with several others severely wounded. "The Indians lost everything. The defeat was unexpected—a surprise, complete and crushing. Followed by a great victory over them in the following October, near where Colorado City now stands, won by Colonel John H. Moore and his brave volunteers, the Comanches were taught lessons hitherto unknown to them."[14]

Curiously enough, the victors of the Battle of Plum Creek drew lots for the captured plunder rather than returning the property to its rightful owners. Brown received for his share ". . . a horse, a fine mule, $27 worth of silk and about $50 worth of other goods for ladies' use. . . ."[15]

The southern Comanches, their vaunted power broken by the massacre at Council House and their reversal at Plum Creek, were never again to mount large-scale attacks against the whites, even though they would continue to raid outlying settlements. But the bold warriors of the Arkansas, Canadian, and Washita rivers were to contest the white man for another thirty-five years for possession of the land. The battle for Comanchería had only begun.

3

THE CAPTURE OF NAUDAH*

[The raid leader] always travels first—he goes to the first camp first and when he camps he looks back at the others one after the other—when they have all arrived he holds a council and says, "Back in the village I decided to go to war—everybody knows it, women and children—now I see you here I feel glad a big party—we are going to war."

— Quanah Parker, 1897[1]

When Quanah was born, Cynthia Ann Parker was the wife of Peta Nocona, whose name in English means He who Travels Alone and Returns. Since the Comanches practiced polygamy, she was one of several wives, one of whom was reported to be Spanish. Late in his life, Quanah wrote, "From the best information I have I was born about 1850 on Elk Creek just below the Wichita Mountains."[2] This estimate is supported by the account hunters gave of their encounter with Cynthia Ann when she was caring for Quanah and his brother Pee-nah (sometimes referred to as Pecos) at Nocona's camp along the Canadian River in 1851. When asked if she would like to return to her people, she "... shook her head ... and pointed to her little, naked barbarians sporting at her feet. ..."[3]

---

* "Someone Found"—Cynthia Ann Parker's Comanche name.

It is evident that Cynthia Ann had ". . . adopted all the habits and peculiarities of the Comanches; [she had] an Indian husband and children and [could not] be persuaded to leave them. [Her] brother, who had been ransomed* by a trader and brought home to his relatives, was sent back by his mother for the purpose of endeavoring to prevail upon his sister to leave the Indians and return to her family; but he stated . . . that on his arrival she refused to listen to the proposition, saying that her husband, children, and all that she held most dear, were with the Indians, and there she should remain."[4]

At the time of Cynthia Ann's capture at Parker's Fort in 1836, the Comanches were near the peak of their power. George Catlin estimates their number then at between thirty and forty thousand, with some six to seven thousand well-armed, well-mounted warriors. With buffalo in the millions and antelope and wild horses in the tens of thousands, The People had ready access to their favorite foods. Their enemies, particularly the Utes and Apaches, continued to extract a toll of Comanche warriors killed in battle, but their main enemy was the white man's diseases. Frequent raids to Mexico exposed warriors to venereal diseases, smallpox, and cholera. To the north, peaceful contact with traders, as well as hostile action against travelers on the Santa Fe Trail, enabled disease to spread through the Comanche bands. With no natural resistance to alien diseases, the Comanches suffered heavy losses in the smallpox epidemics of 1818 and 1839–1840 and the cholera outbreak of 1849, brought on by travelers crossing from the East on their way to California. Colonel W. S. Nye, in his *Carbine and Lance*, states that a ". . . tragic by-product of the gold rush was the introduction of Asiatic Cholera into the plains. The

---

* John Parker was a Comanche warrior in his early teens before being ransomed by his family.

disease spread to the Kiowas and Comanches. They say that 1849 was the most terrible period which they can remember. More than half of them perished, and survivors were utterly terrified."[5]

The principal human enemy of the Comanches after 1840 was still the Texas Ranger; nevertheless, the northern bands continued to raid into Mexico and along the western fringes of the expanding white settlements. The elusive Quahadas and other Comanche bands made many such raids, but could always return to the safety of their wilderness home along the thinly timbered valleys of the Canadian, Red, Pease, Washita, Pecos, and Arkansas rivers.

A significant change in white–Indian relations took place in 1845; Texas became a state, and the U.S. Army assumed primary responsibility for the protection of the frontier—much to the delight, no doubt, of the Comanches. The hated Tejanos were now relegated to a secondary role in policing the territory they claimed as their own. So for a time, the lightning-like raids of the Rangers gave way to a new government policy for dealing with the Indians— defense instead of offense. This meant a return to the centuries-old Spanish practice of building *presidios*, or forts, at wide intervals across the frontier. Instead of launching strikes into enemy territory as the Rangers had been doing for the past decade, the U.S. military began a policy of conciliation toward the Indians. Fearing that the Texas Indians would side with Mexico in the war raging at that time between that country and the United States, the federal government created a special commission whose job it was to offer the Indians of Texas and the southwestern prairies alternatives to battle.

By 1860, the U.S. government had convinced a number of Indians to settle on reservations but it would be another seven years before some of the Comanche bands would make a treaty with the United States. Meanwhile, the Comanches, under the leadership of Peta Nocona, continued their depredations along the western fringes of Anglo-Celtic settlement in Texas. According to James T. DeShields, the condition of the frontier in 1859–60 was

> . . . truly deplorable, [the settlers] were obliged to stand in a continued posture of defense, and were in continual alarm and hazard of their lives, never daring to stir abroad unarmed, for small bodies of savages, quick-sighted and accustomed to perpetual watchfulness, hovered on the outskirts, and springing from behind bush or rock, surprising [their] enemy before he was aware of danger . . . [they] sent tidings of [their] presence in the fatal blow, and after execution of the bloody work, by superior knowledge of the country and rapid movements, safely retired to their inaccessible deserts.
>
> In the autumn of 1860 the indomitable and fearless Peta Nocona led a raiding party of Comanches through Parker County, so named in honor of the family of his wife, Cynthia Ann, committing great depredations as they passed through. The venerable Isaac Parker was at the time a resident of the town of Weatherford, the county seat; and little did he imagine that the chief of the ruthless savages who spread desolation and death on every side as far as their arms could reach, was the husband of his long lost niece; and that the comingled blood of the murdered Parkers and the atrocious Comanche now courses in the veins of a second generation—bound equally by ties of consanguinity to murderer and murdered; that the son of Peta Nocona and Cynthia Ann Parker would become the chief of the proud Comanches, whose boast it is that their constitutional settlement of government is the purest democracy ever originated and administered among man. It certainly conserved the object of its institution—for a longer period, and much more satisfactorily than has that of any other Indian tribe. . . . The Comanche is the most qualified by nature for receiving education and for adapting himself to the requirements of civilization, of all the southern tribes, not excepting even the Cherokees, with their churches, schoolhouses and farms . . . it is a shame to the civilization of the

age that a people so susceptible of a high degree of development should be allowed to grovel in the depths of heathenism and savagery. But we are digressing.[6]

DeShields's digression led him away from his discussion of Peta Nocona's fierce leadership in his efforts to block further settlement of the buffalo plains. Every year since the intrusion of aliens into Comanchería, the buffalo range had constricted in size as a result of encroachment from all sides. The raiders' cruelty in frequently subjecting their victims to lingering deaths had root, at least in part, in their hatred of men who had invaded the buffalo lands and in the process had butchered Comanche women and children. And it probably explains the motivation for a Comanche revenge raid in 1860 that put an end to conciliation and resulted in all-out war between Indians and whites that led, among other events, to the recapture of Cynthia Ann and her return to her relatives.

Revenge raids were common among the Indians, and they were characterized by the specification that a certain number of whites would die. An example is a raid by the Kiowas, as described by Colonel Nye:

> After the last rays of the sun had painted scarlet and gold stripes across the sky, and purple shadows were blackening in the canyon, the people climbed the slope to the lodge of the medicine man. They seated themselves respectfully before it. Soon the rustle of wings was heard, followed by the eerie cry of the hoot owl. Maman-ti [the medicine man] emerged from the darkened tepee. "The revenge raid will be a success," he announced solemnly. "At least one enemy will be killed. None of us will die."[7]

After leaving Indian territory, the war party of fifty men cached some supplies just north of the present town of Quanah, Texas, and continued toward the settlements. They camped on a hill east of Seymour, where Maman-ti again consulted his medicine. He told the warriors that the next morning one or two whites would be killed by men mounted on gray horses and that Hunting Horse, the youngest member of the party, would receive a fine bay.

It was a hot July sun that greeted the Kiowas the next day. Maman-ti led his men to one of the favorite raiding areas of the Southern Plains Indians—the Butterfield Stage road between Jacksboro and Fort Griffin. There they chased four cowboys who managed to escape. From a hilltop, the Kiowas later saw a party of Rangers following a trail that, unknown to the Kiowas at that time, had been left by a raiding party of Comanches on their way back to Indian territory. Maman-ti and Loud Talker rode down the slope in sight of the Rangers, who pursued the wily Kiowas into a trap, where two lines of warriors attacked the whites from both sides. At the conclusion of the battle, two Rangers lay dead, killed by Kiowas riding gray horses, and Chief Tahbone-mah gave Hunting Horse a fine bay ridden by one of the dead. In the aftermath of the battle, according to Nye, "Presently Lone Wolf stood back to make a speech. He said, 'Thank you, oh thank you, for what has been done today. My poor son has been paid back. His spirit is satisfied.' "[8]

Whites also sought revenge, not only a life for a life, but on at least one occasion a scalp for a scalp. Shortly before the Kiowa revenge raid, a band of Comanches killed Josephus Browning and severely wounded his son in an attack on the Browning ranch on the Clear Fork of the Brazos near Weatherford. A party was quickly formed by John R. Baylor and Walter Reynolds, and the men rode in pursuit of the Indians. On June 28, the Texans overtook the Comanches on Paint Creek and killed thirteen warriors. After scalping the dead Indians, the ranchers returned to Weatherford with the Indian scalps and the scalp of a white woman whom the Comanches had killed on their raid. The townspeople of Weatherford proceeded to stage a macabre celebration:

The occasion was celebrated by a public barbecue on the square in Weatherford, at which stirring speeches were listened to by a vast assemblage from every portion of the surrounding county. In the evening a dance was given at the court house, and on a rope stretched diagonally across the large room were hung the arms and equipments captured by the party and also the scalp of the white woman, as well as those of the slain warriors—gruesome decorations for a scene of festivity. General Baker exhibited these trophies of the Paint Creek fight in many other places, and everywhere among the settlers arose the cry, "Exterminate the Indians."[9]

John Baylor was one of the more outspoken foes of the red man. Although he had once served as on-site agent for the Penateka Comanches at the reserve on the Brazos River, Baylor had left the Texas Indian Bureau after being accused of incompetence in the keeping of records of receipts and expenditures. By the time of his dismissal, he had already lost the small measure of rapport he had once had with the Indians, and after his removal as agent, he went on the offensive against Major Robert S. Neighbors, his former boss. Baylor asserted that Neighbors habitually protected agency Indians from accusations by area whites that they had stolen stock. In the fall of 1860, *The White Man*, a local Weatherford newspaper, editorialized in support of Baylor's position: "The most desperate effort has been made by Governor Houston [of Texas] and his friends to create the impression that there is a large, well-organized band of thieves and murderers [rather than Indians] on the frontier, who are committing most of the depredations on our citizens."[10] According to other sources, unscrupulous whites did indeed profit from horse stealing, robbery, and murder, while taking great care to cast blame on the reservation Indians. "Even those settlers of some conscience were not above planting evidence to incriminate the agency Indians and force their removal."[11]

Baylor's agitation to have the Indians removed from Texas resulted in the Reservation War, in which law-abiding citizens witnessed to the fact that vigilantes were killing helpless and aged Indians. Without the protection of United States troops, the mob of armed men surrounding the Texas Indian Reserve would have massacred all of them.

John Baylor's partner on *The White Man,* a journalist named Hamner, was himself adept at stirring up public opinion. In the September 13, 1860, issue he wrote:

> The present condition of the frontier is truly alarming. Not a week passes that we do not hear of fresh depredations by Indians. In Palo Pinto county we learn that near one hundred head of horses have been stolen within the last two weeks; but a short time since a negro man, the property of a Mr. Craven, was killed by Indians in sight of the town of Palo Pinto, in fact not a light moon has passed since last Fall, but some portion of the frontier has been annoyed by Indians. The road is lined with movers from the different frontier counties, who have at last determined to quit the country and seek protection in the older states, where they can at least know that they are free from the annoyances they have been subjected to. For three years past the frontier people have begged, prayed, and supplicated both State and Federal governments for protection, and the Federal government has displayed a cold blooded indifference to our condition, that would do credit to the Czar of Russia.[12]

It was in the midst of this tinderbox of racist hatred that the Comanches carried out a raid that shocked even the already outraged frontier. It may or may not have been a revenge raid, but a Mrs. Sherman was brutally murdered, while her husband and children were spared; in this case, the behavior of the Comanches was very strange. It is possible that the Comanche who killed Mrs. Sherman on the western fringes of Parker County did so in revenge for the loss of a wife, sweetheart, mother, or sister in a Ranger attack or, most probably, in one by U.S. soldiers and Tonkawa scouts. If this was a revenge raid in which a certain number of people were to die, it might explain the Indians' not capturing Mr. Sherman for purposes of torture or bondage. Leaving the children behind was also unusual; each child represented many horses and trade goods as ransom, even though the Indians often became attached to the little ones, as in the case of Cynthia Ann Parker, in which case mountains of goods and a herd of ponies could not ransom them.

The Shermans, neighbors of frontier scout and cattleman Charles Goodnight, had moved to the rolling grassland of Parker County totally ignorant of the dangers awaiting them on the Great Plains. Goodnight, who had come to Texas from Illinois at the age of nine, had lived since childhood on the edge of the plains. By 1860, he and others like him were customarily armed with one or two Colt six-shooters, a rifle, and a Bowie knife. They knew the land and all the plants and animals it supported; they knew where to find water; they could communicate in English, Spanish, and, in some cases, Comanche and French. And, amazingly, like their Spanish predecessors, they managed to acquire minutely detailed knowledge of the region even though they were surrounded by myriad hostile enemies.

Young Mr. Sherman, on the contrary, did not even own a gun. He had brought his pregnant wife and two children to the edge of what was then known in all geographies as the Great American Desert, and he was ill prepared for what was to befall them. Goodnight gives this account of the Comanche raid on the Shermans:

> . . . Sherman, with his wife and two children, had settled in
> the east end of Stag Prairie, in the western edge of Parker
> County, at which place the Indians stopped about noon as

they went back westward. . . . The Indians were carrying a
large herd of horses out with them. As they came in to Stag
Prairie, the rain was descending in torrents. They dismounted,
came into the Shermans' cabin where the family was eating
dinner, and drove them out. The family started to cross to
the east side of a narrow prairie where a neighbor by the
name of Stevens lived, a quarter or half a mile away. The
Indians followed the Shermans and overtook them about a
hundred yards from their cabin. They drove Sherman and the
two children away and badly mistreated Mrs. Sherman. After
shooting two or three arrows through her body and scalping
her, they left her near the house still alive. She lived until
the next day, giving birth to a dead child.[13]

The Anglo-Celts who viewed the body of the dead mother,
violated, tortured, and left to die a lingering death, were ready for
their own revenge. Foremost among them were Charles Goodnight, the Shermans' neighbor, who was years later to become
Quanah's friend, and Captain Lawrence Sullivan ("Sul") Ross.

Young Sul Ross was among those who had applied to Governor Sam Houston for a commission to raise a company of Rangers to combat the Comanches. Despite Houston's efforts at
conciliation, he was by now all too aware that the elusive Comanche warriors, some of whom had recently been forced from
their reserve on the Brazos River, continued to raid the scattered
farms and ranches along the edge of the Great Plains, usually
escaping with minimal losses. The peace policy Houston had
advocated all of his public life was now a failure, and so he had
ordered the enlistment of state troops to assist the settlers in
protecting the frontier. They obviously needed help; not only were
their cabins vulnerable to Indian attack, but since there was little
fencing on the plains, the ranchers' stock ran loose and was easy
prey for Comanche and Kiowa raiders. The ferocity of the Indians'
attacks had root in what they considered to be the perfidy of the

Texans in driving the Penateka Comanches away from their Brazos reserve,* and, even more, the continued intrusion of whites into the buffalo range of The People.

The Comanches and their allies had also achieved a significant measure of success far to the southwest of Parker, Palo Pinto, and Jack counties. John Williams had written to Governor Runnells two years prior to the Sherman murder that many settlers in Brown, Lampasas, and San Saba counties had fled the frontier, while the more stubborn had sought protection by congregating behind log or stone walls. Williams said, "The people will retreat still further unless immediate protection is afforded."[14]

Sul Ross had graduated from Florence Wesleyan, where he had studied military science. When he returned from Alabama to Texas, he found that what had once been a relatively friendly relationship between whites and the Indians on the reserve had given way to suspicion and hostility. The raiding by the nonreserve Indians, which included all of the Comanche bands except the Penatekas, had inflamed many of the settlers in northwest Texas against all Indians, even though nonreserve Indians frequently attacked the reserve Indians as punishment for cooperating with the whites. Some whites were taking advantage of the situation by disguising themselves as Indians and stealing stock. Many Texans, John R. Baylor among them, despised the red men on principle, while others coveted land allotted for the reservation. Sul Ross's return from Alabama required a shift in attitude, and though he did not share Baylor's extreme prejudice, he was an able and willing candidate for a commission with the Rangers.

So, with angry Texans and the governor of Texas on the offensive, the battle that would lead to Cynthia Ann's recapture

---

* The Texas Indian Reserve had been established by the state legislature in 1855 to provide 23,400 acres for the Penateka (or southern) Comanches.

began, with Peta Nocona the especial quarry not only of Charles Goodnight, but of the Rangers and Sul Ross. After the murder, the twenty-four-year-old Goodnight rode all night in a driving rain to enlist his neighbors' aid in avenging Mrs. Sherman's death. The cabin of a Mr. Lynn was designated as their meeting place. The unfortunate Mr. Lynn had recently lost his daughter and son-in-law to the Indians. When Goodnight reached his place, he ". . . found Mr. Lynn sitting before a large log fire in the old fashioned fireplace with a long forked dogwood stick on which was an Indian scalp thoroughly salted . . . after the murder of Mr. Lynn's daughter and son-in-law he had a great craving to kill Indians, and asked all us boys in the neighborhood to bring him the scalps of any Indians we killed."[15]

Goodnight's little group of men rode into the inner reaches of Comanchería, following the enemy into his natural sanctuary. The heart of Comanchería had long been too formidable for white intrusion, except for frontier guides and scouts like Goodnight, who had learned to hunt and track from an Indian named Caddo Jake as a small boy in the Brazos River bottoms. In spite of the reputation of the territory they were entering, the Parker cowboys were bent on vengeance. Riding with Goodnight were I. W. Sheek, Sam Ham, Solon Loving, Chap Loving, and three other men.

The Texans headed in a westerly direction, hoping to intercept the Indians on a northwesterly course toward Red River. They soon arrived at the place where the Indians had left the scene of the Sherman murder. That day they followed the trail and were gaining on the Indians, who were slowed by their herd of approximately 150 horses, composed mostly of stolen stock. By the end of the second day, Goodnight and his men had tracked the Comanches to Pease River, a few miles above the present town of Vernon. At that point, all trails converged into one broad one, as all the Indians and horses were now moving together. It was a sure sign that the warriors felt secure and were in close proximity to their own people. At this point, Goodnight and his men, hopelessly outnumbered, retreated to their camp in the Keechi Valley of Parker County.

Ranger Captain Sul Ross, with the ink on his new commission from Governor Sam Houston hardly dry, was near the frontier when Goodnight and his companions returned from their foray. The young Parker County rancher told Ross what had happened. Ross, under fire from some of the hotheads on the frontier calling for annihilation of red men, seized the opportunity to punish the murderers of Mrs. Sherman. He appointed Goodnight scout and guide of the expedition. The command included Ross's twenty-five regular U.S. troops and eighty frontiersmen volunteers. With Goodnight in the lead, Ross and his men set out from Fort Belknap in Young County to the Sherman cabin, then along the trail the Indians had left. As "head scout," Goodnight was to "keep course." If he saw something that needed a closer look, he would leave the trail and his second in command would keep course until he returned. A rancher/lawyer named Mosely was Goodnight's backup on the Ross expedition.

Just east and south of the Pease River, the scouts picked up Mrs. Sherman's Bible. Since it had fallen with the covers closed, the rain had not penetrated the paper. It was customary for Indians to take books on their raids of settlers' cabins because they knew paper was almost bulletproof when stuffed inside a Comanche bull-hide shield. The discovery of the Bible was ample proof not only that the warriors whom Ross and his men were following were the ones who had murdered Mrs. Sherman, but that they had recently been on the sloping watershed of the narrow Pease.

Shortly after finding the Bible, Goodnight spotted some chittum trees in the sand hills to the south. From his account written much later, "I told Mosely to keep the course and I would go out to the chittum grove, probably half a mile to the south, and see if there had been any Indians there. I knew if there had been any in the vicinity they would be there getting the berries. When I reached the chittum grove, it looked as though the Indians had not been gone ten minutes."[16]

Goodnight then remembered a freshwater creek nearby that emptied into the salt and gyp water of the Pease. Feeling certain that the Indians would be camped there, he loped out to the edge of the sand hills and signaled Captain Cureton, commander of the volunteers, to charge. Ross's Rangers were already on the attack; the volunteers had been traveling slightly behind and to one side of them. Again from Goodnight's account:

> Ross seemed to conceive the idea that the Indians were just beyond the little divide or sand dunes that came down from the hills to the creek. Anyway, at random he had ordered a charge and when he got to the top of the sand dune, the Indians were about a hundred yards from him just mounting to break camp, with all their packs and outfits. He ordered a sergeant to detour to the right, thinking the Indians would attack into the sand hills. Instead they lost their heads, crossed a little creek twice, as Rangers followed them up at full speed, passing through the squaws who were heavily loaded, shooting Indians [the warriors] as they came to them. The sergeant on seeing this fell in behind and killed all the squaws. The Texas boys didn't shoot any of the squaws.
>
> The fight continued on this plain until the Indians were all killed [except two, as it turned out], Ross having a hand to hand fight with the chief who was the head of them. Now it so happened that the woman Cynthia Ann had a good horse and [was] carrying an infant 3 or 4 months old* and she was well up with the chief. For some cause I have never known Ross ordered his lieutenant to take charge of her. I had always supposed that he did it to save her life as he must have heard the guns of the sergeant killing the squaws behind. Anyhow,

---

* The infant was a daughter named Prairie Flower.

the lieutenant took charge of the ponies and brought her back to where we camped just where the fight began.[17]

The campsite was a grove of cottonwoods along the stream. Goodnight reflected on the cruelty of their riding over Naudah's (Cynthia Ann's) dead and dying friends as he, along with Ross and Ross's lieutenant, escorted the captured woman to the campsite in the timber. He continues:

> When we reached the timber where the Indians had been camped, we had Cynthia Ann and also a little Comanche boy, who [Captain] Ross had picked up during the fight and set behind him when his horse was on a dead run . . . Ross took this boy home to raise and educate. The boy accompanied him through the Civil War, cared for his horse, and fought like the devil . . . Cynthia Ann and the little boy were seated at the foot of a large cottonwood tree. The boy did not show any great concern, but Cynthia was in terrible grief and distress. Through sympathy for her, thinking her distress would be the same as that of our white women under similar circumstances, I thought I would try to console her and make her understand she would not be hurt. When I got near her I noticed she had blue eyes and light hair which had been cut off very short. It was the custom of the Comanches for the squaws to cut their hair as a token of grief when any of their family was killed. We had killed some of her relatives prior to this. . . . When I came to the Palo Duro Canyon and established my ranch in 1876 I found enough Indian hair there to make "cinches." It was a little difficult to distinguish Cynthia Ann's blond German features, as her face and hands were extremely dirty from handling so much meat. The Indians adhered very little to cleanliness.
>
> After speaking a few words to her, I turned back to the creek, where there was great excitement. There I came in contact with Judge Pollard, who was one of our volunteers and at that time county judge of Palo Pinto County. I told him we had captured a white woman instead of an Indian. His reply was no. I said; "Go see for yourself." He did, and

in five minutes it had been reported among the entire crowd. I have never believed and do not yet believe that anyone knew until then that she was white, though. I have never verified this statement with . . . Ross. Her grief was distressing and intense, and I shall never forget the impression it made on me. We had a Mexican acting as a very poor interpreter . . . I think here is where . . . Ross got the wrong impression that he had killed her husband, Nocona, as she was saying a great deal about Nocona, meaning, however, that she was in the Nocona band of Indians. . . . To substantiate the information that Ross did not kill Nocona, I had an old Indian friend, George Hunt, look up some old member of the tribe and this is what he wrote:

My dear friend:

I have made the trip to the Comanche country south and east of Lawton and have visited two or three older members of the Comanches and have found the name of the chief that was killed at the battle when Chief Parker's mother was re-captured.

The name of the chief was No-bah. They said that he was the leader or a chief of the Party. The Comanches that tell me the name of the chief are all old men and tell me that No Cone never was killed at the battle on Pease River several miles south of Quanah, Texas and said that you are right to disapprove of Chief No Cone being killed at this battle for he lived several years afterward. . . .

Your friend,
Geo. Hunt[18]

At this time, Quanah was about ten or eleven, and the reason Nocona was not with Cynthia Ann when the Rangers attacked was that he, Quanah, and Pee-nah were hunting several miles away when the attack took place. In the personal treaty Goodnight made with Quanah in the winter of 1877–1878 in Palo Duro Canyon, Quanah confirmed that Nobah was the chief killed by Sul Ross in the Pease River massacre. Quanah said that the little band of hunters and women Ross had killed had been keeping a "swing station" or supply depot for the many war bands passing to and from the settlements during the fall of 1860. Peta Nocona was normally the chief of the band that Ross attacked, but he had left Nobah in command during his brief absence. At the time, most of the Comanches and Kiowas were moving south in an attempt to keep pace with the migrating buffalo, intending to winter there. The use of Nobah's small band as a hunting and supply camp could explain why two of Peta Nocona's wives (the Spanish woman who was killed and Naudah) were in the party. Peta Nocona very likely expected to pass through the camp on his way to or from a raid.

After the battle and the taking of Cynthia Ann, Goodnight succeeded in trailing two other warriors, who had somehow survived, from the confluence of Mule Creek and Pease River to a canyon near the foot of the Staked Plains, fifty or sixty miles away. As he and his men entered the canyon through which the river coursed, they found exhausted ponies put out to graze. Goodnight, the most knowledgeable man in Anglo Texas about the wild haunts of the Comanches, told the ten scouts under his command that they were near the main camp:

> Fortunately, the Indians had not seen us approaching, and it is a mystery to me yet why they had not kept a better lookout. . . . as the spies had reached the camp to report the battle. There were approximately a thousand Indians in this camp, and it appeared that they were prepared to move. We scoured back up the canyon to where I found a sharp curve. The water had cut quite a distance into the rock cliff. Here we could be seen only in front of this curve. I threw the men into it to wait until dark, fearing we would be discovered and knowing we would have no show to live if we were. . . . In 1878 I got the facts from Quanah. When the two Indian guides, who had escaped from the party killed by Ross, had reached the main body of Indians, they reported that there were ten thousand

of us. As I previously stated, it did look like a regiment of us with the tin cups glistening in the sun and with the company strung out such a long distance. Thus, as soon as the main body of Indians could get ready they moved back north where Quanah stated they wintered from the Washita to the Wichita mountains. They suffered much from provisions, as they were entirely north of the buffalo. I am confident Quanah's statement was correct, as I know that in all of our scouting and hunting over the foot of the plains we did not find them again until the next summer, when the war parties had commenced to drift south. That year I joined the Texas Rangers.[19]

So Goodnight and the emerging young warrior Quanah, meaning "fragrant," were to ride on opposing sides for the remainder of the conflict. It was not until 1878 that Charles Goodnight, the new owner of Palo Duro and its running water, timbered slopes, and game, made a peace treaty with Quanah, the previous master. The two could share in their understanding of the heroic struggle now ending between courageous men of the Stone Age and determined, organized European-American men whose benefit from the inventions of the rapidly advancing Industrial Revolution resulted in the their possessing powerful guns that hit on target at great distances, or repeating rifles that guaranteed the U.S. soldier and the Texas Ranger a decided advantage over Comanche warriors, however brave.

Throughout the night after the bloody massacre at Pease River had ended, Naudah cried. Captain Ross had his Mexican servant, a former captive of the Comanches, tell her that the captain recognized her as one of his own people and would not harm her. "At last the Mexican interpreter succeeded in extracting the information that she feared for the lives of her two sons, Quanah and Pee-Nah, who [she thought] had been with her in the camp at the time of the Ranger attack. The whites assured her that no boys had been killed, and thereafter she became more tractable."[20]

As Quanah himself stated to Goodnight, he was not present at Pease River when Ross attacked the camp, which was composed, according to Goodnight's report, primarily of Comanche women who had followed the hunters, moving in only after the buffalo had been felled to butcher and pack the meat. Doubtless there were hunters still in the area when the attack began, but the Indians' estimate of ten thousand soldiers explains why any warriors nearby would have hesitated to enter the fray.

In regard to Cynthia Ann's comments to Ross, Goodnight had the explanation: "We had a Mexican acting as a very poor interpreter."[21] So historians will probably never know for sure what the bereft woman was saying. Surely she must have sought to convey the desire that burned in her heart for the duration of her few remaining years that she be reunited with her two sons.

After the Pease River massacre, Ross returned to Camp Cooper with Cynthia Ann by his side. The news of his capture of a white "squaw" quickly spread among the settlements, reaching Isaac Parker at Weatherford, and Parker journeyed to the frontier to see her. Having forgotten her English during her twenty-four years with the Comanches, Naudah did not respond to her uncle's questioning until he said to the interpreter, "The girl's name is Cynthia Ann." The moment she heard her name, the young woman jumped to her feet and exclaimed, "Me Cincee Ann!"[22] Her uncle was then convinced he had at last found his long-lost niece.

The State of Texas granted her a pension of one hundred dollars a year for five years beginning in 1861, and one league of land. A year later she moved from Birdville to Van Zandt County and lived with her younger brother, Silas Parker Jr., one of two of Silas Parker's children who had escaped capture in the Comanche raid on Parker's Fort. Later she lived with various relatives in Henderson and Anderson counties. T. J. Cates, a neighbor at the community of Ben Wheeler, said of the twice-captured woman, "I well remember Cynthia Ann and her little girl, Tecks

Ann [Prairie Flower]; she lived at the time about six miles south of Ben Wheeler, with her brother-in-law, Ruff O'Quinn, near Slater's Creek. She looked to be stout and weighed about 140 pounds, well made and liked to work. She had a wild expression and would look down when people looked at her. . . . She was an expert in tanning hides with the hair on them, or plaiting or knitting either ropes or whips."[23]

Sometime after her recapture and forced sojourn with her white relatives, Cynthia Ann explained to Coho Smith, also a former Comanche captive, that she longed to be with her boys. In his words:

> When we got to the house we sat down to dinner. Cynthia Ann sat opposite to me. I said to Cynthia Ann the first word that occurred to me, "ee-wunee-keem" [meaning "come here"]. She sprang up with a scream and knocked about half the dishes off the table. She ran to me and fell on the floor and caught me around both ankles, crying in Comanche, "ee-ma, mi mearo, ee-ma mearo" [I am going with you]. . . . She was so excited I really thought she would go into a fit. Cynthia held me by one arm and talking all the time to me in Comanche and Spanish, mixing the two languages all the time. . . . She said to me in Spanish, "You will take us, won't you?" I told her the legislature had granted her a league of land and if I was to take her to the Indians that I would never dare come back to Texas any more. I said, "You have no horse, and this pony of mine is not fit for such a long journey about the head waters of the Arkansas River." "Horses! That is nothing," she said. "There is some first rate horses and whenever I get my hand on their mane they are mine. Don't hesitate a moment about horses. Oh, I tell you mi Corazón está llorando todo el tiempo por mis dos hijos."*[24]

---

* . . . my heart is crying out all the time for my two sons.

Cynthia Ann continued to implore Coho Smith to take her with him to the Comanches. Coho told her he had just married a young wife, to which she replied, "That is nothing. . . . Only take me to my people and they will give you as many wives as you want. Our people are not like the white man, they take as many wives as they wish." Smith asked her why she did not go to the Comanches. She said, "We might start and when we got away up in the Indian country we might be staking a horse or getting wood and we would be killed and I would be made a slave and I would never get to see my boys nor my people never, never, never." She told Smith that she did not know if she could find her people. Though she was an expert horsewoman, she did not completely know the route. She told Smith she would go to Prairie Dog and then from there to the Cimarron and the Arkansas. "But I could not go alone," she said. "I could not hunt game like a man to support myself and child. You must go, don't say no. See now I will give you par-lin pe-ah-et, par-lin-tehe-yah, par-lin esposas."*[25] To Cynthia Ann's dismay, Smith left the next day for business in Dallas.

In spite of her blood relatives' constant efforts to make her happy, Cynthia Ann had long ago merged into the psyche of a new identity, Naudah, Someone Found, the name given to her by her captor, Chief Peta Nocona. The rest of her days she spent assisting with the domestic chores of her white family. She learned to spin and weave, activities that proved useful to the Confederate war effort but which brought little solace to her grieving heart. She died at her brother's home in Anderson County, Texas, in 1864, preceded a short time by her little daughter, Prairie Flower. The Parkers had promised to let her visit her sons after the war

---

* *Esposas* is Spanish for wives. *Par-lin* is Comanche for ten. The whole expression means "ten guns, ten horses, ten wives."

was over, but her spirit, cut off from the nourishment of her Comanche family and friends, left her body at the age of thirty-seven.

Meanwhile, Peta Nocona (who, according to his son Quanah, "knew nothing" of the fight at Pease River until the two survivors returned to camp and informed the war chief "of the great disaster which had befallen his people") lost his warlike fervor. Weakened by a wound he had received before the attack on Parker's Fort, the veteran warrior of the Comanches became "very morose and unhappy." Quanah saw him "shed many tears" over the death of his Spanish wife and the capture of Naudah. Peta Nocona died "two or three years later. I was with him," wrote Quanah, "and saw him die . . . he was buried near the Antelope Hills . . . near the south bank of the Canadian River. . . . Before the death of my father, he told me that my mother was a white woman, that he took her into captivity from central or east Texas, when she was a child."[26]

Thus ended the union of Comanche and Parker, as warrior and wife died within months of each other. Their elder son, however, remained alive to fight for the rights of The People.

4

THE COMANCHE WAR TRAIL

"My people have never first drawn a bow or fired a gun against the whites. There has been trouble on the line between us, and my young men have danced the war dance. But it was not begun by us. It was you who sent out the first soldier and we who sent out the second . . . since that time there has been a noise like that of a thunderstorm."

— Ten Bears, Comanche chief, 1867 [1]

After the death of his father, Quanah "rapidly rose to commanding influence."[2] Since Peta Nocona died two or three years after Naudah's capture in December 1860, it can be assumed that Quanah became a warrior in late 1862 or early in 1863, when he was between fourteen and sixteen years old. By that age, a young warrior's skills on horseback and with the lance, shield, and bow would be known by all the other warriors in the band. And every man would know the physical prowess of each of his fellow warriors, for wrestling and mock hand-to-hand combat were part of a Comanche boy's training from early childhood.

Because fathers were usually hunting, warring, racing horses, playing cards, or making or repairing weapons, they had little time to train their sons, so grandfathers took on that task. They taught the boys to make their own shields, bows, and arrows; they instilled in them the belief that their very existence was based on war and the hunt; and they encouraged competition for leadership. They taught that courage and generosity earned respect, and that valor in war and success in the hunt were qualities prized in Comanche society; the result was that every boy sought to develop these values in himself.

Many lessons on values took the form of stories told to the younger children, girls and boys alike, by parents, grandparents, aunts and uncles. The coyote was a favorite subject of these tales because it was thought of as a brother to the Comanche. The coyote was considered a lookout for a band on the move; if a warrior or priest had coyote medicine,* he was able to see into the future. An example of a coyote story is the following, translated word for word from *Comanche Texts:*

> Long ago it is said somewhere there in the big prairie, prairie dogs had a town. Those ones, having gathered together, were dancing much. As they were continuing that way, Coyote arrived among them.
> That one said, —You all are dancing—
> —Yes,— they said.
> —All of you shut your house tightly. We will dance. All keep coming, all keep coming,— said the coyote. —All of you dancing, holding hands with each other, come with your eyes tightly closed.—
> Then, as they began to dance, that one takes a big club. From one end that one came clubbing them. One of them peeping saw the coyote. That one said, —Everyone run. He is coming clubbing us.—
> Those ones ran to their houses. As they are still unable to open their door, that coyote clubbed many. Then that one, making a big fire, roasted in ashes those prairie dogs. There that one ate good of the clubbing.[4]

---

* "Medicine" was power over natural and supernatural forces, derived from obedience to a source such as the coyote that was revealed through an individual's spiritual vision.[3]

The ability to deceive, as evidenced by the preceding story, was a valued trait. To trick one's enemy was often to pave the way to victory. In another story Coyote chances upon Turtle, who is busy roasting prairie dogs. Coyote convinces Turtle to race to see who gets to eat the prairie dogs. Turtle agrees only after Coyote ties a big rock to his own leg. Then they both start the race, with Coyote soon outdistancing Turtle and disappearing over a hill. Turtle instantly runs back to the fire, pulls the prairie dogs out by their tails, and eats them as quickly as he can. Soon all the meat is gone and only the tails are left. Coyote returns, very tired. He pulls the tails out of the fire. Turtle laughs as Coyote goes to the lake where Turtle has discarded the bones. Coyote says as he gnaws on the bones, "I can't be cheated myself, I thought. . . . you, little turtle, cheated me, beat me." Turtle laughs loudly at him. "I did beat you by cheating," he says.[5]

Clearly, the ability to deceive was desirable, but being over-confident in one's skill in deception could result in embarrassment, as it did for Coyote. On such occasions, The People laughed.

Born and raised a Comanche whose mother, though white, had been thoroughly assimilated into the culture, and whose father was a renowned chief, it is not surprising that Quanah, like most Comanche boys, was a warrior by the time he had lived fifteen winters. Some white boys captured by the Indians also became warriors when very young. Herman Lehmann was made a war chief among the Apaches, his original captors, in his early teens. Two years later, he was a leading warrior of the Comanches, having escaped from the Apaches after a feud developed within his band that forced him to defend himself against the principal medicine man, killing him. White captives Clinton Smith and Dot Babb were Comanche warriors at an unusually early age because at the time they were captured, veteran warriors were being killed at an alarming rate in raids by other Indians, Texas cowboys, Mexican vaqueros, U.S. troops, and buffalo hunters. Babb, taken from his home near Decatur in northwest Texas at the age of thirteen, became a warrior almost immediately. Smith was twelve when he went on horse stealing raids, and he rode into battle when he was thirteen. Smith said, "As I grew older my chief pushed me to the front with the warriors, and it seemed the longer I stayed with them the more fights they had, and I was forced to do my share of the fighting."[6]

Both the continuous warfare and disease were indeed taking a heavy toll of all Indians as Quanah was learning to be a warrior; however, The People continued to fight. They had always fought, and they knew that war was the only means of claiming and maintaining control of their hunting grounds. Despite their losses, by the time Quanah became a war leader, The People were once again expanding their frontiers, driving the line of settlement back. Land gained by conquest over other tribes was, of course, nothing new; it had been taking place long before the incursion of white settlers into Comanchería. In the early 1850s, for example, bands of Comanches and Apaches exacted a grisly toll of each other's warriors in a battle for control over land in northern Mexico (or possibly the Trans-Pecos region of Texas). Nelson Lee, at that time a captive of the Comanches, provided an eye-witness account of the battle:

> As yet . . . I had seen nothing of an enemy, and only drew the inference there was one present from the cries I had heard, and the general commotion that prevailed. In the course of two or three minutes after our line formed on the ridge, the air was rent with the noise of the war whoop, and up the opposite ascent, at full speed, came the Apaches in solid body, like a black cloud. As they approached, a shower of arrows were discharged from both lines, when they rushed upon each other in a hand-to-hand encounter.
>
> From the position I occupied I had a fair, unobstructed view of the battle. It was fierce and terrible. The horses reared, and plunged, and fell upon each other, their riders dealing

blow for blow, and thrust for thrust, some falling from their saddles to the ground, and others trampling madly over them.

The Comanches outnumbered the enemy; nevertheless, they were forced to retreat, falling back down the hill almost to my position; but still they were not pursued, the Apaches appearing to be content to hold possession of the ground. Soon, the tribe of the Spotted Leopard again rallied and dashed once more to the attack. If possible, this contest was severer, as it was longer than the first. Again the fierce blow was given and returned; again horses and men intermingled in the melee—stumbled, fell, and rolled upon the ground, while the wide heavens resounded with their hideous shrieks and cries.[7]

Soon after this battle, the Comanche band with whom Lee lived in captivity made peace with the Apaches in that region. Faced with the necessity of fighting the white man, the Indian bands had begun to realize that they could not afford to maintain the regular losses of manpower they suffered when they fought against each other. These Comanche and Apache bands now chose to live in harmony in the arid mountains of the Chihuahuan Desert.

Yet the Comanches were confident that they would drive the whites out of Comanchería. As proof of this confidence, Chief Rolling Thunder showed his white captive, Nelson Lee, the ruins of a former civilization built by giant white people. Rolling Thunder told Lee this legend about the abandoned village:

> . . . innumerable moons ago, a race of white men, ten feet high, and far more rich and powerful than any white people now living, here inhabited a large range of country, extending from the rising to the setting sun. . . . They excelled every other nation which has flourished, either before or since, in all manner of cunning handicraft—were brave and warlike. . . . At length, in the height of their power and glory, when they remembered justice and mercy no more and became

proud and lifted up, the Great Spirit descended from above, sweeping them with fire and deluge from the face of the earth. In like manner the day will surely come when the present white race, which is driving the Indians before it, and despoiling them of their inheritance, and which, in the confidence of its strength, has become arrogant and boastful and forgotten God, will be swept from existence.[8]

The Comanches had been suspicious of the aggressiveness of the Anglo-American settlers on the edge of Comanchería from the beginning, yet their natural compassion (and, in 1818, their ignorance of what was to follow) led them to allow David G. Burnet to live near them and among them while he regained his health after more than a year of roaming the prairies, living as the Indians did, eating only buffalo and other wild meats and sleeping in the open. By the time he reached West Texas, he was so weak it was difficult for him to mount his horse unaided. Without the help of the Comanches he would likely have died. Yet in a prophetic letter he wrote in Nacogdoches in 1818, he said, "It would not be altogether visionary to predict, that in the course of a few years, these obscure and unnoticed savages will evince their claims to our attention by the massacres and devastations of a border warfare."[9] Having lived among the Comanches, Burnet (later to become first President of the Republic of Texas) knew their culture better than any Anglo-Texan leader would know it until the advent of Sam Houston. And he realized that they waged war for two reasons only: plunder and revenge.

Other insights into the Indians' struggle to adjust to their changing circumstances come from Colonel Edward Stiff, who made a fact-finding trip to Texas in the mid-1830s. He described the Comanches as "uncommon fine looking men and women; some of them exhibiting the most perfect symmetry united with a muscular and athletic frame; the countenances strongly marked; indicative of intelligence and generosity; while that of others bespeak the wily knave, and cunning lurks in every feature."[10] He was very much impressed with their extraordinary horseman- ship, and described them to be "mostly honest in their intercourse with the whites, and would scorn an act of perfidy, particularly in small affairs; they are kind and generous to a fault."[11] In a clear warning to the Texans, however, Stiff wrote, "Were this tribe provoked to hostilities, or induced to believe that peace was not for their interest and honor, the present population of Texas would be exterminated and their homes made desolate in a brief space of time. So, ye wise ones, beware."[12]

At about the same time that Colonel Stiff was collecting his data, the northern Comanches and several allied bands from the Plains were having a big powwow on the headwaters of the Arkansas River. Rachel Plummer, captured in the attack on Park- er's Fort, by this time had lived with the Indians long enough to have learned the Comanche tongue. Mrs. Plummer was pres- ent at the council, enduring the blows of the warriors as they sought to keep her away from the proceedings. Still hoping to escape or to be ransomed,* Mrs. Plummer thought it important to listen to the speeches of the various Indian leaders. Here is her description of the great encampment and what was discussed in council:

> The council was held upon a high eminence, descending every way. The encampments were as close as they could stand, and how far they extended I know not; for I could not see the outer edge of them with my naked eye. . . . A number of traditional ceremonies were performed, such as would be of little interest to the reader. This ceremony occupied about three days, after which they came to a determination to invade and take possession of Texas. It was agreed that those tribes

---

* Rachel Plummer was later ransomed, after a captivity of twenty-one months, by traders from New Mexico.

of Indians who were in the habit of raising corn, should cultivate the farms of the people of Texas; the prairie Indians were to have entire control of the prairies, each party to defend each other. After having taken Texas, killed and driven out the inhabitants, and the corn growing Indians had raised a good supply, they were to attack Mexico. There they expected to be joined by a large number of Mexicans who are disaffected with the government, as also a number that would or could be coerced into measures of subordination, they would soon possess themselves of Mexico. They would then attack the United States.[13]

Probably thousands of Plains Indians were in attendance at this great war council, but the independence of scattered bands, especially among the Comanches; the constant movement from one camp site to another; and, perhaps, the absence of one great war leader, doomed the grand plan to failure. As much as The People hated the white intruders, their lack of organization precluded their annihilation of the whites. White men would have to be killed one by one by warriors claiming individual heroism. Terror would be the Indians' ally, but most of the whites they hoped to eliminate were, as the Spanish had been in their first two centuries in the American Southwest, desperate men of courage and drive who thought their moment in history had arrived. Their lust for land and sense of racial superiority equipped the Anglo-Celtic settlers to endure all manner of hardships for the ultimate goal of possessing land. As Arthur K. Moore describes them in *The Frontier Mind,* these frontiersmen were

Unquestionably primitive, nature's noblemen . . . outraged romantics by their violence and animality. While readily approving that part of the progressivist program leading to luxury, they debased the concept of progress by rejecting the arts and sciences. . . . This is not altogether to withhold credit from the picturesque barbarians who harassed the Indians from Kentucky to the Pacific.[14]

Quanah, as a Comanche, had no understanding of the whites
who wanted to usurp the land, whose world view was based upon
the changing of nature. Such an idea, such an approach to living,
was unthinkable to a Comanche. His whole being—his very existence—depended upon Mother Earth as the Great Spirit had created her. Could the white man make a better world than the
Creator himself? The idea was contemptible. So were the people
whose lives revolved around such a principle. He was to become
a warrior and a chief to defend his people against the whites—and,
ironically, he was also to become one of those who bridged the
gap in cultures with conciliation and diplomacy.

That was a lifetime later. Quanah the child had rejoiced with
the rest of the band when his father returned from his many
successful raids into Texas and Mexico, and the night would be
filled with the glow of firelight and the echo of rhythmic drumming as Comanche warriors chanted their triumphs and danced
until dawn lightened the eastern sky. The Noconis (Wanderers),
Kotsotekas (Buffalo Eaters), and Quahadas (Antelope Eaters)*
would fill the canyons of Comanchería with sounds of pristine
exultation.

To become one of these warriors, according to Comanche
custom, Quanah had first to dance the Eagle Dance, sponsored
by Peta Nocona, who had named him Eagle after the massacre at
Pease River.† This amounted to a religious rite, although, unlike
other Plains tribes, the Comanches had no religious organization
or priestly class. According to the historian Ernest Wallace, "Every
man was his own priest and his own prophet—the individual

* There were no boundaries between bands, and any Comanche was free to live with
and hunt with whichever band he chose.
† Aubrey Birdsong, Quanah's son-in-law, wrote in his "Reminiscences of Quanah
Parker" that Peta Nocona renamed Quanah "Tseeta," the Eagle, after Ross's victory
at Pease River. Thereafter, he had two names, but was known mainly as Quanah.

interpreter of the wills and ways of the spirits. . . . Power came in mystic visitations, a dream phenomenon or hallucinatory experience. Its authority was absolute; psychic experiences were socially recognized and regarded as the very cornerstone of Comanche cultural life."[15]

A medicine man with strong power was the leader of the Eagle Dance. "He and the dancers arose before daylight, went to the creek, bathed, stripped to the breechclout, put on war paint, let their hair down and put eagle feathers in it, and rubbed themselves with sage. After that they sat in a semicircle with the opening toward the east and smoked ceremonially."[16] After each participant had smoked, the medicine man led the young dancers to a nearby camp, where they "captured" a girl, who was in reality a captive adopted by an Indian family. The girl's family made a show of protecting her, but allowed the "raiders" to take the captive to their camp, where the participants entered a tepee. All sat close together facing east, the direction from which the sun first appeared to start the new day. The girl sat beside the leader, while the dancers formed a circle around the drummers, who numbered two, four, or six, never an odd number.

"Each dancer," Wallace writes, "carried in his right hand a rattle, decorated with feathers, paint, and beads, and in his left hand carried a wand or fan prepared from the wing feathers of an eagle. The dancers were young eagles attempting to leave their nest and parental care in order to soar away, masters of the sky," and instead of singing they imitated the cry of the young eagle. Between dances, individual warriors rushed into the circle and told of outstanding coups they had performed. Their recital of heroic deeds had to be true, because "the power of eagle medicine was so strong that misfortune would result to any who on this solemn occasion falsified the facts. Spectators looked on in reverential silence."[17]

After the failure of the captive girl's family to recapture her, they brought gifts and put them in front of her. The medicine man took some of the gifts and gave the remainder to the dancers. Eagle dancers frequently received horses as gifts, and it is likely that Quanah received a fine war horse from his father, great war chief of The People.

As powerful as was the Eagle Dance in the life of a young warrior, his own personal vision was paramount in a Comanche's life. All young warriors sought such a vision, for through it would come the source of the power they believed would be their sustenance. In an interview at Fort Sill years later, Quanah said, "Sometimes a Comanche man dreams and a big bear comes and tells him you do this—you paint your face this way. I help you—if he sees bear in his dreams then he makes medicine* that way."[18] (Quanah was described as wearing a necklace of bear claws in the Battle of Cañon Blanco in 1871.) All of the dances had spiritual significance, especially the Eagle Dance, but bear medicine was clearly the source of Quanah's power.

The young Eagle of the Comanches was soon exhibiting his power and courage on the war trail, usually with bands of Quahadas, striking out from their strongholds along the Canadian River, Tule Canyon, the headwaters of the Brazos and Red Rivers of northwest Texas, to targets in Mexico, even though raids there were becoming more difficult.

There was a long history of Comanche raids on Mexico, although other tribes contented themselves with other areas. Late in the eighteenth century, the pressure the Comanche warriors had been exerting on the Apaches resulted in The People's taking over prairies rich in buffalo and driving the Apaches into the mountains of New Mexico, where they delighted in raiding the

---

*That is, he derives power from obedience to the bear's instructions, which, if followed correctly, will give great power through the bear's spiritual strength.

Spanish colonists and sedentary Pueblo cultures up and down the Rio Grande. In 1786, the Governor of Santa Fe, Don Juan Bautista de Anza, after a successful military campaign, effected a treaty with the northern bands of The People that called for fairs and free trade at Pecos Pueblo, Santa Fe, and Taos, but northern Mexico had no protection from Comanche raids. It had been the favorite target for marauding Comanches for generations. On the vast, thinly populated *ranchos* of the Mexican north grazed thousands of cattle and horses. Widely spaced adobe huts were home to many a family set upon by Comanches in the nights when there was a full moon. Men were either killed or captured for torture and slavery; women were raped, and, if strong enough, taken captive. Children were almost always made captives. By the mid-1800s, every Comanche village held Mexicans captive. No wonder the Mexican town crier called out "Los Bárbaros! Los Bárbaros!" whenever Comanche warriors rode into a settlement. Historian Carl Coke Rister presents an example of the Mexicans' fear:

> Captain John Pope, in 1853, told of an incident in which a single Comanche, even at mid-day, had dashed at full speed into the square of Durango, and by his mere presence had caused the hasty closing of the stores and public places and the rapid retreat of a population of 30,000 souls to their barred houses.[19]

In 1868, Quanah was one of the Comanches who still raided Mexican as well as Texan settlements; in 1867, over one-third of the Comanches, including the Quahadas, had refused to put their "mark" on the Treaty of Medicine Lodge. In June of that year, Congress had authorized a commission to secure a lasting peace with the Indians, and on October 21, 1867, the Treaty of Medicine Lodge was signed by a considerable portion of the Kiowas and Comanches, including the reluctant Chief Ten Bears. Article I of the treaty stated that "From this day forward all wars between the parties to this agreement shall forever cease."[20] In addition to giving up most of the hunting grounds the two tribes had shared for generations, the Indians were to ". . . have the privilege to select, in the presence and with the assistance of the agent then in charge, a tract of land within said reservation, not exceeding three hundred and twenty acres in extent . . . and held in the exclusive possession of the person selecting it, and of his family, so long as he or they may continue to cultivate it."[21]

To till the soil upon which the grass and trees grew was against the most basic of Plains Indians' beliefs. As nomadic hunters and gatherers, the Comanches and Kiowas had always harvested the fruits of the land the Creator had made for them. The idea of an individual Indian owning land was as incomprehensible to a Comanche or a Kiowa as was the tilling of the soil. Tribal life was based upon the welfare of the whole. Individual honors could be won in war or in the hunt alone, and the sharing of possessions with one's neighbors was an integral part of the culture.

Article X of the treaty promised the Indians $25,000 worth of clothing to be issued on each 15th of October for the next thirty years. "For each male person over fourteen years of age, a suit of good, substantial woolen clothing, consisting of coat, pantaloons, flannel shirt, hat, and a pair of homemade socks."[22] Clothes were also pledged to women and to children under the age of fourteen.

In addition to the promises to clothe them, make farmers of them, and school them, none of which the Indians wanted, Article XI was particularly onerous. It stated that "In consideration of the advantages and benefits conferred by this treaty and the many pledges of friendship by the United States, the tribes who are parties to this agreement, hereby stipulate that they will relinquish all right to occupy, permanently, the territory, outside of their reservation, as herein defined, but they yet reserve the right to hunt on any lands south of the Arkansas River, so long as the buffalo may range thereon in such numbers as to justify the chase."[23]

The real intent of the treaty was to exact from the tribes their agreement not to attack "any persons at home, or traveling, nor molest or disturb any wagon trains, coaches, mules or cattle belonging to the people of the United States. . . . They will never kill nor scalp white men nor attempt to do them harm."[24]

Quanah attended the council at Medicine Lodge, and afterward he said, "I went and heard it—there were many soldiers there—the council was an immense one 'a great many rows.' The soldier chief said . . . you must remember one thing and hold fast to it and that is you must stop going on the war path. . . ."[25]

As unrealistic as were the promises to clothe the Indians in the garb of the whites and to make farmers of them, were the exacting of promises from them to cease their raiding. The buffalo range of Comanchería had constricted considerably since the Texans' successful War of Independence against Mexico in 1836, and while the Comanches had succeeded in pushing back the line of white settlement in the 1860s, the abandoned ranches and blackened chimneys of burned cabins offered them little solace. Their success served only to enrich them in stolen livestock and to adorn their scalp poles with the hair of white men and women; the buffalo had vacated the area, never to return. The warfare between tribes that had raged on the southern plains long before the advent of the white man had been inspired by the need for food and individual achievement. Washington, therefore, was naive in the extreme to expect men of a nomadic warrior society dependent upon the buffalo for food and shelter to acquiesce to the provisions of the Treaty of Medicine Lodge. Certainly the Quahadas, led by Bull Elk, Wild Horse, Parra-o-coom, and the young Quanah, did not accede to the provisions of the treaty. And they certainly had no intentions of sparing Mexico.

In 1868, just one year after the Treaty of Medicine Lodge, Kiowa chief Tohausen led a raid to Chihuahua. According to Quanah, who was one of the nine who made up Tohausen's war party, a leader on a raid had a lot of responsibility. In 1897, he told Captain Hugh Scott,

> A leader's road is a hard road. Some men are good leaders of war parties. Everybody knows who they are. Sometimes he meets a man and tells him he is going on warpath and wants him to go along—then another and another and after a while he calls a council and says he is going on warpath against the Pawnees and fills a pipe and offers it to a man to smoke—if the man smokes the pipe he say yes he will go on war path with him—one night they go into a big lodge . . . they sit down in a circle sing—one man beating on a lodge pole—on a drum with a stick for a little while not long—then they take a hard hide, men and women holding, all carried it drumming and singing until the middle of the night and then stop—this is done the night before they start out—a war party usually goes at the full of the moon as to have the moon to travel by— they want moonlight when they get there so as to see to find horses . . . at night—if near a mountain they climb up and remain hidden in the timber looking about during day and come down at night—they usually attack at daylight if they are in sufficient force to make a bold attack. When the leader starts out he mounts his horse and holds his pipe with stem down in his left hand with his reins.[26]

This is Quanah's own account of the 1868 raid on Chihuahua, one led by a renowned chief, but ultimately doomed to failure:

> . . . Tohausen was holding the pipe . . . and we went to war in Chihuahua on the other side of the big river—there were nine of us all riding mules—that was a long way to go and a horse soon gets tired so we rode mules—the Kiowa camp was on the Canadian River at the Antelope Hills—we went past the head of the Red River [Big Sandy River] up on to the Staked Plains [high flat country] and we were two days without water

twice—we travelled for a month—we did not go fast on account of the mules, and sometimes when we struck a good camp we remained in it 4 or 5 days until the mules got rested until finally we reached an Apache camp [Mescalero] and remained there for some time. Then we went on the warpath across the Rio Grande until we came near some high mountains when the leader said hobble the mules and turn them loose here . . . put your saddles and robes in this tree . . . we could see all around—there were streams running out of the mountains—many white man's house and we could hear the children talking.

Tohausen said you stay here until I come back—I am going to look for horses . . . we went looking for horses but did not find any and pretty soon Tohausen said we must go up on a mountain tired out—we kept going that way for ten nights—where the white man's houses are thick they keep their horses hidden and they are hard to find—on the 10th night we found some horses and were saved—we started back travelling on the horses and one day we killed a calf—we had had nothing to eat for two days and everybody was hungry—we made a fire in a small creek bed and were turning the meat before the flames—everybody hungry and watching the meat when someone looked up and said "here come some Mexicans"—there were 4 Mexicans coming who had not seen us yet—we threw the meat and the fire into the creek and Tohausen said to hide well in the brush and not to kill these men unless they find us—if they find us kill them all and if one gets away and gives the alarm the Mexicans will surround us and kill us all . . . they were laughing and joking—we kept hidden they rode off in a different direction without seeing us and we were saved—we rode on until we got the mules and saddles and travelled back until we met a big Mescalero and Quahada Comanche camp where we stayed for our mules were played out and our moccasins worn out—here we met another Kiowa war party who told us the Kiowa village had moved to the forks of Lone and Beaver Creeks . . . when they started south.

One day our leader said I am going on warpath into Mexico what are you going to do . . . I and two other men said, "we are going back to the Kiowa village," so we started back across the Staked Plains—when we came to the head of Red River my mule played out . . . and I came back on foot . . . I went on then to Salt Fork—that place the Kiowas often went to get salt at a salt spring where I looked for tracks— I saw some old horse tracks and said these were made by a war party. I next went on to Walnut Creek (North Fork of the Red River) beyond the end of the mountains and looked for tracks but did not find any—there I waited for the other two men and we slept there that night—next day when the morning star was rising, I got up and the other two men said you go over toward the Washita and look for tracks on little creek this side and we . . . will join you there . . . then I went over a divide on to the head of a little creek that runs into the Washita . . . there I saw some people—they had no lodges but had horses and I couldn't tell what people they were so I crept down the bed of the stream until I could hear their talk and they were talking Kiowa—then I spoke to them and they were astonished to see me and said you left a long time ago on the warpath and now you have come back. I said, "Where is the Kiowa village?" and they replied you walk on foot down the bed of the river and you will get there before the sun goes down—and they packed their horses and we found a large village and my own lodge was with theirs and that was when I first heard that the Cheyennes had been wiped out on Washita (Black Kettle's band) by white soldiers [Nov. 27, 1868] . . . Two days after the other two men got in and said their mules had been lost for one day and I pretty fast walk.[27]

In a council that preceded Quanah's first notable actions as a warrior, Asa-habi said, "The white soldiers fight us when we try to go across the Rio Grande to raid in Mexico, although they themselves used to fight the Mexicans, and I do not see why they want to help them now. If we slip past them and go, they are on the watch when we come back. We can easily get a great many horses and mules there, but we are likely to lose them if we have to fight the white soldiers."[28] Tabby-nanaka agreed, saying, "There are many white people living below Red River, and toward the rising sun. They do not have big herds. We can get only six or eight at one place, and the white men all have guns and there is more danger of someone getting killed. But I think that is the best way for our young men to go."[29]

The others concurred, and in a few days Quanah was riding with a band of Comanche warriors south and east toward the settlements. They crossed Pease River, where the young Eagle's mother had been captured, and struck the isolated farms and ranches almost to Gainesville. From widely scattered homesteads, the warriors gathered a large herd of horses and mules, then headed home. Fort Richardson near Jacksboro had been alerted in the meantime, and as the warriors rode toward the Staked Plains, the soldiers caught up with them near Red River and opened fire. Bear's Ear, who was leading the raid, was killed in the attack. In the midst of the confusion, Quanah quickly took control. "Spread out!" he shouted to his companions. "Turn the horses north to the river!"[30]

In giving this command, Quanah departed from the original plan of crossing the river farther west. His decisive action undoubtedly saved many of his fellow warriors' lives, for the Indians had a long tradition of losing their sense of direction when their war chief went down. Quanah's companions, "though dismayed by the loss of Bear's Ear, responded bravely to the voice of a new command. They shouted on to those ahead, and they in turn swung the stolen herd about and raced for the stream. Quanah, keeping the rear, urged them on. The ground was rough, and both Indians and horses had to scatter. One of the soldiers almost caught up with Quanah, and a bullet whizzed past his ear. He swung down under his horse's neck and fitted an arrow to his bow. If he turned his pony and exposed its side, the pursuing soldier was sure to shoot it. But a large clump of bushes lay ahead, and circling this, the young warrior drew himself upright and headed back toward his foe. They were less than a hundred feet apart when the soldier fired his revolver, the bullet grazing Quanah's thigh. Quanah's arrow struck the white man's shoulder, causing him to drop his gun and turn back, leaning low in his saddle. Bullets from the other soldiers were singing about him as Quanah wheeled his pony and raced after his companions."[31]

Fortunately, there was no quicksand in the river where Quanah and his fellow warriors were forced to cross. Along with their stolen stock they swam safely to the other side, while the soldiers, after some deliberation, decided not to cross Red River. Thus, the Comanches escaped with their booty, though mourning the loss of Bear's Ear. Because of Quanah's courage, that night when they camped they chose him as their leader.

Quanah was now one of the leaders of the hard-riding bands of Comanches who terrorized the Texas frontier, stealing stock, killing men, and kidnapping women and children. All the women and girls on the frontier preferred death to captivity, as all had heard the horrible stories of what happened to grown women and teen-aged girls held captive and later released by the Indians. The custom among the Comanches and Kiowas had long been to share captive women with each member of the raiding party. When they reached camp, the warrior who had captured a woman would be her master, and he could use her as he saw fit.

The fear of Comanche raiders electrified the imaginations even of those who had not yet been touched by the loss of a family member to death or captivity, and many loaded up their meager possessions and departed for points east. By the time of the Civil War, according to Texas pioneer Floyd Holmes,

> . . . the situation was truly deplorable all along the line of
> frontier. The Indians had stolen nearly all the horses in the
> country, and kept on stealing and committing their barbaric

practices on the whites whenever opportunities presented themselves.

Every day brought to us the sad intelligence of the killing and scalping of some one or more of the settlers and of houses being attacked and robbed and women and children being carried off captives.

Truly it was a gloomy time, for neither life nor property was safe at this time. The few citizens of Comanche were forted up in about three places, to-wit: Comanche, South Leon and Cora, now extinct. Most assuredly we were in a tight [sic]. We were afoot, only a few in number, and whenever one would go out on the range he was either chased in or lost his scalp.[32]

One spring in the mid-1860s, when it was time for the white farmers of Comanche to plant their crops, they sent a messenger to the state government requesting help, but they received no response. The people of Bell County, however, sent to the hungry citizens of Comanche five wagons loaded with flour, pulled by teams of oxen and escorted by forty mounted, well-armed men. But even with these reinforcements the raids continued, and Holmes was set afoot five different times by Indian horse thieves. In addition, he wrote, "I lost three work-oxen killed, and about thirty head of grown hogs, all killed in two beds at one time by the redskins. When spring opened up and the Indians were gone out of the country, I had only one ox that I could call my own. The horses were all gone, the hogs and oxen were killed, and I had abandoned home to save the life of myself and family."[33]

So throughout much of the decade of the 1860s, the Comanches and Kiowas were on the offensive. Cheyenne and Arapahos fought the rugged frontiersmen of Colorado and Kansas, while sweeping down at times to raid with the Comanches and Kiowas into Texas and Mexico. But the last chapter of the Comanches' reign over the southern Plains was to begin with the conclusion of the Civil War. Hungry, tired, wounded Texans straggled home from the great conflict, having sacrificed their best and brightest for a cause they considered worthy. Confederate veterans looked to the vast grasslands of Texas, stretching away in mostly arid landscapes from South Texas through the Hill Country and on to Parker, Jack, and surrounding counties to the west and north of Fort Worth. Wild cattle abounded in the brush country and on the open meadows of the state. Everywhere, cow hunting was a rewarding occupation. When there was no outside pressure on their grazing lands, longhorns and buffalo prospered together. Wild cattle numbered in the millions, furnishing war-weary Texans with instant food and a cash crop on the hoof. Based upon Spanish-Mexican methods of ranching, the Texas cattle industry was on the verge of expanding across the wide reaches of rolling prairie, stark canyons, the level llano, and, far to the west, the arid mountains of the rugged Trans-Pecos. But in order to fully succeed, the Texas cowmen needed the range for the use of their cattle alone. They did not want to share it with Indian raiders. Many favored John Baylor's solution: extermination of the red men. Extermination would stop the raiding, and whites could seize the Indian lands.

Quanah, however, was determined not to make the white man's job an easy one. Like any other Comanche warrior, he was brave and generous, but extremely dangerous when provoked to violence. Such were all the fighting men of his time, white and red alike. In describing the Comanches, Carl Rister writes,

> As is generally true with other people, tradition and environment strongly influenced the virtues, vices, and religious conceptions of the Indians. Their virtues and vices should not be measured by the standards of their white enemies, for they were the products of a primitive culture; nor should it be said that they had no ideas of right and wrong. . . . Perhaps the warrior's propensity to boast, to steal, to vent his rage in cruel torture, and to indulge in sexual improprieties, were the traits

most severely condemned by the border white settler. But under his primitive code these things, under certain circumstances, were permissible. For example, the "eye-for-an-eye" code was accepted by all southern plains warriors.[34]

Just as the white warriors detested certain characteristics of the Comanches and Kiowas, so also did the Indians despise the whites, especially the hated *Tejanos*. "The inconsistencies of the traders and ne'er-do-wells—outlaws and occasional designing agents—with whom the warrior had trade and treaty relations, caused the latter to have little faith in the white man's claim to superior virtue."[35]

But the all-out torture of captured white men that was the norm for most Comanche villages was probably the most inflammatory issue with the Texans. Examples abounded, and although treatment varied from band to band depending on the personality of the leader, most Comanches tortured their white male captives. The Comanches who captured Nelson Lee and three of his comrades on a lonely stretch of trail somewhere between Eagle Pass, Texas, and El Paso were barbarous indeed.

Lee, after serving as a Ranger for several years, had formed a partnership with a man named Aikens to drive horses to California. While he and the other men were sleeping, the lookouts also having fallen asleep, the Comanches attacked. Startled awake by the shrill chorus of war whoops, Lee sprang to his feet, grabbed his rifle, drew the butt of the gun to his shoulder and sought a painted, shrieking target. But a lasso quickly settled over his head, and he was jerked violently to the ground. Instantly, several Indians sprang upon him, one holding him by the throat. In short order he was stripped of his clothes and bound. As the Indians examined his clothes for plunder, Lee's alarm watch, which he had bought in New Orleans not long before, went off. It was three-thirty in the morning, the usual hour for rising and beginning the day's work. The awe with which his captors viewed the watch made Lee an instant curiosity, and thus saved his life. Upon being taken to the Comanches' village, Lee become the vassal of Chief Big Wolf. (Later he would be traded for a large number of furs to the cruel Spotted Leopard and, finally, to the dignified Rolling Thunder, from whom he eventually escaped.)

Chief Big Wolf frequently required Lee to perform his "spiritual" rituals with the alarm.[36] So the watch saved him from the horror that was to befall two of his companions. Here is his description of the torture rite of that band of Comanches:

> On arriving, I found my fellow captives had preceded me, and at once comprehended some terrible scene would ensue. There were Aikens, Martin, and Stewart, stripped entirely naked, and bound as follows: Strong, high posts had been driven in the ground about three feet apart. Standing between them, their arms had been drawn up as far as they could reach, the right hand tied to the stake opposite. Their feet, likewise, were tied to the posts near the ground. Martin and Stewart were thus strung up side by side. Directly in front of them, and within ten feet, was Aikens, in the same situation. A short time sufficed to divest me of my scanty Indian apparel and place me by the side of the latter, and in like condition. Thus we stood, or rather hung. Aikens and myself facing Stewart and Martin, all awaiting in tormenting suspense to learn what diabolical rite was now to be performed.
>
> The Big Wolf and a number of his old men stationed themselves near us, when the war chief, at the head of the warriors, of whom there were probably two hundred, moved forward slowly, silently, and in single file. Their pace was peculiar and difficult to describe, half walk, half shuffle, a spasmodic, nervous motion, like the artificial motion of figures in a puppet show. Each carried in one hand his knife or tomahawk, in the other a flint stone, three inches or more in length and fashioned into the shape of a sharp pointed arrow. The head of the procession as it circled a long way round, first approached Stewart and Martin. As it passed them, two

of the youngest warriors broke from the line, seized them by the hair and scalped them, then resumed their places and moved on. This operation consists of cutting only a portion of the skin which covers the skull, of the dimension of a dollar, and does not necessarily destroy life, as is very generally supposed; on the contrary, I have seen men, resident of the borders of Texas, who had been scalped and yet were alive and well. In this instance, the wounds inflicted were by no means mortal; nevertheless, blood flowed from them in profusion, running down over the face, and trickling from their long beards.

They passed Aikens and myself without molestation, marching round again in the same order as before. Up to this time there had been entire silence, except a yell from the two young men when in the act of scalping, but now the whole party halted a half-minute and slapping their hands upon their mouths, united in a general and energetic war whoop. Then in silence the circuitous march was continued. When they reached Stewart and Martin the second time, the sharp flint arrowheads were brought into requisition. Each man, as he passed, with a wild screech, would brandish his tomahawk in their faces for an instant, and then draw the sharp point of the stone across their bodies, not cutting deep, but penetrating the flesh just far enough to cause the blood to ooze out in great crimson gouts. By the time the line had passed, our poor suffering companions presented an awful spectacle. Still they left Aikens and myself as yet unharmed; nevertheless, we regarded it as a matter of certainty that very soon we would be subjected to similar tortures. We would have been devoutly thankful at that terrible hour—would have hailed it as a grateful privilege—could we have been permitted to choose our own mode of being put to death. How many times they circled round, halting to sound the war whoop, and going through the same demonic exercise, I cannot tell. Suffice it to say, they persisted in the hellish work until every inch of the bodies of the unhappy men was haggled, and hacked and scarified, and covered with clotted blood. It would have been a relief to me, much more to them, could they have only died, but the object of the tormentors was to drain the fountain of their lives by slow degrees.

In the progress of their torture, there occurred an intermission of some quarter of an hour. During this period, some threw themselves on the ground and lighted their pipes, others collected in little groups, all, however, laughing and shouting, and pointing their fingers at the prisoners in derision, as if taunting them as cowards and miscreants . . . I hung down my head and closed my eyes to shut out from sight the heart-sickening scene before me, but this poor comfort was vouchsafed me. They would grasp myself, as well as Aikens, by the hair, drawing our heads back violently, compelling us, however unwillingly, to stare directly at the agonized and writhing sufferers.

At the end of, perhaps, two hours, came the last act of the fearful tragedy. The warriors halted on their last round in the form of a half-circle, when two of them moved out from the center, striking into the war dance, raising the war song, advancing, receding, now moving to the right, now to the left, occupying ten minutes in proceeding as many paces. Finally, they reached the victims, for some time danced before them, as it were, the hideous dance of hell, then threw their hatchets suddenly, and sent the bright blades crashing through their skulls.[37]

Quanah's band treated male prisoners quite differently than did the warriors of Big Wolf. The father of Reverend A. E. Butterfield, pioneer missionary to the Comanches during the early reservation years (1867–1901), was captured along with another soldier near Tahlequah, Oklahoma, by Quanah's band shortly after the close of the Civil War. Having heard the tales of Comanche torture, the white men expected to suffer a slow, painful death. But to their surprise, Quanah informed the prisoners that only an attempt to escape would bring them harm. According to Ben Moore in his *7 Years with the Wild Indians*, this is what happened next:

Butterfield wisely feigned perfect contentment, but after a few days his companion begged to be released, whereupon a proposition was made by the Indians in that they were to form a double line of warriors, one hundred yards in length, one warrior standing every ten feet with bow and only one arrow each. The victim was to be set free provided he emerged alive at the lower end of the gauntlet. Needless to say, he did not return to Texas.[38]

Six months passed, and Butterfield remained in Quanah's constantly migrating camp. He was surprised when one of the Eagle's wives offered him a plan of escape. It is not clear from Moore's account which of Quanah's wives offered to help the white prisoner. At this time, according to pioneer Olive King Dixon, Quanah was already married to Weckeah, daughter of Old Bear. Since Moore mentions "wives" in his narrative, it is not possible to ascertain whether Quanah had more than two wives at the time of Butterfield's captivity, but his second wife, Chony, was surely with Quanah at his camp just after the Civil War.

Olive King Dixon's account of Quanah's marriage to his first wife was taken from conversations with Charles Goodnight and Baldwin Parker, Quanah's son, in the 1920s. Dixon states: "After Quanah was grown he fell in love with Red Bear's daughter.* She and Quanah had grown up together and had been close companions which ripened into love."[39] Chief Old Bear opposed the union (after his father's death Quanah was often spurned by those who hated his white blood), so Quanah, along with several other young braves and their women, "stole the girl and ran away, locating at the headwaters of the Concho River. He remained there several years. Soon other bands of young people would break away from

* According to Quanah's grandson, James Cox, Old Bear was the correct name of the father of the chief's first wife, Weckeah.

their parent tribes and join the new settlement until the number of Quanah's followers was over 100."⁴⁰ Old Bear eventually gave in and went to have council with Quanah over the value of his daughter. The Eagle gave his father-in-law twenty ponies for his daughter. "As he did so, he remarked he knew where he could steal as many more from a nearby ranch the next night. The deal, or treaty, was ratified by feasting and dancing, and both bands rode north-ward toward the Staked Plains together, and Quanah took his place at last among his father's people as a full-fledged chief."⁴¹

Whether the wife who aided Butterfield in escaping from Quanah's band was Weckeah or Chony, or possibly even a third wife, remains unclear, as does her motive. But whoever conceived the plan for his escape was a clever woman. She told the captive white man to feign enjoyment of deer hunts, but to frequently "get lost" and then show great excitement upon reaching camp. Each time Butterfield "got lost" he was supposed to stay out longer before "joyously" returning. Finally, after his longest absence, he did not return at all, but reached the safety of his family and friends.

According to Olive King Dixon's account, Quanah was not only kind to captive men, but also merciful to women and children. She claimed that "he never allowed any women or children to be killed in his battles."⁴² Charles Goodnight also believed Quanah's later assertions that although he had killed several white men, he did not hurt women and children. Certainly, he recalled too well the fate of his own mother, twice captured, by divergent and warring peoples, yet Quanah did not shrink from battle with male opponents.

These came more and more to include buffalo hunters. The wanton slaughter of buffalo for their hides alone so enraged the Indians that they felt compelled to kill every buffalo hunter they could find. Chief Kicking Bird of the Kiowas expressed the attitude of all the Indians: "The buffalo is our money. It is our only resource with which to buy what we need and do not receive from the government. The robes we can prepare and trade. We love them just as the white man does his money. Just as it makes a white man's heart feel to have his money carried away, so it makes us feel to see others killing and stealing our buffalos, which are our cattle given to us by the Great Father above to provide us meat to eat and means to get things to wear."[43] Try as the red men did to stem the flood of white hunters onto their hunting grounds, the outcomes of battles were destined to shift toward the side with the technological edge. The raw courage of the Indians could not alone defeat the big guns of the hunters.

Clearly, The People needed the help of the Spirit World to protect them from the white man's bullets. What medicine man, though, had medicine strong enough to protect not only himself, but all of the warriors in a raiding party as well? Quanah knew such a man. His name was Esa-tai, Rear End of a Wolf.* Missionary/teacher Thomas Battey wrote,

> This young medicine man makes bold pretensions. He claims that he has raised the dead to life. He is reported to have raised from his stomach nearly a wagon-load of cartridges at one time, in the presence of several Comanches. He then swallowed them again, informing the Comanches that they need not fear the expenditure of ammunition in carrying on a war against the whites, as he can supply all their needs in that line. He can make medicine which will render it impossible for a Comanche to be killed, even though he stands just

---

* Esa-tai, Eshiti, and Ishiti are all spellings for the same name. For convenience, the author will use "Esa-tai" except when quoting from other sources. Esa-tai is sometimes translated as Coyote Droppings.

before the muzzle of the white man's guns. He ascends above
the clouds far beyond the sun—the home of the Great Spirit,
with whom he has often conversed.[44]

The majority of the Comanches believed Esa-tai's medicine
was indeed very strong. At last the mystic warriors had a rallying
point against the whites: invincibility.

Because, as adopted Comanche Herman Lehmann said, every
time the Indians killed a white man, seven more took his place,
many of the Comanches were enthusiastic about the optimistic
prophecy of invincibility as propagated by Esa-tai. But missionary
Battey feared Esa-tai's influence on them: "Horseback [a Comanche chief], who has hitherto been friendly, has brought in and
left his ambulance with the agent, and gone to the great medicine
council. Some few are bold enough to brave his [Esa-tai's] medicine, and remain near the Agency. What the result will be is
impossible to forecast; but in all probability the Comanches will
be led by him wheresoever he sees fit. It is seriously to be feared
that he will lead them to destruction, in which many others may
become involved."[45]

Later, Quanah related to Captain Hugh Scott his version of
the councils leading up to the attack against the buffalo hunters
at Adobe Walls, a trading post for hunters built on a wide prairie
sloping gradually to a little creek and south to the Canadian River.
According to Billy Dixon, who took part in the ensuing battle,
Adobe Walls "was scarcely more than a lone island in the vast
sea of the Plains, a solitary refuge uncharted and practically unknown. . . ."[46] Originally, Quanah's intention had been to enlist
warriors for a revenge raid, because he had just lost a boyhood
friend to the Tonkawas, Indians who acted as scouts for whites.
In his own words, this is what happened:

> Tonkawas kill him make my heart hot and I want to make it
> even—that time I little big man—pretty young man but knew
> how to fight pretty good—I wait one month and go to Noconie

THE COMANCHE WAR TRAIL **83**

Comanche camp on head of Cache Creek—call in everybody—I tell him about my friend kill him Texas—I fill pipe—I tell that man, "you want to smoke"—he take pipe and smoke it—I give it to another man—he say I not want to smoke—if he smoke pipe he go on warpath—he not hang back—God kill him [if] he afraid—I go see Kiowas on Elk Creek and Quahadas—then I go to Cheyennes lots of 'em smoke pipe—Cheyenne camp up on Washita near Fort Elliott (before fort was built) lots Comanches there—Otter Belt, He Bear (Parra-o-coom), Taba-nanica and old man White Wolf there—a big village—camps in different places and they ask me "When you go at night—Big Horse dance here—Little Horse dance over there" . . . and I hear somebody, "Quanah—old men want see you over here" and I see old man Otter Belt and White Wolf and lots old men and they said, "you take pipe first against white buffalo hunters—you kill white men make your heart feel good—after that you come back take all young men go to Texas warpath"—then I say to Otter Belt and He Bear you take pipe yourself—after that [Adobe Walls] I take all young men and go warpath Texas and they say all right—Esati make big talk that time—lots white men—I stop the bullets in gun—bullets not penetrate shirts—we kill them just like old women—God told me truth. Before that pretty good medicine Esati—he sit down away listen God talk to him—maybeso fifty miles over there little creek—I see white soldiers we go kill them—pretty soon truce—this time he listen what God tell him.[47]

In Zoe Tilghman's description of the great council on Elk Creek where the Comanches hosted their only sun dance, Esa-tai stood up. His youthful face was unlined by wrinkles, and his body was strong and vigorous. He wore no buffalo skull cap or cere-monial mask, as did most of the older medicine men, but was attired only in breechclout and moccasins and a wide sash of red cloth around his waist. From his hair protruded a red-tipped hawk's feather, and from each ear hung a snake rattle. "Bending over the small fire, he laid upon it a handful of green cedar twigs and in a moment the heavy, pungent smoke rose thickly. With his feather fan, Esa-tai spread and fanned it toward all the circle. A companion who sat just behind him began to beat softly on a small drum. He leaned over the fire and washed his hands in the purifying smoke, bathed his face and breast with it. He sang a low chant, some of it mere syllables, but interspersed with words: 'Great Spirit, have pity on us,' 'Great Spirit, make us strong,' 'Esa, our brother, show us what to do.' "[48] The fire blazed higher, casting a reddish glow on Esa-tai. He stood with arms stretched upward and his face raised in appeal to the Great Spirit. Those who observed him thought the young medicine man grew larger as he stood there with his face uplifted.

Finally Esa-tai motioned to the drummer to cease and spoke to the council:

> O chiefs and brothers, behold me, Esa-tai, son of the wolf. My medicine is strong. My spirit left my body and went far away, up the path of the stars. I came to the place of the great spirit; the Great Father of the Indians, who is greater and higher than the white man's God. I was weary with the far journey. My feet could scarcely move and my tongue was dry with thirst and my belly thin with hunger. My moccasins were strings and my robe could not keep out the terrible cold. But the Great Father said: "Ho, here is a brave man and a strong warrior who could make this journey." A woman gave me food and drink. I was warm and happy. The Great Father talked with me.
>
> He said, "I will take pity on the people. I will make them strong in war and they shall drive all the white men away. The Caddoes and Wichitas, tribes that dig in the ground and have made peace with the white men, they shall very soon pass away. There shall not be any of them left. Those Comanches and Kiowas and the others who stay on the reservation shall pass away just like them. Only the warriors shall be strong and increase. They shall hold all the land, going where they please. The buffalo shall come back everywhere so that there shall be feasting and plenty in the lodges."

That is what he told me to tell the people. He told me how to make paint that will turn away bullets. My medicine is very strong.[49]

Murmurs of excitement came from the council, but White Horse was not fully convinced. "The Chief Quanah," Esa-tai replied, "and the other Quahadas will tell you that I have a strong medicine and do not speak with a crooked tongue. I told them of a great snow that was coming and again, when we wished to come here, and there was little food in the camp, I told them of a rain that would last two days. There were no buffalo near us and I told them that after the rain they would find them. Because they were killing buffalo, the Quahadas were the last to come to the council. I tell you that there will be a great dry time this summer."[50]

Quanah supported the statements of his fellow Quahada. As soon as Quanah had finished speaking, Esa-tai threw back his head and howled like a wolf. Then he grasped a handful of cedar next to where he had been sitting and nodded at the drummer.

As the smoke rose, he began a rhythmic swaying in time to the drum beats, not leaving his place, but now and then throwing up his knees, or making a small leap, bending his body and waving his arms. As the drum changed to short, sharp beats, he stood very still for a moment, his arms folded over his breast. He began a low chanting:

O Great Father, have pity.
O Great Father, make us strong.
Make our arrows swift.
Make our bows powerful.
Give us sharp lances.
Great Father, have pity.

Slowly, Esa-tai stretched his arms upward. Smoke swirled through the lodge as the Quahada medicine man chanted softly and then emitted a loud whoop. In his outstretched hand appeared an arrow. No one saw where it came from. In his other hand appeared a second arrow, and while the astonished chiefs looked on, a third arrow appeared in Esa-tai's hand. As he held them out before him, the wolf prophet proclaimed, "These are medicine arrows sent by the Great Spirit. You saw them come to my hands out of the air. My brothers, the Great Father will give you power. You shall drive out the white men and the Great Father will bring the buffalo back again. He has told me so when I was taken up to see him."[51]

Promising that the white men at Adobe Walls would be killed in their sleep, Esa-tai rode with Quanah at the head of the large war party, along with He Bear (Parra-o-coom) and Tabananaka; Stone Calf and Red Moon of the Cheyennes; and Lone Wolf and Woman's Heart of the Kiowas. Esa-tai rode with pride and confidence. His pony was painted from head to tail with the yellow paint that would repel bullets. Scalps hung from his horse's bridle.

The war party of 250 to 500 men departed Elk Creek when the new moon brightened the night sky. Killing a few hunters as they rode through the northern panhandle of Texas toward the Canadian River, the warriors met along a little creek near the rude buildings of Adobe Walls just north of the river and northeast of present-day Borger, Texas. Esa-tai's words of favor from the Great Spirit had fired the hundreds of red men with new hope that their way of life would continue as they had always known it. They could hardly wait for dawn.

Adobe Walls had been established as a store and supply center near the abandoned Bent's trading post by A. C. Myers, a buffalo hunter turned merchant, who was from Dodge City. Billy Dixon had led the merchants and hunters south from Dodge to the site of the new settlement. Myers and Leonard's Store, of picket construction, was on the extreme north of the little cluster of buildings that had been raised on the windswept prairie. About three hundred feet to the south was Hanrahan's Saloon, made of adobe, as was Rath and Wright's Store, just over two hundred feet south of the saloon. In addition, there were O'Keefe's Blacksmith Shop and two outbuildings.

The inhabitants of this lonely settlement were glum; spring was late arriving, and the buffalo hunters, having drifted south from Dodge City in increasing numbers, were afraid that the big animals would not be grazing northward when the weather finally warmed. The merchants, having invested large sums of money in their businesses, wore long faces. G. Derek West relates that "the hunters slept late in the morning, and whiled away the time at cards, shooting matches, horse races, and Hanrahan's whiskey."[52]

Not far from the new buildings of Adobe Walls, the great mass of moving horses and brightly attired men rendezvoused in a stand of cottonwoods. The long column of men was strung out separately for morning prayers, the making of medicine, and painting for battle, and each warrior looked with an increasing sense of oneness at the tall trees glistening in the early sun and the hills rising from their camp on the little stream. Shadows stretched long across the land, slowly to recede before the noonday sun to a fraction of their former size. Could The People be like the noon shadow? Once they had cast a long shadow over the vast reaches of Comanchería, and then the white man had come.

Esa-tai had warned the warriors not to kill a skunk on the way to Adobe Walls. His medicine had foreseen the hunters asleep; they would not use their big guns, and his antibullet protection would never be put to the test. That Esa-tai was confident in his medicine is clear, but he insisted that the skunk taboo must be strictly enforced. Nevertheless, as he later learned, a group of Cheyenne warriors did kill a skunk on the way to the battle scene. Since skunk meat was a favorite of the southern plains Indians, this was not unusual, for hungry members of a large war party would eat whatever strayed into their path.

Meanwhile, news of the impending attack on Adobe Walls had reached Camp Supply, Indian Territory. The post traders, Lee and Reynolds, sent a warning to Charles Rath. The message was carried by Amos Chapman, a government scout, escorted by a few soldiers. After reaching Adobe Walls, Chapman conferred with the merchants. On orders from those who chose to believe that the message was meant only for the owners or their senior employees, the news of the Indians' plan to attack the buffalo hunters was quickly circumscribed. The merchants were sure that they would lose their investment of time and money if the hunters got wind of an impending attack and left the region.

Myers and Rath* prudently chose not to stay at Adobe Walls, and soon headed for Dodge mounted on good horses. The Mooar brothers, to whom Chapman did reveal the message, also headed north. In fear of his life, Chapman asked J. Wright Mooar if he could sleep in his wagon. Following is Mooar's version of the secret warning as he told it to his brother John:

> There came in that day [two days before attack] a sergeant and six soldiers, and Amos Chapman [half breed Indian] was their scout. This roughneck outfit goes to one of these private soldiers and asks him what they come up there for. The fool, he didn't have no sense . . . and he told them they was looking for horse thieves. There wasn't a thing in the world he could have said worse than that.
>
> This roughneck outfit cussed them out and told them there wasn't no horse thieves there, and finally they got these soldiers pretty badly scared, and these soldiers pulled out and

---

* G. Derek West, in "The Battle of Adobe Walls—1874," indicates that although Mooar recalled Myers and Rath riding past him toward Dodge City prior to the Indians' attack, "there are strong grounds for believing that Rath, at least, left Adobe Walls some weeks earlier." T. Lindsey Baker suggests that neither Rath nor Myers was at Adobe Walls just prior to the attack.

off up the river . . . to camp. They didn't stay, but Amos stayed there, and in the evening Amos got a chance to get Charlie Rath and Charlie Myers and Jim Hanrahan together . . . and deliver the message that he was sent there to deliver. These soldiers was an escort for him. Lee and Reynolds had sent him from Supply, and he delivered the message to them: the day and the hour that they proposed to massacre the Dobe Walls: the morning of the 27th of June, 1874.[53]

If there were a secret warning, it would appear that the Army took a major role in seeing that it was delivered when they sent an escort with Chapman to "the Walls." It would also seem that Mooar was right in concluding that Chapman had carried a message from merchants at Fort Supply, where news of the large attack had leaked out, to the merchants of Adobe Walls. So Chapman did bring a warning, but there was no reason to keep it secret.

Indians had been killing hide hunters in the region since the first greening of the grass. Because he had arrived after Chapman's visit and his information was secondhand, perhaps Mooar did not realize that James E. McAllister had ridden to Adobe Walls with Chapman. McAllister recalled, "I and Amos Chapman were at Adobe Walls two days before the fight took place in 1874. I was working for Lee and Reynolds at Fort Supply, I. T., running a bull train. Amos was a government scout. . . . Two men had stolen a couple of horses from Lee and Reynolds and Amos and I were following them across the plains. We ran upon the men on the head of Wolf Creek, but didn't catch them and we thought they would be by Adobe Walls. We made for that place, but the men we were after did not go by there. . . . The Indians around Fort Supply would be in to the fort every day, and they told us that they were going down to Adobe Walls and kill the buffalo hunters. When we passed there we told the hunters what the Indians had said, and that they were coming, but they wouldn't believe us. They weren't even looking for them when they came."[54]

So everyone who wanted to listen had been warned of an impending attack. It seems, however, that only Hanrahan and two or three other men knew the day and the hour; J. Wright Mooar suggests that Hanrahan certainly did. What he did with that knowledge surely affected the outcome.

The Mooars met the Shadler brothers heading for Adobe Walls and warned them of a possible Indian uprising, but the Shadlers continued on their way undeterred, followed by a party of five hunters, including a young man named Billy Tyler. Tyler told the Mooars that he and his companions had been attacked by Indian warriors the day before on the Cimarron; all were seeking what they hoped would be the security of Adobe Walls.

Myers and Rath, according to Derek West, were able to leave their businesses in the care of unsuspecting employees. Hanrahan, however, was forced to remain in his saloon, as he had sunk all of his capital into the venture. All too aware of the probability that reports of the impending attack were reliable, he approached Billy Dixon, who was an excellent marksman, about joining forces. Since Dixon always killed more buffaloes than his skinners could handle, he was happy to form a partnership with Hanrahan, who had seven skinners.

Dixon's wagons, loaded with enough supplies to last for two months, were ready to roll out the next morning. That evening, the 26th of June, the Indians had a full moon to prepare for the attack. Billy Dixon describes the evening:

> The night was sultry and we sat with open doors. In all that vast wilderness, ours were the only lights save the stars that glittered above us. There was just a handful of us out there on the Plains, each bound to the other by the common tie of standing together in the face of any danger that threatened us. It was a simple code, but about the best I know of. Outside could be heard at intervals the muffled sounds of the stock moving and stumbling around, or a picketed horse shaking

himself as he paused in his hunt for the young grass. In the timber along Adobe Walls Creek to the east owls were hooting. We paid no attention to these things, however, and in our fancied security against all foes frolicked and had a general good time. Hanrahan did a thriving trade.[55]

About two o'clock in the morning of June 27, 1874, the men sleeping in Hanrahan's saloon heard a loud crack like the sharp report of a rifle. Hanrahan jumped up and yelled that the ridgepole was breaking. The men sprang to their feet, fearing the big cottonwood pole had cracked, in which case dirt and logs would cascade down upon everyone in the saloon. According to Billy Dixon, "Some climbed on top and began throwing off the dirt, while others went down to the creek to cut a prop for the ridge pole."[56] The noise woke others, and soon fifteen men were repairing the roof.

"Providential things usually are mysterious," Dixon later wrote, adding, "There has always been something mysterious to me in the loud report that came from that ridge pole in Hanrahan's Saloon. It seems strange that it should have happened at the very time it did, instead of at noon or some other hour, and, above all, that it should have been loud enough to wake men who were fast asleep. Twenty-eight men and one woman would have been slaughtered if the ridge pole in Hanrahan's Saloon had not cracked like a rifle shot."[57] But was it a providential warning that prevented a massacre at Adobe Walls? Dixon wrote in the original draft of his autobiography (later deleted by an editor), "It has been told that the ridge pole broke. As a matter of fact, when [it] was examined afterward, it was sound and firm."[58]

Evidently, Hanrahan had succeeded in rousing the men either by shooting a gun or having someone else do so. It was the only way he could alert them to the attack. If he had wakened the hunters with a verbal warning, he would have risked their wrath if he was wrong. So it appears that his only alternative was to alarm the men with the ridgepole story. By the time they had installed a prop, or props, under the suspect pole, the sky was reddening in the east. Hanrahan asked Dixon if he would make an early start on the day's hunting, since he was already awake. Dixon agreed, and sent Billy Ogg to the creek to get their horses. Some of the men crawled back into their bedrolls. Again, Dixon's narrative:

> Turning to my bed, I rolled it up and threw it on the front of my wagon. As I turned to pick up my gun, which lay on the ground, I looked in the direction of our horses. They were in sight. Something else caught my eye. Just beyond the horses, at the edge of some timber, was a large body of objects advancing vaguely in the dusky dawn toward our stock and in the direction of Adobe Walls. Though keen of vision, I could not make out what the objects were, even by straining my eyes.
>
> Then I was thunderstruck. The black body of moving objects suddenly spread out like a fan, and from it went up one single, solid yell—a warwhoop that seemed to shake the very air of the early morning. Then came the thudding roar of running horses, and the hideous cries of the individual warriors, each embarked in the onslaught. I could see that hundreds of Indians were coming. Had it not been for the ridgepole, all of us would have been asleep.[59]

The Indians, meanwhile, had stopped near Adobe Walls the afternoon before. Quanah said:

> We put saddles and blankets in trees and hobble extra ponies—make medicine paint faces put on warbonnets then travel in columns fours until pretty near a red hill near a little creek where houses were—we walk all the time—hear trot a long way off—when we got pretty near somebody want to go to sleep—He Bear say dismount hold lariats in hand—I call you—mount again—some go to sleep—some smoke tobacco and talk until He Bear and Tabananaka call when we mount again and go until little light—pretty soon we make a line—the

chiefs try to hold young men back—go too fast—no good go too fast—pretty soon they call out 'all right to go ahead' we charge down on houses in wild charge—threw up the dust high—I saw men and horses roll over and over—some men ahead wanted to catch the horses they drove off the horses— I was in middle—I got in [on?] house with other Comanches and poked holes . . . to shoot—we killed two white men in wagon—the white men had big guns that kill a mile away—that pretty hard fight—from sunrise until 12 'clock—then we go back—I had on war bonnet I gave you [Scott] long time ago— that time I got shot in the side—my 1st wife's Father [Old Bear] had his leg broken. . . .[60]

The first mighty war whoop had frightened Dixon's horse frantic. After a great effort, the young buffalo hunter managed to grab the rope and tie the horse to his wagon. He then dashed for his gun, thinking at first that the Indians were only after the hunters' stock. Then he saw the long line of warriors heading straight for the buildings, whipping their horses as they thundered over the prairie. "There was never a more splendidly barbaric sight," said Dixon. "In after years I was glad that I had seen it. Hundreds of warriors, the flower of the fighting men of the southwestern plains tribes, mounted upon their finest horses, armed with guns and lances, and carrying heavy shields of thick buffalo hide, were coming like the wind. Over all was splashed the rich colors of red, vermillion and ochre, on the bodies of the men, on the bodies of the running horses. Scalps dangled from bridles, gorgeous warbonnets fluttered their plumes, bright feathers dangled from the tails and manes of the horses, and the bronzed, half-naked bodies of the riders glittered with ornaments of silver and brass. Behind this head-long charging host stretched the Plains, on whose horizon the rising sun was lifting its morning fires. The warriors seemed to emerge from this glowing background."[61]

Dixon fired one shot and ran for the nearest building, which was Hanrahan's Saloon. The door was closed, but opened as he shouted. At that moment, Billy Ogg also reached the door and fell exhausted on the floor, having run all the way from the creek. With Dixon and Ogg safely inside the adobe building, the hunters scrambled to prepare a defense. They had scattered from their bedrolls outside the post to the nearest building. In Hanrahan's Saloon were the proprietor, "Bat" Masterson, Mike Welch, Shepherd, Hiram Watson, Billy Ogg, James McKinley, "Bermuda" Carlisle, and Billy Dixon. The men holed up in Myers and Leonard's Store were Fred Leonard, James Campbell, Edward Trevor, Frank Brown, Harry Armitage, "Dutch" Henry, Billy Tyler, Old Man Keeler, Mike McCabe, Henry Lease, and "Frenchy." Rath and Wright's Store was the most vulnerable, as only six men—James Langton, George Eddy, Thomas O'Keefe, William Olds, Sam Smith, and Andy Johnson—and Mrs. Olds were there to put up a defense. The men in Hanrahan's were alert and ready to barricade the doors with whatever they could find to stack against them, while hunters in the other buildings had to roll from their beds and get their guns and ammunition. Hurriedly, they pushed furniture and boxes of merchandise against the doors.

Quanah, riding among the leaders in the charge of yelling Indians, lanced one of the unlucky Shadler brothers, who were rousing from sleep in one of their wagons. The Shadlers did not hear the approaching Indians until it was too late.* His brother and their big guard dog were quickly dispatched by other warriors. The scalps of all three were taken. Thus was partially fulfilled Esa-tai's promise of killing the white men in their beds. But the other whites were now very much awake, and further scalps would be hard to come by.

---

*Quanah's killing of one of the Shadlers is depicted on a Comanche deerskin painting. A color photograph of the painting is on pages 116–117 of *The Great Chiefs* (Alexandria, Virginia: Time-Life Books, 1975).

Even as the Indians whooped in their exultation of counting coup on the Shadlers, the grim reality of their situation slowly replaced their euphoria. Behind the two-foot-thick adobe walls, the hunters were firing desperately at the charging warriors. Quanah ordered repeated attacks, and repeatedly had to withdraw as casualties mounted. He often charged at the head of the pack, and once he backed his horse against the door of a building and tried in vain to batter it down. In an act of great courage, Quanah raced his war horse in front of Rath's store, through a hail of bullets, to pick up Ho-we-a, a wounded Comanche. "Lifting the body with what seemed miraculous strength, he clung with foot and arm to the pony and swept past to safety. His friend was dead, but the enemy must be given no change to scalp him and doom his spirit to eternal wandering.[62]

But soon Quanah himself was to feel the sting of a bullet penetrate the shield of medicine paint that Esa-tai had prepared for him. In one more charge his horse was shot out from under him. Thrown free, Quanah crawled to cover behind a buffalo carcass, only to be shot in the side. Quanah told Goodnight in later years that "his life had been saved in battle when a bullet was deflected by the buffalo powder horn that he wore swinging from his shoulder."[63] After he was wounded he made his way to a plum thicket where he remained hidden until he was rescued, mounted behind another warrior. When Quanah was taken out of the battle, the Indians lost their most able war leader, and with him their thrust. They did not charge again as before, but only circled the adobe buildings.

A council was called by the older chiefs, who were not actively engaged in the fighting, to try to determine who had shot Quanah. All of the warriors who had been in the vicinity were questioned, and it was soon established that none of them had shot the Eagle. Esa-tai and the other members of the council began to wonder whether the white men had some new gun or gift of powerful medicine by which they could make bullets strike from behind as well as from in front. For a moment the Indians' courage faltered. In the natural world, they could face the greatest dangers and even give their lives to prove their mettle, but they could not fight the supernatural.

In spite of their misgivings, however, they decided to continue the attack against the well-fortified, well-armed whites. While acrid smoke from the huge buffalo guns filled the small enclosures, the hunters' eyes burned, they were very thirsty, and they had trouble breathing, but these were minor annoyances compared to the alternative; torture and death at the hands of hundreds of angry Indians.

"Time and again," according to Billy Dixon, "with the fury of a whirlwind, the Indians charged upon the building, only to sustain greater losses than they were able to inflict. This was a losing game, and if the Indians kept it up we stood a fair chance of killing most of them. I am sure we surprised the Indians as badly as they surprised us. They expected to find us asleep, unprepared for an attack. Their 'medicine' man had told them that all they would have to do would be to come to Adobe Walls and knock us on the head with sticks, and that our bullets would not be strong enough to break an Indian's skin."[64]

The whites were also surprised from early in the battle to hear a military bugle orchestrating the charges and retreats of the Indians. Bat Masterson, then a young man in his twenties, said of the bugler, "We had in the building I was in [Hanrahan's Saloon] two men who had served in the United States army, and understood all the bugle calls. The first call blown was a rally, which our men instantly understood. The next was a charge, and that also was understood, and immediately the Indians came rushing forward to a fresh attack. Every bugle call he blew was understood by the ex-soldiers and orders were carried out to the letter by the Indians, showing that the bugler had the Indians thoroughly drilled. The bugler was killed late in the afternoon of the first day's fighting as he was running away from a wagon owned by the Shadler brothers, both of whom were killed in this same wagon. . . . Armitage shot him through the back with a 50-caliber Sharp's rifle, as he was making his escape."[65] The bugler was a black soldier who was thought to have deserted from the 10th Cavalry.

During the course of the fighting, Dixon acquired the use of a "big .50" from a man named Shepherd, Hanrahan's bartender. As the ammunition for the buffalo hunter's own gun was in Rath's store, Dixon wanted a .50 caliber Sharps because there was some ammunition for it in the saloon. According to Dixon, "He [Shepherd] was so glad to turn loose of it, and handed it to me so quickly that he almost dropped it. I had the reputation of a good shot and it was rather to the interest of all of us that I should have a powerful gun. We had no way of telling what was happening to the men in the other buildings, and they were equally ignorant of what was happening to us. Not a man in our building had been hit. I could never see how we escaped, for at times the bullets poured in like hail and made us hug the sod walls like gophers when a hawk was swooping past."[66] If the Indians had organized early in the battle and breached the doors, as Quanah had tried to do, there would have been a massacre.

Soon Dixon's supply of ammunition ran low, and he and Hanrahan made a desperate run for Rath's store. "I have no idea how many guns were cracking away at us," said Dixon, "but I do know that bullets rattled round us like hail. Providence seemed to be looking after the boys at Adobe Walls that day, and we got inside without a scratch, though badly winded."[67] Hanrahan urged Dixon to return to the saloon with him, but the men at Rath's store begged this expert marksman to stay with them. Besides, as Dixon said, "There were fewer men at Rath's than at any other place, and their anxiety was increased by the presence of a woman,

Mrs. Olds. If the latter fact should be learned by the Indians there was no telling what they might attempt, and a determined attack . . . would have meant death for everybody in the store, for none would have suffered themselves to be taken alive nor permitted Mrs. Olds to be captured."[68]

Dixon's courage was unquestioned, and also his honesty, on the basis of his admitting to having missed—twice—an Indian crawling through the grass at no great distance. On his third try with the Sharps .50, he hit his target.

By midafternoon the Indians were firing from an increasingly wider circle, forced to move ever farther from the deadly guns of the hunters. All of the white men, according to Dixon, thanked their lucky stars that they were behind walls of adobe; otherwise, they would have been burned alive. "Still there was no telling how desperate the Indians might become, rather than abandon the fight; it was easily possible for them to overwhelm us with the brute force of superior numbers by pressing the attack until they had broken down the doors, and which probably would have been attempted, however great the individual sacrifice, had the enemy been white men."[69]

About four o'clock that afternoon, Dixon and some of the men ventured out to pick up Indian relics. It was then that he heard that Billy Tyler had been killed while attempting to aid the distressed animals in the corral near Myers and Leonard's store. The hunters soon discovered that they were afoot, as the Indians had killed all of their horses. "For the time we were at the end of the world," said Dixon, "our desperate extremity pressing heavily upon us, and our friends and comrades to the north ignorant of what was taking place."[70]

After burying the Shadlers and Billy Tyler, the hunters beheaded the Indian bodies and put the heads on stakes outside "the Walls." Then they rolled the thirteen decapitated bodies onto buffalo robes and dragged them away from the buildings. They removed several dead horses the same way, and buried twelve animals that had died in a pile.

On the second day, the hunters fired at several Indians on a bluff across the valley east of Adobe Walls. The Indians vanished. "Our situation looked rather gloomy," Dixon later said. "With every horse dead or captured, we felt pretty sore all round. The Indians were somewhere close at hand, watching our every movement. We were depressed with the melancholy feeling that probably all the hunters out in the camps had been killed. Late that afternoon our spirits leaped up when we saw a team coming up the valley from the direction of the Canadian."[71]

It was George Bellfield and his crew of hunters and skinners. That same day Jim and Bob Cator came in to Adobe Walls from their camp to the north. It was decided to send a rider to Dodge City for help. Bellfield furnished a horse, and Henry Lease volunteered to make the dangerous journey to Dodge. Lease was to wait until cover of darkness before attempting this.

Also on the second day, the Indians held a council. In the face of their anger, Esa-tai defended his medicine by saying that the power of his magic paint had been nullified when some of the warriors on the way to Adobe Walls had killed a skunk. According to Zoe Tilghman, "The council was assembled on a lower slope, with the crest of the ridge between them and the fort, out of sight, and, as they considered, too far for effective gunfire, even if on a level. The pony of Esa-tai, wearing the protective painting that its owner declared would ward off arrows or bullets, stood by. Suddenly it jerked its head, staggered and fell, blood oozing from a hole in its forehead. In a moment it was dead. The mark of the heavy buffalo slug was unmistakable. The pony had been killed by a shot from the plainsmen's guns, coming over the hill."[72] It was the end of Esa-tai's spiritual hold over the Indians.

Brandishing a quirt, an angry Cheyenne warrior named Hippy approached Esa-tai, but the chiefs intervened to spare the disgraced medicine man a thorough flogging. Quanah said, ". . . the Cheyennes were pretty mad at Esati—what's the matter you medicine . . . 'pole cat medicine' [a term of derision]. . . ."[73]

A few bands slipped away that night. In the middle of the afternoon of the third day, the chiefs held another council. Afterward, Quanah, Stone Calf, White Shield, and about twenty other warriors rode to the top of the butte beyond East Adobe Walls Creek. Billy Dixon and his companions saw them silhouetted against the eastern sky. The sun hung in the sky behind the little cluster of adobe buildings. Dixon wrote:

> . . . some of the boys suggested that I try my big .50 on them. The distance was not far from three-fourths of a mile. A number of exaggerated accounts have been written about this incident. I took careful aim, and pulled the trigger. We saw an Indian fall from his horse. The others dashed out of sight behind a clump of timber. A few moments later two Indians ran quickly on foot to where the dead Indian lay, seized his body and scurried to cover. They had risked their lives, as we had frequently observed, to rescue a comrade who might be not only wounded but dead. I was admittedly a good marksman, yet this was what might be called a "scratch shot."[74]

The Indian had not been killed, however. Co-hay-yah, an aged Comanche veteran of the battle, later described the effect of Dixon's long shot to Colonel Nye:

> We lost the fight. The buffalo hunters were too much for us. They stood behind Adobe Walls. They had telescopes on their guns. Sometimes we would be standing 'way off, resting and hardly thinking of the fight, and they would kill our horses. One of our men was knocked off his horse by a spent bullet fired at a range of about a mile. It stunned, but did not kill him.[75]

Thus ended the battle of Adobe Walls. The white man's medicine was too strong for the Indians to risk the loss of any more
warriors. "Pretty soon," Quanah said, "all go back, get saddles
and bridles and go to village—I take all young men, go warpath
to Texas."[76]

5

THE BATTLE OF CAÑON BLANCO

A large and powerfully built chief led the bunch, on a coal-black racing pony. Leaning forward upon his mane, his heels nervously working in the animal's side, with six-shooter poised in air, he seemed the incarnation of savage brutal joy.

— Captain R. G. Carter, 1935[1]

In the fall of 1871, three years before the Battle of Adobe Walls, Colonel Ranald Slidell Mackenzie led a column of six hundred men into the inner reaches of the home range of the Quahadas. His aim was to punish Quanah, He Bear, Wild Horse, Bull Elk, and the other war chiefs of this fiercest band of the Comanches, whose raids into the settlements along the Texas frontier had prompted even Quaker Indian Agent Lawrie Tatum at Fort Sill to request the aid of the U.S. Army in finding and attacking the elusive warriors of the plains. Although committed to the Peace Policy of the Quakers, which advocated negotiation and education over guns and swords, Agent Tatum believed there could be no peace until all the Comanches and Kiowas had been settled on the reservation set aside for them in the Treaty of Medicine Lodge in 1867, a treaty none of the Quahadas had agreed to. Over a third of all the Comanches had refused to put their "mark" on the treaty, and now they were to pay for what the United States government considered to be their intransigence.

Colonel Mackenzie's recent attempt to catch Chief Kicking Bird of the Kiowas off the Kiowa–Comanche reservation near Fort Sill had been unsuccessful, since Kicking Bird had drawn back within its boundaries, but this failure had whetted the appetites of his fighting men for a real battle. So it was with high spirits that the 4th Cavalry, with a scouting party of Tonkawa Indians, departed Fort Richardson near Jacksboro, Texas, on the morning of September 19, 1871, in search of the Quahada warriors. Their path lay along the stretch of road between Jacksboro and Camp Cooper to the west, from which they would launch out into the unmapped wilderness that was Comanchería.

The Tonkawa scouts employed by Mackenzie had for generations hated the more numerous and powerful Comanches. Herman Lehmann, a white captive who had become a Comanche warrior, had this to say about their blood feud:

> The hatred the Tonkawa had for the Comanches was fierce, for they blamed the Comanches for all of their misfortunes and eventually made a treaty with the white people and combined with them to exterminate the Comanche, acting as scouts and trailers and warriors for the whites.[2]

Lehmann went on to explain the revulsion all Comanches in their turn felt for the Tonkawas. After trailing a band of Tonkawa warriors who had attacked and overcome a much smaller Comanche force, Lehmann's band found them in their camp eating the leg of a Comanche warrior. No wonder that after a desperate hand-to-hand battle, in which the Comanches overpowered the cannibals, Lehmann reported, "A great many of the dying enemy [Tonkawas] were gasping for water, but we heeded not their pleadings. We scalped them, amputated their arms, cut off their legs, cut out their tongues, and threw their mangled bodies and limbs upon their own campfire, put on more brush wood and piled the living, dying and dead Tonkawas on the fire."[3]

Past history, then, had given the Tonkawa scouts employed by Colonel Mackenzie a blood lust to hunt down and kill Comanches. Mackenzie himself had plenty of reasons for wanting to quell the Quahadas, for as long as they were free on the prairies, their kinsmen and allies on the Kiowa–Comanche–Apache Reservation in southwestern Indian Territory would be disinclined to stop raiding the settlements of Texas. The Peace Policy of the Quakers in the late 1860s and early 1870s provided a "City of Refuge," as Colonel Nye described this particular reservation in his *Carbine and Lance,* whose regulations precluded Mackenzie's pursuing Comanche and Kiowa warriors over its borders (and had prevented him from capturing Kicking Bird); if he could not catch and punish raiding parties before they crossed the Red River from Texas into Indian Territory, he was powerless to press further. But although he had failed to catch Kicking Bird, he had at least succeeded in chasing him onto the reservation, a feat he hoped to duplicate with the Quahadas.

The Quahadas, however, wanted no refuge other than the land the Great Spirit had given them. Although they had not spoken at the council at Medicine Lodge Creek, their sentiments were the same as those Yamparika Comanche Chief Ten Bears expressed on that occasion in a passionate and eloquent speech to the delegation from Washington:

> The Comanches are not weak and blind like the pups of a dog when seven sleeps old. They are strong and farsighted, like grown horses. We took their road and we went on it. The white women cried and our women laughed. But there are things which you have said to me which I do not like. They are not sweet like sugar, but bitter like gourds. You said you wanted to put us upon a reservation, to build us houses and make us Medicine Lodges. I do not want them. I was born upon the prairie, where the wind blew free and there was nothing to break the light of the sun. I was born where there were no enclosures and where everything drew a free breath.

I want to die there and not within walls. I know every stream
and every wood between the Rio Grande and the Arkansas.
I have hunted and lived over that country. I lived like my
fathers before me and, like them, I lived happily. . . . If the
Texans had stayed out of my country, there might have been
peace. But that which you now say we must live on is too
small. The Texans have taken away the places where the grass
grew the thickest and the timber was the best. Had we kept
that, we might have done the things you ask. But it is too
late. The white man has the country which we loved, and we
only wish to wander on the prairie until we die.[4]

That the Quahadas were willing to die fighting for their land,
Mackenzie had no doubt. Their raids against outlying ranches
and settlements on the Texas frontier had been so successful that
the population of Wise County, for example, had dwindled from
3,160 in 1860 to 1,450 in 1870. General Philip H. Sheridan had
sent an inspector to the frontier to investigate conditions there,
authorizing the use of troops should there be a need for armed
protection, which proved to be the case. The 6th Cavalry had
arrived at Fort Richardson near Jacksboro in January 1867, but
the Indian raids only increased. Governor James W. Throckmor-
ton had reported in August of 1867 that from May to July the
Indians had killed 162 persons, wounded 24, and carried 43 into
captivity. Those figures did not include Wise and Young counties,
both of which were on the edge of the frontier and suffered constantly from Indian raids.

Colonel Mackenzie understood the nature of the Quahadas.
In many respects they resembled his own Scottish warrior for-
bears. His father was a naval commander, his uncle was a Confederate commissioner, and his mother was the granddaughter of
patriots of the Revolutionary War. One of his brothers had served
in the Civil War, had attained the rank of lieutenant commander,
and had been killed leading a charge in a battle on Formosa in
1867. Another brother was to become a rear admiral in the navy.

Less than three years after graduating from West Point, Mackenzie himself had received seven brevets for gallantry, and he had suffered six wounds during action for the Union forces against the Confederacy. So it was in keeping with his heritage that Mackenzie was considered by General Ulysses S. Grant to be "the most promising young officer in the army."[5]

Prior to Mackenzie's arrival on the frontier, the reservation Comanches and Kiowas had raided with impunity from the City of Refuge. When admonished by Agent Tatum, many of the raiders arrogantly and boastfully admitted their acts of violence against the citizens of Texas. In fact, Mackenzie's campaign against young Quanah and the other Quahada warriors was prompted by the Indians' killing of seven teamsters who were hauling corn from the railroad at Weatherford, Texas, to Fort Griffin. Led by Mamanti, owl prophet of the Kiowas, a band of one hundred Kiowa, Comanche, and Apache warriors had left the reservation and attacked the wagon train on an open stretch of ground known as Salt Creek Prairie. Swooping down from their hiding place in the oak timber on the slopes of Cox Mountain, the Indians charged the teamsters, who quickly drew their wagons into a circle and opened fire. After a desperate battle from inside the corral of wagons, five of the teamsters had escaped into the timber two miles to the east while the Indians were busy mutilating the bodies of the fallen whites and dividing the plunder contained in the wagon train.

This incident provided Mackenzie with his first glimpse of Plains Indian warfare; he was greeted with the sickening sight of the bodies of the teamsters, swollen and bloated beyond recognition, lying in a pool of water. One of the corpses had been hung upside down over a fire and burned; Mackenzie's surgeon could not determine whether the man had died before being burned or afterward.

The effects of the massacre of the teamsters were far reaching. General William T. Sherman himself had barely escaped almost certain death at the time; he was on a fact-finding mission in the area, and the ambulance in which he was riding with an escort of fifteen mounted troopers had passed nearby along the Butterfield Trail under the hostile gaze of Maman-ti's warriors only hours before the attack on the wagon train. Many of these warriors wanted to attack Sherman's small detachment, but the medicine that Maman-ti had received the preceding night had foretold the passing of two groups of whites and had clearly shown success if they attacked the second party only. The owl prophet managed to restrain his warriors, and the general passed in safety.

The attack on the wagon train a few hours later, however successful it might have seemed to the Kiowas, would contribute to the Indians' undoing. Sherman's presence in the region was in response to the Texans' demands that something be done to curb the constant raiding; an all-out effort to control the situation was already under way.

Inspector General Randolph Marcy, who accompanied Sherman on the fact-finding expedition, was a veteran of the frontier. It was he who had laid out the route below Cox Mountain, later known as the Butterfield Trail, in the early 1850s. As Sherman and Marcy passed through the frontier forts and outlying ranches, they saw landscapes of blackened chimneys surrounded by the charred logs of burned-out cabins and weed-infested fields. Marcy observed that the Texans "expose women and children singly on the road and in cabins far off from others as though they were safe in Illinois. . . . If the Comanches don't steal horses it is because they cannot be tempted."[6] In his journal, Marcy later noted, "This rich and beautiful section does not contain today so many white people as it did when I visited it eighteen years ago, and if the Indian marauders are not punished, the whole country seems to be in a fair way of becoming totally depopulated."[7]

The massacre of the teamsters at Salt Creek Prairie resulted in the arrest of Satanta, Satank, and Big Tree, the Kiowa chiefs who had boasted of their role in the attack. Upon learning that Agent Tatum was cooperating with General Sherman, and that after two years of a hands-off attitude toward Indian raiders seeking refuge on the reservation the Army was now determined to punish them for their forays into the settlements, the three Kiowa chiefs quickly changed their story, but to no avail. Sherman ordered Mackenzie to take Satanta, Satank, and Big Tree from Fort Sill to Jacksboro, Texas, for trial. Satank was shot by Corporal John B. Charlton while attempting to escape, but the other two chiefs, closely guarded, reached Jacksboro without further incident.

As Mackenzie and his troopers rode into the sun-drenched settlement on June 15, 1871, they were greeted by the garrison band and the whole population of the little ranching community. Three weeks later, Satanta and Big Tree were tried by a jury of cowboys and sentenced to be hanged. But supporters of the Quaker Peace Policy across the country protested the sentence, and Agent Tatum's superior, Superintendent Hoag, wrote President Grant that executing the two Kiowa chiefs would trigger an Indian war. Acting on Tatum's advice, Governor Davis of Texas commuted the sentences to life imprisonment.

The day of his triumphant entry into Jacksboro with Satanta and Big Tree, Colonel Mackenzie wrote a letter to General Sherman suggesting a campaign against all Kiowas and Comanches who were not cooperating fully with Agent Tatum, saying, "It is of the very first importance that the action which has been taken in sending these Indians to this post [Fort Richardson] be sustained. The Kiowa and Comanches are entirely beyond any control and have been for a long time. I spoke of this both to the President and Commissioner of Indian Affairs while in Washington last winter. Mr. Tatum understands the matter. He appears to be very straightforward, resolute and capable. He is anxious that the Kiowa and Comanches now out of control be brought under. This can only be accomplished by the Army. . . . It is not very important who are dealt with first, the Staked Plains people, or those of the reserve."[8]

MacKenzie received approval for the campaign against the Quahadas, and with high spirits the men of the 4th Cavalry departed from their bivouac at Camp Cooper on the Clear Fork of the Brazos, singing with six hundred voices strong, "Come home, John, don't stay long; Come home soon to your own Chick-a-biddy!" The blue coats, weary of chasing reservation Indians in the vicinity of the City of Refuge, were after bigger game. The Comanches of the Staked Plains, led by Bull Elk, Mow-way (Hand-shaker), Parra-o-coom (He Bear), and Quanah, the youngest of the war chiefs, were their targets. These Quahadas persisted in considering the land to be theirs; in fact, Mow-way and Parra-o-coom had told Agent Tatum on several occasions that not until the soldiers had come into their country and defeated them in battle would the Quahadas consent to move onto the reservation and "walk the white man's road."[9] And not until they were beaten in battle would the Comanches release their white captives, many of whom, like Quanah's mother, had been adopted into the tribe. In a letter to Colonel Grierson, commander at Fort Sill, Agent Tatum expressed concern for the welfare of Clinton Smith, captured along with his younger brother Jeff two years before by a band of Comanches. "I should be very glad indeed," he wrote, "if thee and General Mackenzie could get that little captive and induce Mow-way and his band to come into the reservation and behave. Mow-way does not appear likely to bring in that poor little captive child of his own volition."[10]

And so the column of men and animals of the 4th Cavalry left Camp Cooper strong in their mission. Their route lay over a rolling prairie dotted with mesquite and cedar and cut with ravines. They crossed Paint and California creeks and eventually made camp on the banks of the Clear Fork of the Brazos River in Cañon Blanco, or White River Canyon, east of present-day Crosbyton, Texas.

In the wilderness, with the exception of Comanche traders from New Mexico, only the Tonkawa scouts could hope to find the men who made their home in the rugged canyons and shallow streams below the caprock, the slopes of which fall from the level plains down precipices of rock and cedar to the undulating grassland below, the final range of the buffalo on the southern plains. So a day's march before reaching Cañon Blanco, when the column stopped to camp for the night, Colonel Mackenzie sent the Tonkawas out on a night scout with the hope of locating the Indians and making a surprise attack under the cover of darkness. The Tonkawas, reluctant at first to venture out into a strange country inhabited by a mortal enemy, rode out into the night only to return after finding no sign of the Comanches.

The next day, however, the scouts rode down a deep ravine and surprised a small number of Comanche spies studying the advance of the soldiers into the heart of their hunting grounds. Only the superiority of the Comanches' mounts saved their lives as the Tonkawas pursued them. After a fruitless chase, the Tonkawas returned to camp to report what had happened. When they had feasted on buffalo meat, Mackenzie ordered his troops forward, intent on following the Quahadas to their village and striking his blow before they could dismantle their tepees, load their possessions, and flee. After sloshing through the treacherous, quicksand-riddled Freshwater Fork of the Brazos River, the column spread out and headed deeper into the canyon, when a shot was heard, causing Mackenzie to turn back, on the assumption that the men left at the camp were being attacked, only to discover that the shot had been fired by one of his own nervous soldiers.

Angrily, Mackenzie ordered another about-face. Clearly the white soldiers were as edgy in Quahada country as the Tonkawa scouts had been the night before.

By this time Quanah, Parra-o-coom, Wild Horse, and the other Quahada war chiefs had ascertained the number of men in Mackenzie's command, as well as the number of horses and mules and their condition. Mackenzie himself was riding a gray pacer, a magnificent animal he had acquired just before leaving Fort Richardson, but most of the other horses were in relatively poor condition, not having had time to recover from the campaign against Kicking Bird.

According to Captain R. G. Carter, the soldiers bivouacked before dark in a narrow canyon with small bluffs on one side and a stream with quicksand on the other. In an error of judgment no experienced Indian fighter would have made, Mackenzie allowed the men to start fires. A generation earlier the Texas Rangers had learned to stop two hours before dark, build fires to cook their supper, then ride on for an hour before making camp. After dark, fires were forbidden.

Around midnight, the horses were grazing at the end of their lariats, stamping and snorting, switching their tails in an effort to drive away the pesky insects of early fall, when suddenly the night echoed with a shot and several shots followed. "Then a succession of unearthly, blood curdling yells . . . and, in an instant, our whole camp was aroused,"[11] wrote Captain Carter. As the rear squadron fired pistols and carbines at the ridges on one side of the camp, their flares revealed the hills to be swarming with Comanches "riding by at full speed, shaking dried buffalo robes [raw hides], ringing bells, yelling like demons, and by every other possible device trying to stampede our animals."[12] Officers shouted over the din, "Get to your horses!"–for to be on foot in the heart of Comanchería would almost surely be a sentence of death. The horses were plunging wildly, falling and twisting, tangling their lariats. Iron picket pins were pulled out of the ground by frantic horses, and they whizzed around in the near darkness, endangering the crouching soldiers as they fought desperately to hold on to their mounts. In spite of all their efforts, however, the Quahadas drove off seventy horses and mules, including Mackenzie's valuable gray pacer. "The hissing and spitting of the bullets sounded viciously," Carter said, "and the yells of the retreating Indians from the distance came back on the midnight air with a peculiar, taunting ring, telling all too plainly that the Quahadas, Quanah's wild band of Comanches, had been among us."[13]

Quanah's version of this episode, recorded later, tells a slightly different story. According to Quanah, he led a few young men toward the soldiers' camp, then he and his friend Sankadota crept along the picket lines where the enemy's horses were secured and cut the halter ropes. Leaping on two of the horses, the Quahada warriors emitted a war whoop and stampeded seventy horses, including Mackenzie's gray pacer. Their jubilation was to be short-lived, because the soldiers for the first time were to ride up the canyon to one of the Quahadas' favorite camping grounds. Never before had the band experienced a direct attack by soldiers, and clearly the women and children had to be protected at all costs. Quanah was placed in charge of the retreat of the village, and his courage and skill as a chief were to become all too evident to Colonel Mackenzie in the next few days, and earned him widespread fame among the Comanches. According to Zoe Tilghman in *Quanah, the Eagle of the Comanches*, "Ambitious young men came from other bands, and from the reservation, to join the Quahadas and follow him in raids. They were a sort of Robin Hood company, the boldest and wildest bucks of the whole Comanche tribe and Quanah himself said in later years, 'We stole horses all over Texas.' "[14]

After the stampede, it was dawn before Captain Carter could calm his own horse, unhobble and saddle him, and ride along the picket lines to assess the damage. At the nearest post he asked a Dutch corporal what had happened. In Carter's version, the corporal said, "I vas lying down, sir, ven I hears a shot. I shoomps up, dries to get my bicket pin as de horses roosh by, and de next ding I knows de Injuns dey rode all over me."[15]

While Captain Carter was checking the losses incurred by the stampede, a shot rang out in the valley, echoing in the slowly yellowing air. Two detachments of K and G troops galloped up to him just as several Indians were making off with another dozen or so horses down the river valley. Carter and the K and G troops took chase, keeping the Quahadas in sight and slowly gaining on them in the lingering darkness of the deep, narrow valley. When the soldiers were almost within pistol range, the Comanches abandoned the stolen horses, plunged into an arroyo, and were soon scrambling up the other bank with Carter, Captain Heyl, and ten troopers in hot pursuit.

As Captain Carter and the others ascended the ridge rising from the arroyo, he saw at the base of a bluff a swarm of mounted, yelling Indians galloping toward them. In his words, "It was like an electric shock. . . . For a moment the blood seemed fairly congealed for we realized what the ruse of the Indians had been and knew now that their purpose had been to lead us into the ambuscade."[16]

Along with five men of G troop, Carter dismounted and began to fire on the attacking Indians from an open stretch of prairie. To one side Captain Heyl and seven troopers were also firing. "The well directed fire of our little handful of men," Carter wrote, "covering now a considerable line, caused the savages to scatter out still more, to falter and hesitate, and to commence their curious custom of circling. They were naked to the waist; were arrayed in all their war paint and trinkets, with head dress or war bonnets of fur or feathers fantastically ornamented. Their ponies, especially the white, cream, dun, and clay banks [sic], were striped and otherwise artistically painted and decorated with gaudy stripes of flannel and calico. Bells were jingling, feathers waving, and with jubilant, discordant yells that would have put to blush any Confederate brigade of the Civil War, and uttering taunting shouts, they pressed on to what they surely considered to be their legitimate prey."[17]

Added to the din was the high-pitched tremolo of the Quahada women as they cheered on their warriors from the safety of the caprock wall; all were mounted, no doubt, for a quick exit if the battle should go against their men. Carter saw two scalp poles that contained several long scalp locks probably taken from women victims. Mirrors flashed in the early light as the Comanches signaled each other for advances and retreats. "It was a most terrifying spectacle to our little band," Carter said, "yet wild, grand, novel [to look back upon] in the extreme."[18]

Captain Heyl's men were raw recruits, and Carter, then a lieutenant, quickly noticed Heyl's reluctance to fight. Soon it was apparent that Carter and his handful of seasoned troopers would have to bear the brunt of the battle. After firing several rounds at the circling, yelling Comanches, Heyl and his men made a sudden dash for Mackenzie's main camp down the valley. At that moment the Comanches let out a great howl of satisfaction and began to close in on Carter and his five veteran soldiers. Slowly moving back toward the ravine they had so foolishly crossed in pursuit of the Comanches, the six soldiers fired sparingly, then just before reaching the arroyo they let loose a fusillade of shots at the circling Indians, driving them back long enough to enable them to mount their horses and make a dash for safety.

The gray horse belonging to a trooper named Gregg, which was still in bad condition from the campaign against Kicking Bird, stumbled, and Quanah swept in to finish off Gregg. He was riding a coal-black thoroughbred that Carter later learned was named Running Deer. Carter described Quanah in this way:

His face was smeared with black war paint, which gave his features a satanic look. A large, cruel mouth added to his ferocious appearance. A full-length head-dress or war bonnet of eagle's feathers, spreading out as he rode, and descending from his forehead, over head and back, to his pony's tail, almost swept the ground. Large brass hoops were in his ears; he was naked to the waist, wearing simply leggings, moccasins and a breech-clout. A necklace of bear's claws hung about his neck. His scalp lock was carefully braided in with otter fur and tied with bright red flannel. His horse's bridle was profoundly ornamented with bits of silver, and red flannel was also braided in his mane and tail, but being black, he was not painted. Bells jingled as he rode at headlong speed, followed by the leading warriors, all eager to out-strip him in the race. It was Quanah, principal war chief of the wild Quahadas.[19]

Since Gregg's horse had already faltered, the only chance the soldier had of saving his life was to win a hand-to-hand encounter with Quanah. Gregg's fellow troopers fired vainly, but as the fast-charging Quanah was on the other side of Gregg, zigzagging his pony, making a shield of the soldier he intended to kill, Gregg was probably in more danger from his defenders' bullets than was Quanah. Carter shouted to Gregg to use his carbine, but his pull on the lever was too weak to force a cartridge into its chamber. Just as Carter screamed at him to use his six-shooter, a shot from Quanah's pistol ended Gregg's life.

Without scalping the fallen Gregg, Quanah whirled and, followed by his warriors, galloped toward the canyon wall, which rose in undulating folds of rock, sparse grass, and scrub timber from the river. Carter, in wonder that his life and those of the remaining troopers had been spared, looked back down the river to see the Tonkawas coming fast toward the battle scene. It was not the "Tonks," however, that had caused the Comanche retreat; behind them rode Mackenzie's troopers, and Quanah's keen eyes had seen their dust in the distance.

Supplied with fresh mounts by their women, the Comanches slowly moved back, exchanging curses, challenges, and shots with the also circling Tonkawas. Up the walls of Cañon Blanco they went, while the women kept up their ululation. Just as Mackenzie's main column drew near, the Indians disappeared on fresh horses onto the level Llano Estacado, or Staked Plains. Colonel Mackenzie had found the Quahadas, but keeping them in one place long enough to "punish" them was to prove a considerable challenge.

As the soldiers continued their pursuit, they saw evidence of Indian life along the sloping walls of the canyon rising abruptly from the valley several hundred feet away. Carter gave this description:

> Scattered all along were many of the small "wicky-ups," still intact, put up for the use of the Indian herders, usually half-grown boys and girls. Every few miles the canyon widened out into more or less broad valleys bounded by almost impassable bluffs. We also saw numerous ravines and sand hills, as well as many small herds of buffalo. Here and there the creek . . . widened out, [creating] beautiful ponds or lagoons, clear as crystal, out of which swarmed immense flocks of wild ducks and curlew, and occasionally a majestic swan, whose trumpet notes sounded strange to our hunters who had rarely, if ever, seen such game.[20]

All day following the early morning battle, the soldiers rode along over the rough terrain, unmapped and unspoiled by Western man. Feeling watched at all times in the unfamiliar country, they found the Comanche village, but all that was left of it were the holes in the ground where the lodge poles had been driven. The People had vanished.

Following the clear trail made by lodge poles and the immense number of horses, mules, and cattle, the "Tonks" led the soldiers on the trail heading up the canyon. Quanah, however, used every trick he knew to keep the noncombatants safe, never forgetting his mother's capture and the slaughter of Indian women at Pease River eleven years before. In one attempt to confuse his pursuers, he and the other chiefs divided the people and animals into two groups and had them cross and recross paths as they went forward to throw off the Tonkawa trackers. "For the first time," Carter said, "our sharp-eyed scouts seemed 'at fault.' After much parleying and time lost, they concluded that the wily enemy had 'doubled' on us and gone back upon the same trail."[21]

Mackenzie turned the column around and countermarched on their back trail until dark, then bivouacked near the location of the recently abandoned village. The next morning, the scouts signaled from the edge of the bluff on the plains above Cañon Blanco that they had found the trail leading out over a seemingly impassable barrier. "There was a long delay," according to Carter, "in scaling with horses the steep ascent, but, at length, after toiling over many rocky bluffs and floundering around in the 'breaks' and 'arroyos', all were over and out of the canyon upon what appeared to be a vast, almost illimitable expanse of prairie. As far as the eye could reach, not a bush or tree, a twig or stone, not an object of any kind or a living thing, was in sight. It stretched out before us—one uninterrupted plain, only to be compared to the ocean in its vastness."[22]

Mackenzie and his troops soon had to face the vagaries of weather on the Llano in mid-October. Across the wide expanse of the treeless plain blew a gathering wind, coming straight from the north with an unmistakable chill. The soldiers, hot on the trail of the Quahada village, were experiencing their first "norther" on the Llano. The elevation of over three thousand feet and the increasingly cold wind shocked these troops; they had been campaigning for months on the hot plains hundreds of feet below the level of the Llano, and they were clothed for summer and totally unprepared for the sudden change in the weather.

Mackenzie had not foreseen the need for warm clothing. It was another in a series of mistakes on this, his first military expedition against the Quahadas.

After trailing the Indians across the prairie for some time, the Tonkawa scouts finally realized that the Comanches had once more doubled back and had gone again into the canyon. Mackenzie led his men, slipping and sliding, single file down the dangerous descent from the Llano into Cañon Blanco. In the valley the soldiers discovered fresh trails going in different directions, some leading up, others down, while still others leading straight across the valley at right angles. "Again in our supreme disgust," said Captain Carter, "we felt that we had been completely foiled. The 'Tonks' scattered and rode rapidly all over the valley, and before the rear of the column had got fairly down into the canyon and closed up, they were waving us on. It [the trail] had been found going out again over the bluff, this time, however, on the opposite side of the canyon. We were soon ascending for the second time that day the steep precipitous sides of the rocky barriers."[23]

The tenacious Mackenzie was now more determined than ever, for all of Quanah's ruses had taken time, and by Carter's estimate the Comanches were driving two to three thousand head of horses, mules, and cattle. When one takes into account the fact that women and children and the elderly were also riding up and down the steep walls of the canyon and back and forth over the valley in an effort to confuse their pursuers, it was a maneuver of great tactical brilliance that they had escaped thus far the six hundred soldiers and cannibal scouts on their trail. Quanah knew all too well what would happen to the women and children and old people if the Indians were forced to take a stand.

His greatest challenge now faced him. The hated Tonkawas had at last found the true trail, and the soldiers were riding across the windswept prairie toward a confrontation. A different tactic was called for to slow them down and gain time for the fleeing noncombatants. Carter described the Comanches' next action as follows:

> As we "rose" or "lifted" a slight ridge in the almost level prairie, we observed, in the far distance, moving figures, silhouetted against the skyline, as of mounted men galloping along the horizon, here as distinct as the sea line that limits the boundless ocean. First, two or three, then a dozen or more, until finally, on both sides of our now swiftly speeding column there seemed to be hundreds. The "Tonks" said they were the Comanches, and we knew ourselves that at last we were on the right track! We had them! Or, at least, we thought we did . . . the Comanches began to swarm on the right and left of the trail, like angry bees, circling here and there in an effort to divert us from their women and children. Every preparation was made for a fight, for we firmly believed that, failing to throw us off the lodge-pole trail of their fleeing village, the red scoundrels had gathered all of their warriors for a determined resistance and a supreme effort should we overtake their families. We knew that it is then that an Indian will fight with all the ferocity of a wild animal, blind to everything except the preservation of his squaws and papooses.[24]

Mackenzie was not to be baited by the groups of Comanches advancing, taunting, and retreating, hoping thereby to draw the soldiers away from the main trail of the fleeing village. Doggedly, the troops pursued the women and children, expecting an all-out attack at any moment, even though the Indians were outnumbered. Mounted skirmishers were sent out to the front and on both flanks to contest the threatening Comanches.

The Tonkawa scouts, meanwhile, had paused to paint themselves and their horses for battle. "Our gallant allies," Captain Carter continued, "then pranced alongside the columns, posturing, moving their heads from side to side, brandishing their carbines, and evidently feeling all the pride of conquering monarchs, so self-conscious were they of all the dignity which all the display of paint, feathers, gew-gaws, etc. gave them."[25]

Show it was, and nothing more, for the Quahadas would not close in battle as long as their noncombatants were in the lead. Darkness was coming on, and a cold rain mixed with sleet and snow began to blow on the rising wind, chilling the soldiers to the bone. The freshening trail revealed fires the women had built to warm themselves, some of which were still burning when the soldiers reached them. Mesquite roots and other firewood were strewn along the trail, indicating a lightening of the horses' burdens. Lodge poles, iron and stone hammers, mortars, pestles, and even the cured buffalo skins used to cover the lodge poles of the tepees were also scattered along the trail.

Only a mile ahead, the fleeing village was now visible to the soldiers. Just at that moment Captain Carter thought the order to trot, gallop, and charge would be given, but Mackenzie hesitated. Whether he feared sustaining heavy casualties one hundred miles from his supply camp or whether he was reluctant to attack the women and children, Carter could not know, for the colonel kept his own counsel. Whatever Mackenzie's reasons for not attacking the Quahada village, it is doubtful that the soldiers could have won a decisive victory, because the elements were smiling on the Comanches. Suddenly an inky darkness, hastened by the storm, hid them from view. It was as though they had disappeared.

Throughout the night, the soldiers huddled before the storm. Someone took Colonel Mackenzie a buffalo robe. He had not brought an overcoat, and without the robe he could scarcely have withstood that night of rain, snow, and raging wind. He had received several wounds in the Civil War, and according to Captain Carter, they "had disabled him and rendered him incapable of enduring such dreadful exposure."[26]

The next morning a clear day dawned, and the men, cold and tired, their spirits flagging, began again to follow the trail, now etched clearly in the snow. Colonel Mackenzie concluded from his maps that the Pecos River lay due west of his position. The nearest post was Fort Sumner, New Mexico, a considerable distance away. Rations were low, and the horses' strength was deteriorating. As the chances of catching up with the Quahada village diminished due to the several hours' head start given the Indians by the storm, Mackenzie decided to return to Fort Richardson.

As the column dropped once again into Cañon Blanco, which Captain Carter described as an "Indian paradise," the cry of "Indians! Indians!" rang out, alerting the sleepy soldiers to action. The Tonkawa scouts, who were ahead of the troops, were running at breakneck speed toward a small ravine. Two Comanches had been discovered leading their horses along the soldiers' trail up the canyon. When Captain Carter reached the scene, he saw that the entrances to the ravine were blocked. Mackenzie ordered fifteen of the Tonkawas to dismount and go into the ravine on foot to finish off the Comanches. After some time had passed, he became impatient, dismounted, and got behind Lieutenant Boehm of the Tonkawas to oversee the operation. "Just then," according to Carter, "a sharp swish, a thud, and a spiked arrow buried itself in the upper, fleshy part of Mackenzie's leg. He hurried back to the rear and had the spike cut out and the wound dressed. Soon all firing ceased, and we knew the two Comanches were dead. . . . One was shot several times through the body, the other through the head. One had been shot in the hand while firing his pistol. The bullet had shattered the pistol butt. A bloody bowstring showed that he had used his bow later. With the strength necessary to draw the string, it must have proved very painful, and a clear test of the Indians' wonderful courage, tenacity, and stoical nature under such circumstances."[27]

That night, Dr. Rufus Choate, Lieutenant Wentz C. Miller, and two black cooks went to the ravine and decapitated the dead Quahadas, placing their heads in gunny sacks for what Carter termed "future scientific knowledge." The next day, Captain Carter was called by Lieutenant Miller to join him for lunch. Two kettles were strung on a pole over a fire. Carter took his cup to one of the kettles anticipating a cup of hot soup, but just as he was about to dip in, he saw to his horror the heads of the two Comanches killed the day before. He promptly had his camp moved farther down the canyon, some distance from the sickening sight.

In spite of his pain, Colonel Mackenzie was still determined to find Quanah, and he sent orders for Lieutenant Henry W. Lawton to bring supplies from Duck Creek near present-day Spur to the Fresh Fork of the Brazos. Many of the troops' horses had died and others had had to be shot. All disabled men were sent to Duck Creek, but Mackenzie himself led part of the command on a scouting trip toward Pease River, thinking that Quanah might have doubled back from his westward course on the Llano Estacado. After five days in the field, however, Mackenzie's wound was so painful he was forced to return to the supply camp. Carter described him as "irritable, irascible, mean and 'onery." On November 6, the command under Major Clarence Mauck returned in a snowstorm from their search along the Pease River without having found any Comanches.

On the 18th, the entire command straggled into Fort Richardson in the midst of a blizzard, cold and exhausted. Mackenzie and his men had been in the field since May 1. They had succeeded in driving Kicking Bird onto the reservation, but Quanah and the Quahadas were still free on the plains.[28]

According to Colonel Nye, the Quahadas were not only free, but "did not slow down at all. The northern and western counties of Texas were favored by their presence to such an extent that

Colonel Mackenzie reported that . . . 'the outrages committed by Indians have been more frequent than I have known them here or at any other point. . . .' "[29] Herman Lehmann wrote that even though the Comanches' numbers grew steadily smaller as a result of almost constant conflicts with the Army, Texas Rangers, and buffalo hunters, the Comanches "held a great council, in which other tribes participated, and pledged ourselves to kill all of the whites as they came into our territory; kill them as they destroyed our game; kill them as they slew our warriors; kill them as they killed our squaws and children; to follow them and kill them so long as any of us remained, and on the break-up of the council we had a big war dance."[30]

In the fall of 1872, Mackenzie returned to Quahada country, only to be foiled again in his attempt to catch the Eagle of the Comanches. The Scottish warrior, however, did surprise Mow-way's camp of Kotsotekas and Quahadas on McClellan Creek in a beautiful valley near what is now Lefors, Texas. Ironically, Mow-way, who had once told Agent Lawrie Tatum at Fort Sill that when Indians on the reservation were treated better than the ones in the wild, he would go in, had gone to talk with the "peace" people when Mackenzie attacked. Although Quanah was not present, as a leader of The People, he was affected by the outcome of the battle. Over two hundred tepees were destroyed in the attack, along with stores of meat, equipment, and clothing. Even worse, 52 Comanches were killed and 124 women and children were taken prisoner. Also, Mackenzie rounded up between 800 and 3,000 horses and mules, which he entrusted to the care of the Tonkawas. Sergeant Boehm and the other cannibal scouts herded the horses to a sink [sic] in the prairie about a mile from the burned village. "The Tonkawas felt so secure that they rolled into their blankets and fell asleep."[31] The next morning, according to Sergeant Charlton, the "faithful Tonks" sheepishly straggled into the soldiers' camp leading a small burro, upon which they had piled their saddles. In spite of the fact that they had retrieved their stock, the Comanches were demoralized by the loss, through death or captivity, of over a hundred of their women and children.

In the aftermath of the fight, adopted Comanche Herman Lehmann reflected on his deep-seated hatred of the white man:

> When we reached our camp we found it had been attacked by a body of soldiers and some Tonkaway Indians, and a number of our women were among the slain. Several women and children were made captives. . . . When the attack was made on the camp most of the squaws ran away and hid, but five of them were killed while escaping and we found the dead bodies scattered about. I remember finding the body of Batsena, a very brave warrior, lying mutilated and scalped, and alongside of him the horribly mangled remains of his daughter, Nooki, a beautiful Indian maiden, who had been disemboweled and scalped. The bodies presented a revolting sight. . . . Other bodies were mutilated, too, which showed the hand of the Tonkaway in the bloody battle. . . . We soon found our scattered women and children and old men, and heard the sad details of the attack, and our rage knew no bounds. . . . In our council we swore to take ten captive white women and twice as many white children, and to avenge the death of our squaws, especially Nooki; we vowed to kill a white woman for every year of her age (she was about 18 years old), and that we would disembowel every one we killed.[32]

Everywhere, the tempo of hostilities accelerated. Clinton Smith, who was a captive member of the Kotsoteka and Quahada bands at McClellan Creek, had cause to fear for his life because of Mackenzie's attack on the village. "On account of General Mackenzie's killing so many of our band and taking others captive, a lot of the squaws who lost sons in that fight, had brooded a grudge against all of the white boys in the tribe, and had made threats that if they ever caught us out of camp they would kill us.

My old foster mother, Limpia, the chief's wife, had told us of these threats and had warned us that if any squaw or buck came to us in the woods that we should be on our guard and not let them get too close, but to watch them always. Tasacowadi had given us arms and told us to tell them to keep away, but if they would not, for us to kill them if we could, for we were not to blame for what had been done."[33]

Clearly, the subjugation of the Quahadas would not be an easy task for Mackenzie, for among nature's inhospitable streams of quicksand, precipitous canyon walls, and howling blizzards, Quanah, Eagle of the Comanches, now rode the war trail on Mackenzie's gray pacer. The young Quahada chief, according to adopted Comanche Lehmann, "continued to raid and kill and pillage,"[34] defiantly waiting for the white warriors to return.

6

FORT SILL

We saw somebody coming on the prairie crying one day and we said, "There he is, Quanah!"

— Iseeo, Warrior who rode with Quanah, 1897[1]

The white warriors returned in force in 1874, among them Ranald S. Mackenzie (whose men called him simply The General), to take part in what was to become a full-fledged effort to either drive the Indians back onto the reservation or exterminate them. Despite their losses, and in many ways because of them, the Indians had remained on the war trail. While Quanah and the young warriors who followed him to Texas were raiding the Tejanos, other parties of Cheyenne, Kiowa, Arapaho, and Comanche raiders were attacking settlers in New Mexico, Kansas, and Colorado. Because most of the warriors rode out on their missions of vengeance and death from camps along tributaries of the Red River, the war now flaming on the southern Plains came to be known as the Red River War of 1874–1875. Perhaps it would be more appropriate to refer to the conflict as the Buffalo War, for it was largely in response to the slaughter of the big animals that the Indians were fighting the buffalo hunters, the Army, and the Texas Rangers. One example supplies a clue as to why their efforts were doomed to eventual failure. In an engagement following the Battle of Adobe Walls, a large party of Kiowas under Lone Wolf attacked twenty-seven Texas Rangers in Lost Valley, near Jacksboro. The Indians kept the Rangers pinned down in a ravine for much of the day before withdrawing. Even so, the outcome of the fight was only one Ranger dead and three wounded, while the Kiowas lost three men and suffered many injuries. In spite of the fact that they far outnumbered the Rangers on this day, the arithmetic was against the Indians, and the superior firepower of the whites was the deciding factor.

"Clearly faced with a serious outbreak the Army began preparations for the most extensive and comprehensive campaign ever undertaken on the southern Plains. The architects of the operation were Lieutenant General Philip H. Sheridan, commander of the Division of Missouri, and his ranking subordinates on the Southern Plains frontier."[2] Brigadier General John Pope and Brigadier General Christopher C. Augur helped to formulate a plan that featured a five-pronged attack converging on the Indians' strongholds along the area drained by the Canadian, Red, and Brazos rivers. Colonel Nelson A. Miles was to march from Dodge City, Kansas, to Camp Supply, Indian Territory, and thence southwestward; Major William R. Price was to march toward the east from Fort Union, New Mexico Territory; and north from Fort Concho, Texas, would come Quanah's chief antagonist, General Mackenzie, who was by now a veteran Indian campaigner. Lieutenant Colonel John W. Davidson was to move west from Fort Sill, Indian Territory, while Lieutenant Colonel George P. Buell was to head northwest from Fort Griffin, Texas. The very heart of the targeted area was Quanah's Quahada homeland, no doubt a source of much satisfaction to Mackenzie.

Warnings were given to Indians enrolled at the agencies, and many of them, including most of the Arapahos and Apaches, elected to remain under the protection of the Indian agents. But the Quahadas, Kotsotekas, and many Comanches from other bands chose, as always, the only course they knew: war. Cheyennes and Kiowas in the hundreds also painted their faces, danced the war dance, and tied up their horses' tails for battle.

General Miles's troopers were to see the greatest action of the five columns of well-mounted, well-armed soldiers now scouring what was left of Comanchería. Miles's scouts, among whom was Bat Masterson, discovered the fresh trail of an Indian village on the move on Sweetwater Creek, near the future site of Fort Elliott in present-day Wheeler County, Texas. Following the trail southward, the soldiers knew that the Indians were fleeing in great haste because of the amount of goods and the number of old horses they had abandoned along the way. After crossing the Salt Fork of Red River, Miles's column of over seven hundred men rode down the Prairie Dog Town Fork, the headwaters of the Red River, into Palo Duro Canyon, where they were attacked by about seventy-five Cheyennes. Soon the soldiers' organized firepower drove the Indians back to a steep wall of the canyon, where five hundred well-armed warriors made a stand. "Covered by three light field guns and two or more Gatling guns, the soldiers advanced to the attack against positions which seemed almost impregnable. And yet the Cheyennes were unable to hold fast in the face of the hard-charging troops and their superior firepower. Miles's soldiers pushed the Indians from one crest to another."[3]

After repeated charges had driven the Indians from their positions, the warriors slowly retreated toward their camp along Tule Creek, which emptied into the Prairie Dog Town Fork of Red River. The next day, August 31, 1874, dawned hot and dry, something the once-discredited Esa-tai had correctly foreseen. The scouting party Miles sent out rode up the narrow gorge of Tule Canyon for eighteen miles before discovering that the Cheyennes had climbed the rugged bluffs of the canyon walls onto the level Llano Estacado, east of what is now Tulia, Texas, much as Quanah had done in 1871 to outwit Mackenzie. The troops followed the trail some thirty miles before Miles decided to abandon the chase; enough damage had been done for now. The Indians' casualties were an estimated twenty-five killed and, more importantly, the women had lost most of their supplies. The dry summer would make the buffalo harder to find, and there would be hunger in the Cheyenne camps.

Quanah himself, although he did not figure in the Cheyennes' engagement with General Miles, could not help but be affected by their defeat. It was obvious that with their growing understanding of the geography and topography of the land, the Army's white and Indian scouts could now more easily discern the locations of the Indians' favorite camping grounds; areas that had once been known only to the Comanches, Kiowas, Apaches, Cheyennes, and Comancheros were now becoming known to the white enemy.

Mackenzie, who had chased Quanah onto the Staked Plains in 1871 and 1872, now rode north from Fort Concho. Instead of pursuing Indians running away from him, the Scottish general now found himself facing Indians running away from Miles and Davidson *toward* him. After reaching the all too familiar Cañon Blanco, Mackenzie set up a supply camp on the west side of White River, the Freshwater Fork of the Brazos River, and from there he departed in late September for Tule Canyon, where a party of Kiowas and Comanches, which in all likelihood included Quanah, attacked the soldiers during the night.

According to Captain Carter, also by this time a veteran, "It was about 10:30 when the first attack came and a large body of mounted Indians charged along our lines, in fact, all around us, firing and yelling, to try and start our horses. The latter were securely anchored."[4] Obviously, Mackenzie had learned a valuable lesson from Quanah's previously successful effort to stampede the soldiers' horses three autumns earlier.

About five o'clock the next morning, the Indians again fired into the 4th Cavalry's camp. "Orders were sent to each troop commander to 'saddle up,' which was done in quick time. 'E' troop being nearest the General, was mounted and started off towards the position held by the Indians, who, when they saw the troop coming towards them, ran to their ponies, mounted and galloped off in a body on to the high and level ground, there being, at a rough guess, about 300 of them. . . . The entire 2nd Battalion was out on the high ground by this time, but the Indians had disappeared as completely as if the ground had swallowed them."[5] Woman's Heart of the Kiowas and fifteen other warriors were killed in this action.

After having fought most of the night in Tule Canyon, Mackenzie's men were allowed a few hours' sleep the next night, then marched for twelve tiring hours before settling down for some badly needed rest, which did not last long, because Sergeant John B. Charlton and two Tonkawa Indians came riding into camp to report a fresh trail. Captain Carter's account:

> We mounted and moved out quickly, every man alert. It was yet dark about 4 o'clock A.M. when we resumed our march, still going North, and just as the first faint streaks of daylight came in the East we suddenly came to a wide and yawning chasm or cañon, which proved to be Palo Duro Cañon.
>
> In the dim light of the dawn, away down hundreds of feet we could see the Indian "tepees" or lodges, and as we had to march along the edge of the cañon some distance before we could find any path or trail to descend by, the morning had become quite light and the Indians, who had now discovered us, rushed out of their lodges and began gathering their herds of ponies and driving them off towards the head of the Cañon. How we got down into the Cañon was, and always will be, to the few surviving members of the old 4th Cavalry, who participated in the Palo Duro fight, a great mystery.
>
> The whole command dismounted and each officer and man, leading his horse in single file, took the narrow, zig-zag path, which was apparently used by nothing but Indian ponies

and buffalo. Men and horses slipping down the steepest places, stumbling and sliding, one by one we reached the bottom.[6]

The Indians nearest the soldiers amassing on the floor of the canyon fled with their horses upriver. Most of the Indians escaped up the steep cedar-lined walls of Prairie Dog, but their means of transport, their shelter, and their clothing were left behind. Carter described the colorful scene of soldiers charging behind General Mackenzie as follows:

> As we galloped along we passed village after village of Indian lodges both on the right and left, all empty and totally abandoned. The ground was strewn with buffalo robes, blankets, and every imaginable thing, in fact, that the Indians had in the way of property—all of which had been hastily collected and a vain attempt made by the squaws to gather up and save, but finding the troops coming up so rapidly they were forced to drop their goods and chattels and suddenly take to the almost inaccessible sides of the Cañon to save themselves from capture. Numbers of their pack animals were running around loose with their packs on, while others stood tied to trees—all having been abandoned by their owners, who were pressed so hard by our command that they had to hastily flee to the friendly shelter of the rocks that towered above us to the right and left.[7]

As their women and children escaped, the warriors entrenched themselves behind boulders and clumps of cedar on the rugged canyon walls and began to fire on the soldiers. "At a time when the fire was the hottest," wrote Captain Carter, "one of the men said on seeing that the command was nearly surrounded, 'How will we ever get out of here?' The General on hearing him said, 'I brought you in, I will take you out.' Most of the men did not question when he led, we knew we could depend on his care and guidance."[8]

About noon, Mackenzie saw a group of warriors on top of the south rim of the canyon riding toward the place where the soldiers had descended to the canyon floor. He ordered Captain Gunther to take H Company and secure the pathway. As Gunther and his men spurred their horses toward the steep slope down which the men and animals had made their daring entrance to Palo Duro, Captain Carter saw the Indians racing to reach the trail before the soldiers could ascend the canyon. Fortunately for Captain Gunther, the Indians had to skirt a side canyon, which slowed their progress. Once Gunther had secured the trail, the Indians swerved off onto the prairie.

With one company guarding their escape route, Mackenzie sent a detachment to round up the warriors' horses. Since the Indians' desultory fire from the canyon walls continued throughout the afternoon, "The General" gave orders for the men still fighting to keep them pinned down.

After reaching the plain above the canyon, "the whole command now assembled, with the immense herd of captured ponies, on the high prairie. A 'hollow square' or huge parallelogram was formed as follows: One troop in line of battle rode in advance; on either side marched two troops in columns of twos; and one troop, in line, rode in rear. In the center of this huge hollow square the captured herd of about 2,000 was driven along. One troop marched in rear of all as rear guard. It was a living corral and our march was nearly 20 miles."[9]

Immediately after breakfast on September 29, 1874, a detail was assigned to shoot the captured horses now corralled in Tule Canyon. Mackenzie wrote to his superiors a month later explaining his actions in killing the horses. He said, "The ponies captured by my command on the 28th of September were disposed of at the time in various ways. I had promised one of the Guides forty if he found or was the means of my finding a camp and they were given him as promised. He afterwards sold most of them to Officers of the Command and others. . . . There were but a few good ponies

Portrait photo of Quanah Parker, about 1880. (Courtesy of the Panhandle–Plains Historical Museum, Canyon, Texas)

Cynthia Ann Parker and Prairie Flower, about 1861. (Courtesy of the Panhandle–Plains Historical Museum, Canyon, Texas)

Quanah Parker in ceremonial regalia, about 1885. (Photo by Lanney; courtesy of the Panhandle–Plains Historical Museum, Canyon, Texas)

Quanah (lower right) lancing one of the Shadler brothers, as depicted on a Comanche hide painting of the 1874 Battle of Adobe Walls. (Courtesy of the Museum of the Great Plains, Lawton, Oklahoma)

arles Goodnight. (Courtesy of the
nhandle–Plains Historical Museum,
nyon, Texas)

Brevet General Ranald S. Mackenzie, circa 1880. (Courtesy of the Crosby County Historical Committee, Crosbytown, Texas)

Quanah with one of his wives, about 1880.
(Courtesy of Wayne Parker family)

Side portrait of Quanah Parker in
ceremonial regalia, about 1880.
(Courtesy of the Panhandle–Plains
Historical Museum, Canyon, Texas)

Chief Quanah Parker in a studio portrait, about 1880. (Courtesy of the University of Oklahoma Library, Norman)

Quanah Parker on a U.S. Cavalry mount, about 1890. (Courtesy of the Panhandle–Plains Historical Museum, Canyon, Texas)

Quanah Parker and two of his wives, (left) Tonarcy and (right) Topay, about 1890. (Courtesy of the Panhandle–Plains Historical Museum, Canyon, Texas)

Quanah Parker and Tonarcy, about 1900. (Courtesy of the Panhandle–Plains Historical Museum, Canyon, Texas)

Quanah Parker in business attire, about 1890. (Courtesy of the Fort Sill Museum, Fort Sill, Oklahoma)

Quanah Parker (second from left, bottom row) after a peyote ceremony, about 1890. (Courtesy of the Panhandle–Plains Historical Museum, Canyon, Texas)

Quanah Parker and his family, Fort Sill, Oklahoma, 1892. (Courtesy of the University of Oklahoma Library, Norman)

Quanah Parker's summer arbor, near Fort Sill, Oklahoma. (Courtesy of the University of Oklahoma Library, Norman)

Quanah Parker and Tom Burnett, about 1900. (Courtesy of the Panhandle–Plains Historical Museum, Canyon, Texas)

Grave of Cynthia Ann Parker at Post Oak Cemetery near Cache, Oklahoma. The grave was moved to the Army Cemetery at Fort Sill, Oklahoma, in the 1950s. (Courtesy of the Panhandle–Plains Historical Museum, Canyon, Texas)

Comanches performing a war dance at the Comanche County Fair in Lawton, Oklahoma, about 1905. (Courtesy of the Panhandle–Plains Historical Museum, Canyon, Texas)

Quanah Parker riding in the parade at the Comanche County Fair in Lawton, Oklahoma, about 1905. (Courtesy of the Panhandle–Plains Historical Museum, Canyon, Texas)

Quanah Parker's stagecoach. (Courtesy of the Fort Sill Museum, Fort Sill, Oklahoma)

Star House, Quanah Parker's spacious home near Cache, Oklahoma. (Courtesy of the Panhandle–Plains Historical Museum, Canyon, Texas)

Quanah Parker and his family at Star House. (Courtesy of the Fort Sill Museum, Fort Sill, Oklahoma)

Quanah Parker and his family on the porch of Star House, about 1908. (Courtesy of the Fort Sill Museum, Fort Sill, Oklahoma)

Quanah Parker (kneeling) with cattlemen and President Theodore Roosevelt (standing, second from right) on a wolf hunt east of Frederick, Oklahoma, in 1905; Burk Burnett is to the president's right. (Courtesy of the Panhandle–Plains Historical Museum, Canyon, Texas)

Quanah Parker and Andrew Jackson Houston, about 1900. (Courtesy of the Panhandle–Plains Historical Museum, Canyon, Texas)

Quanah Parker's grave at the Post Oak Cemetery near Cache, Oklahoma.
It was moved in the 1950s to the Army Cemetery at Fort Sill, Oklahoma.
(Courtesy of the Panhandle–Plains Historical Museum, Canyon, Texas)

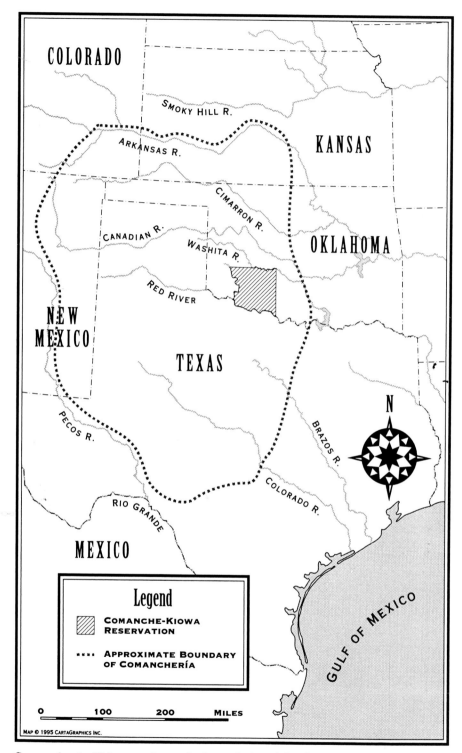

Comanchería. This map shows the boundaries of the Comanche country at its greatest extent and the reservation on which the Comanches later lived.

among them and I had all killed except which I thought would satisfy these people. . . . Men are frequently such forty miles away from the command without the prospect of large rewards, no officer can get it done."[10] The Tonkawa scouts were permitted to select the best of the horses formerly belonging to the three leaders of the Indians attacked in Palo Duro Canyon: Kiowa Ma-Manti, Comanche Oh-ma-tai, and Cheyenne Iron Shirt. Captain Carter wrote, "It took Lawton the most of one day, with one troop, to pile these bodies up on the plains. They were still there—on the 'Tex' Rogers ranch [midway between Tulia and Silverton on Tule Creek] some years ago—an enigma to the average Texas boy who looked upon them with wondering eyes."[11]

Again, Mackenzie had failed to catch Quanah, but the Eagle's Comanche, Kiowa, and Cheyenne allies had suffered a defeat perhaps more chilling than the warriors' failure to destroy the hunters at Adobe Walls. Could it be possible that the old ways of The People were slipping away forever? After the destruction of the herd of horses and the loss of provisions necessary for a nomadic life, many of the Indians whom Mackenzie had attacked in Palo Duro Canyon went back to their reservations and surrendered. So while the five columns sent by General Sheridan into Comanchería fought relatively few engagements, their presence in the country was alarming to warriors who had to hunt for provisions in the midst of dry weather in an attempt to feed their women and children. There were no safe places anymore. Comanchería had once been a refuge for Numunu, The People, but now the whites had come in great numbers and were destroying their game and hunting down the fleeing villagers.

The fight had not yet gone out of the Indians still in the wild, however, as evidenced by the following excerpt from the *Daily Commercial* of Leavenworth, Kansas, entitled "The Present Outlook from Ft. Sill," and dated November 10, 1874:

Gen. Davidson has just been out after the reds and come in without much success attending his trip. He has gone out again with his cavalry (colored) and supplies for thirty days. He was last heard from one hundred and sixty miles distant westward on the trail of the Cheyennes, and will undoubtedly "camp" too frequently to strike them effectually. Our present army had rather be in a comfortable camp or pleasant quarters than be in close proximity to the fighting savage.

The Government is making great exertions to completely whip the Indians and bring them in subjection, but so far without permanent success. The military has undoubtedly "rounded up" a great many worthless horses, that is, regarded by the Indians as worthless, for their present war purposes. These horses of the government were superfluous to the reds' rapid movements, and impeded their progress. Their numerous war horses they still retain, but when the army gets possession of them, they will capture the red devils mounted upon them in full battle array. Major Schofield of the tenth made a very splendid movement—he has taken 67 men prisoners some 350 women and children, and nearly 2,000 unridable ponies; he deserves credit. These Indians belonged to what is called the Nocosinois Comanches, they were endeavoring to get in, but before they got in fifteen miles of their agency, the soldiers made their appearance and the reds raised a white flag in token of their submission. The army confiscated their horses and effects and these are now under the guns of the sentinels. Now the question arises how will the government dispose of so many horses, they are not serviceable for the cavalry use—only for breeding purposes. It is not likely that Uncle Sam will go into stock raising, for the United States. To sell them under the hammer, they would not bring the small sum of two dollars and-a-half a head; we would suggest that the government give them to the many whites who have been stolen out by the reds in the past five years. The whites have been robbed from the Arkansas to the Rio Grande; burnt, stolen and killed out.[12]

If this inflammatory article against the Indians reflects the thinking of whites on the Kansas frontier, it is quite apparent that Kansans in 1874 concurred with Texans influenced by *The White Man,* the anti-Indian newspaper in Weatherford, Texas, in 1860. Leavenworth and Weatherford were distant from each other in a geographical sense, but the journalists' attitudes toward native Americans were identical.

Quanah had thus far evaded the soldiers, but it was not for lack of effort by General Mackenzie and his 4th Cavalry. For three days after the engagement in Palo Duro Canyon, Mackenzie rested his men and allowed the horses to graze on the rich grass along Tule Creek; then he ordered his command to circle the head of the canyon and take an easterly course, amidst heavy rains that lasted for twenty-four hours. On October 7, they encountered fifteen Mexicans driving six ox carts loaded with provisions. Three of the Mexicans, perhaps in fear of their lives, joined the expedition as scouts, while their compatriots, claiming that they were on a buffalo hunt, went on to deliver their goods to the Indians.

On October 16, 1874, only four months after the Battle of Adobe Walls, Mackenzie's command camped along Quitaque Creek between present-day Quitaque and Turkey, Texas. The area, with its rugged canyons, running water, and stands of cedar and cottonwood, was a favorite camping spot of the Quahadas, but Mackenzie found no signs that they had recently camped or passed through there. Next, he moved his troops to a campsite near what is now Matador, Texas, where the soldiers received a long-needed boost in morale in the form of mail, rations, and forage brought by a wagon escorted by troopers. The night of October 23 the men camped on the Freshwater Fork of the Brazos. "In thirty-four days [Mackenzie's] men had traveled more than 400 miles, had captured 1,445 horses, and had killed at least 4 Indians."[13]

After scouting the area around present-day Brownfield, Post, and Tahoka, where the soldiers had a brief engagement with Indians, Mackenzie returned to his supply camp in Cañon Blanco. When a wagon train loaded with corn arrived on November 16, he was again ready to give chase to the widely scattered bands of "hostiles." But weather conditions in the form of severe sleet storms delayed his departure. On the 22nd, the weather cleared, and "The General" moved out with a force of 13 officers, 265 cavalrymen, 38 infantrymen, and 14 scouts, in search of Indians. Mackenzie sent the scouts in different directions, hoping to find fresh signs, but they returned to report that few Indians were to be found to the north and west of Cañon Blanco. So Mackenzie decided to move south and scout the Mucha-que Valley on the headwaters of the Colorado River near what is now Gail, Texas. En route his command was again stalled by the weather, this time in the form of a blizzard on the prairie three miles northwest of Lake Tahoka. The storm was so severe that several horses froze to death standing in the picket lines. Could the elements again be smiling on Quanah?

Mucha-que was one of the last remaining campgrounds that afforded ample water and forage for Quanah's vast herd of horses. Also, antelope were plentiful in the area, and although all Comanches preferred buffalo or wild horse meat to any other, the Quahadas were known to be antelope eaters. And buffalo, though scarce, were not yet gone from the region.

As Mackenzie drew nearer to Mucha-que, he camped east of present-day Lamesa on the boundary of Dawson and Borden counties, where his men spotted five Comanche scouts; they chased down and killed three, but two escaped to warn other Indians in the area. If Quanah were camped at Mucha-que, it is certain that Mackenzie's heralded approach prompted him to strike camp and move southwest. Whatever occurred, when the 4th Cavalry reached Mucha-que on December 10, they found no

Indians. "Frequent rains and the condition of the men and animals made further scouting impossible. Lack of forage, long marches, and inclement weather had left the horses too weak to continue, and the men, now subsisting on a small amount of buffalo meat each day, were continually hungry. Clothing was in disrepair; some of the troopers were almost barefoot; and the rains again turned into snow and ice."[14]

Frustrated yet again in dealing a crushing blow to Quahada warriors, Mackenzie, whose intention had been to surprise them, had to return to his temporary supply camp on Duck Creek, from where he made one last short scouting trip around the area before meeting his supply train at the junction of Duck Creek and the Salt Fork of the Brazos ten miles west of present-day Jayton, Texas. There he received orders to report to Departmental Headquarters in San Antonio for further instructions.

Thus, Quanah, Esa-tai, and other members of their band were spared the horror of having their families attacked, their lodges and provisions burned, and their beloved horses destroyed. Although it is not certain how Quanah evaded the soldiers, it is likely that he camped for a while at Lagunas Sabinas, or Cedar Lake, between present-day Brownfield and Seminole, Texas. Lagunas Sabinas had long been a favorite camping site for bands traveling the Comanche war trail to Mexico. The likelihood of Quanah's band having camped at various sites between Muchaque and what is now Fort Stockton is very great when one considers the extreme difficulty of their escaping hundreds of hated Tonkawa and white frontiersmen who were constantly scouting for the five columns sent out by General Sheridan. The only avenues of escape would have been to the northwest or southwest of the area targeted by Sheridan and his staff. Since Quanah said, following the Battle of Adobe Walls, "I take all men, go warpath to Texas,"[15] it is clear that he did not choose a course to the northwest. Instead, the vast sand-speckled, rock-strewn landscape

of the area west of present-day Odessa-Midland would have offered much more security from the converging columns. Huge
sand dunes rose (and still rise) from a prehistoric ocean floor in
an area bordered by present-day Andrews, Kermit, and Monahans,
Texas. Although this seeming wasteland was forbidding to whites
who attempted to cross it in wagons, the Indians could ride their
horses and pull travois loaded with lodges and provisions across
the shifting sands, and it was virtually impossible to follow their
trail through the dunes because the tracks of horses and the ruts
left by the dragging travois soon filled up with wind-blown sand.
As for water, it lay underneath the surface in places the Indians
had known through generations of following the Comanche war
trail to Mexico's northern *ranchos.*

One branch of the war trail originated along the Arkansas
River near present-day Pueblo, Colorado, passed through what is
now northeastern New Mexico and down the rolling grasslands of
New Mexico's eastern plains to present-day Roosevelt County, and
entered Texas near what is now Bledsoe in Cochran County.*
From there, the trail swung out to what is now Brownfield and
then to Lamesa, where it turned south, passing between present-
day Stanton and Midland, and went southwest to Comanche
Springs, later known as Fort Stockton, where the Indians would
fill their water containers before they followed their quest of death,
rape, and bondage to the Chisos Mountains and on to Mexico.

Mackenzie believed the Quahadas were heading toward the
Pecos River, which they would probably ford at Horsehead Crossing if they were on their way to Comanche Springs. He also
thought Quanah might have headed for the Guadalupe Mountains

---

* According to Harlie and Maxine Adams of Bledsoe, Texas, arrowheads, spear points,
and other Indian artifacts have been collected by generations of arrowhead hunters
around a spring-fed lake just east of Bledsoe.

between present-day Carlsbad, New Mexico, and El Paso, Texas. In either case, the Indians would find safety if they chose to pass through the sand hills on their way. Whatever happened, Quanah's escape was especially frustrating for Mackenzie and fortuitous for Quanah, for the Scottish warrior was not destined ever to take the field against the Eagle of the Comanches again. Mackenzie had received orders from General Sheridan to assume command at Fort Sill, Indian Territory. The Red River War was over.

Before Mackenzie's arrival at Fort Sill on March 16, 1875, Lieutenant Colonel J. W. Davidson had sent messengers to the Comanches in an effort to coax them onto the reservation. In compliance with Davidson's offer, Mow-way, Long Hungry, Wild Horse, and 35 warriors, along with 140 women and children, surrendered themselves and their 700 horses to Davidson on April 18, 1875. In an attempt to induce Quanah's band, also, to give up the war trail and come into the reservation, Mackenzie sent as an emissary Dr. Jacob J. Sturm, physician and post interpreter, who had married a Caddo woman and lived with her people. Following are excerpts from Sturm's journal:

> On the 23rd of April in company of three Comanche Indians: to wit, Wild Horse, Watebi-with-Kit, and To-vi-ah, I left Fort Sill and camped the first night out at West Cache Creek, called by the Comanches To-zo-passa-honovit.* 24th we travelled to Otter Creek called by the Comanches Exa-pana-conich-honovit.† This is a creek of good size and plenty Timber and is called Turkey Creek by the Indians on account of the vast number of Turkeys found here in winter time. We crossed North Fork called by the Comanche Movee-tah-honovit, or Shin Oak. After travelling briskly for some hours we crossed

---

* About 16 miles west of Fort Sill near present-day Cache, Oklahoma.
† Five miles southwest of present Altus, Oklahoma.

the Salt Fork called by the Indians Pah-uah-cup . . . where we found fair grass and plenty of wood and water, here we passed a comfortable night, being only interrupted by the constant howling of Wolves.

25th Soon after we got up this morning a raven flew around our camp and with many cah, cahs let the Indians know that we were close to Buffalo of which we have yet seen none. We got an early start and travelled over Light Prairie with scarcely a stick of timber in sight occasionally crossing deep ravines, the heads of streams running into Red River, a travel of four or five hours brought us in sight of plenty of Buffalo Bulls . . . as soon as the Indians saw them they told me that our morning visitor, the Raven, never lied and was a good friend to the red man, always letting him know when he was in the neighborhood of Buffalos. A short time after finding the first Buffalo we came in sight of immense herds . . . some of the cows having calves, we killed two cows and stopped at noon to rest and eat at a large boiling spring in the broad prairie. . . .

26th An early start, country very broken, small rocky hills and rough broken Prairie, immense herds of Buffalo in every direction . . . after a hard half days ride we moved on a small stream which I suppose is a tributary of Pease River. The water is Plenty but almost unbearable on account of the buffalo. This creek has a good deal of timber. Cottonwood and hack berry. . . . This whole country is very destitute of grass and timber and in mid-summer there is hardly no water to be found, so that it will perhaps never be inhabited by civilized men. . . . I will remark that the whole streak of land laying between the Red River and Pease River through which we passed is a barren waste unfit for habitation of civilized men.[16]

After noting that the Comanche name for Pease River is Wah-pit or Cedar, named after the lush growth of scented cedars lining the narrow stream, Sturm wrote that he and the small company of Comanches followed Wah-pit-honovit until they reached a campsite on Middle Pease River, near what is now Matador, in the heart of Quahada country. "The country we have travelled over today is much better than we have seen for some days," he said. "There is plenty of Short Oaks and the Prairie is covered with various flowers, some of which are very beautiful."[17]

The Comanches riding with Sturm resorted to their habit of taking food from nature's harvest, which now, to the most profound heartache of the Indians, was slowly yielding to the rapine of the advancing whites as they pressed farther west, heartened by the news that hostilities between Indians and whites on the southern plains had virtually ceased. The Red River War over, aggressive white men, many of them poor, and in proportion to their poverty, desperate, were rushing into the abandoned country to possess the land—a practice long denied to common people throughout European history. These frontier people were largely ignorant in terms of book learning, but were very resourceful and ingenious in making the most of their tools and, like the Indians, living off the land. Former Texas planters destroyed by the collapse of the slave-based agricultural economy—the Southern planters had more in common with Mexican hacendados (owners of vast ranches in the north of Mexico) than with Northern industrialists—were forced to start over again as cattlemen. Even some of the poorest of the untutored masses were becoming landed and self-supporting. The wild cattle available throughout the settled areas near the Texas frontier made instant money a reality, for a large northern market clamored for Texas beef.

While the longhorn cattle of Ibero-African origins were making it possible for the defeated Texans to rise on the energy and courage of the emerging Anglo cowboy, the buffalo were being slaughtered by the millions for their hides alone. When Charles Goodnight (who as a young man had pursued Quanah's father after the murder of Mrs. Sherman) first settled in Palo Duro Canyon in 1876, he heard the thundering boom of the big Sharps rifles. He said, "I have seen great piles of the carcasses, and in riding out here, when I first settled here, I would hardly ever be out of the sound of the guns from sun-up to sun-down."[18]

The Indians guiding Dr. Sturm on his journey to the Quahadas' camps enjoyed one of the last hunts by free-moving Indians in Comanchería. Wild Horse and his companions killed a calf and drank the milk from its stomach, which they regarded as *te-bits-su-ehalt,* or "very good." "They destroy an immense number of calfs," wrote Dr. Sturm, "only for the milk to be found in the stomach of them. It is their custom also to eat the Phisnegs of the calfs now dipping them into the warm blood of the calf which they pronounce delicious."[19]

On the 29th of April, Dr. Sturm followed Wild Horse and the other two Quahadas into Black Beard's camp of fifteen to twenty lodges near present-day Roaring Springs. The chief said he was tired of fighting and anxious for peace. After learning that the main camp was two sleeps, or nights, away, Dr. Sturm continued his journey, calling Black Beard "a jolly good fellow."[20] Wild Horse led the way from the small Quahada camp to Tosah-Honovit, or White River, one of Quanah's favorite campsites. The Eagle, however, was not there, so the party headed west-southwest across the Llano Estacado. Eighteen miles north of what is now Post, Texas, the Indians pointed to a butte that they called Wa-we-ohr, Blowing Mountain.

Near sundown they camped on a large creek the Indians knew as Tah-tem-a-reie, Trader's Creek. This was the North Fork of Double Mountain Fork of the Brazos, which led into Yellow House Canyon at present-day Lubbock, Texas. The Spanish called this stream Rescate, or Ransom, because of the many Anglo and Hispanic captives exchanged there by the Comanches to New Mexican traders for trade goods. On May 1, Dr. Sturm and his Quahada guides entered Quanah's camp along a small stream near the present town of Gail in Borden County, Texas. He wrote:

On our arrival in camp the Indians rode up from every direction to see who we were and finding we were peace messengers they invited us to alight from our horses, which were taken care of by the squaws while we were escorted to a large tent (tipi) by the men. Here we divided our tobacco, coffee, and sugar with them which pleased them immensely, having had none of the luxuries for a long time. After they had drunk some coffee we proceeded to their council house. After the usual preliminary smoking I delivered the message sent out by Col. [sic] Mackenzie, with which they all seemed pleased. . . . After the talk was over I was invited to the tent of their great medicine man Isah-tite [Esa-tai] with whom I had a big talk. He told me that he would go with me and that all his people must go. He is a very young man but has a good deal of influence among his people.[21]

Dr. Sturm wrote on May 2, "We are again in counsel, and Quanah, a young man of much influence with his people, made a speech in favor of coming in here. The medicine man then told his people they must all prepare to come in to Fort Sill and as his authority seems to be absolute, they all agreed to start tomorrow. . . . They have agreed to surrender everything but hope to be allowed to retain a portion of their horses for the use of their families. The people have treated us with the utmost kindness for which I must feel grateful and hope that General Mackenzie will treat them as leniently as possible."[22]

Whether he was to be treated leniently or not, Quanah knew that the time had come for him to impress upon his people the necessity of going to Fort Sill. Even before Dr. Sturm's expedition had reached his camp near Mucha-que, the Eagle had struggled with the most momentous decision of his life. Only the natural world could provide the answer. Accordingly, Quanah rode out from camp to Cañon Blanco and climbed a large mesa. With a buffalo robe drawn over his head, he fought his greatest battle. For himself, he would rather die than surrender. But should he lead his people to their death? He despised the reservation Indians who planted crops and drew subsistence from the agency, but he thought of his mother. She had been white and had learned to live the Indian way. Perhaps he could learn the white man's way. Down on the flat ground below the mesa, a rangy wolf turned his head toward Quanah and howled, then trotted off to the northeast, toward Fort Sill. Above him an eagle glided lazily and then whipped his wings in the direction of Fort Sill. These were signs from the Great Spirit, and Quanah obeyed.

Esa-tai told Dr. Sturm that although he (Esa-Tai) was no chief, he exercised great influence over the people because he treated them kindly and never abused them. "He says he has a big heart, loves everybody and every living thing, that he never gets mad or strikes even a beast," wrote Sturm.[23]

On May 4, while en route to Fort Sill, the Indians camped on either Sand Creek or on the south fork of the Double Mountain Fork of the Brazos. From Sturm's journal, "The Indians are having a big dance tonight and make it to be the last Medicine dance they ever expect to have on these broad Plains. They say that they will abandon their roving life and try to learn to live as white people do. They are anxious to raise stock and show a great preference to sheep-raising."[24]

One can only imagine the feeling of loss the Indians experienced, for in addition to losing their freedom to move about, Quanah and his fellow Quahadas were leaving the sacred burial ground of their ancestors to the white man's cattle, and, later, to the plow. But leave they did, keeping to a leisurely pace, chasing and killing three wild horses and capturing one, on their way to Fort Sill. Sturm stayed in Esa-tai's lodge throughout the journey, noting in his journal that the Wolf Prophet was in charge of the movements of the village. "When he says move, we move and when he says stop we stop. If I ask any one when we will start they refer me to him always." Quanah, then, was clearly the chief of war, deferring to Esa-tai in civil matters.

On May 11, 1875, the Quahadas camped on upper Tepee Creek, a few miles south of present-day Matador. The Indians' obvious love for the campsite prompted Sturm to write, "I know these Indians bid adieu to these their old haunts with many regrets. Some offered pretty stern resistance to going in and I can not much blame them for it. They were always watchful and Troops would never have overtaken them. But they are learning the ways of their white brothers and sisters and are fond of dress, feathers, and ribbons, coffee and sugar and they have given up their old haunts, leaving their great vast plains to go down to live in the lower ground and learn the ways, virtues and vices, of their white brothers."[25] That same day, a party of several Comanches, including Quanah and Black Beard, rode on toward Fort Sill with a message from Dr. Sturm to Mackenzie. It was Sturm's first communication with "The General" in three weeks.

On May 17, the Quahadas and their white companion camped on a little creek southwest of the town later to be named after Quanah in what was to become Hardeman County, Texas. The water in the creek, which ran northward toward Red River, was so mixed with buffalo urine that they had to dig for potable water. "The Indians have killed a large number of Buffalo today and we will be detained here drying the meat," Sturm wrote. "The Children had fine sport chasing chaparral hens. . . . Occasionally a buffalo will dash into camp and create quite a stir . . . the old women howling and the little ones crying and the larger boys and girls joining the chase."[26]

On May 23, Sturm wrote to Mackenzie that there was "no discontent among the Indians. I have told them the first time I met them, that all the Warriors would have to go into the Ice House and this they all expect to do."[27] After crossing the flooding

North Fork of Red River and Otter Creek, the Quahadas camped about twelve miles west of Fort Sill on June 1st. Sturm said in his journal:

> From this camp I dispatched a messenger to let General Mackenzie know that the Indians would be ready to meet the troops opposite the Signal Station there to surrender themselves and their arms to the military authorities of the United States. According to appointment about noon of the 2nd of June the Indians were met by the Troops and quietly surrendered themselves and their arms, and were escorted by the Troops to Fort Sill. Arriving there they marched to their place of confinement and all the warriors were put under guard. The old men and the squaws proceeded to their appointed camping ground and quietly encamped. Their horses and mules were turned over to the Troops and here ended my labor in bringing the Quah-de-res band of Comanches from the Staked Plains, their former home, into the Indian Reservation.[28]

At last Quanah met his old enemy, General Mackenzie, face to face. Ernest Wallace describes it as "a brief and undramatic meeting; they were both too proud to make overtures or to reveal their feelings at a moment that must have been deeply stirring to each of them. Thus, the Comanche war chief began his second life—as a peaceful reservation Indian."[29]

Nearly eight years after the Treaty of Medicine Lodge, on which the Quahadas had refused to place their "mark," the warriors of Quanah's band spent their first night on the little island of the reservation in a roofless ice house with a stone floor. Outside, soldiers stood guard. Once a day an army wagon loaded with raw meat stopped in front of the carefully guarded door, and two soldiers threw chunks of meat over the high walls to the Indians. Gotebo, a Kiowa warrior who was imprisoned before Quanah's arrival, told Colonel Nye, "They fed us like we were lions."[30]

Since Quanah had spoken in favor of coming in, and because he was immediately assigned to seek scattered bands of Indians still in the wild, it is unlikely that he had to stay in the ice house. Quanah himself told Goodnight that Mackenzie took an intense interest in him from the moment he arrived at Fort Sill.

This would not be surprising; the man who was to lead The People on the "white man's road" was, according to Nye, blessed with native dignity, "superior intelligence, shrewdness, and force."[31] Using all his skills, Quanah quickly went about consolidating his influence over the Comanches. William T. Hagan, in *American Indian Leaders*, writes, "The shift of the Quahadis to the reservation environment markedly accelerated Quanah's rise to prominence among the Comanches by introducing new political conditions. The problems inherent in administering an Indian reservation encouraged agents to foster a degree of political unity among the Comanches previously unknown to them. Clearly it was easier to treat with them as a single group and through only a few chiefs, or preferably a single chief, than to deal with several autonomous bands and their leaders."[32]

In the weeks immediately following the surrender of the Quahadas and the other bands who fought the soldiers to the last, the authorities at Fort Sill focused on Mow-way (Shaking Hand) and Esa-tai as the two leading candidates for principal chief of the Comanches. Toshaway (Silver Brooch) and Esahabbe (Milky Way), both Penateka chiefs, were respected by the whites for their early efforts to make peace with the dominant culture, but the Penatekas were joined to the Wichita agency, having been moved there from their reserve in Texas by Agent Neighbors in 1859 as a result of pressure exerted by John R. Baylor and his constituents. Even if Toshaway and Esahabbe had not been separated from the Comanches now occupying the reservation adjoining the Wichita agency on the south, members of the Quahada, Yamparika, Noconi, Kotsoteka, and other bands who had fought the white man to the bitter end would probably not have followed the Penateka chiefs. Other chiefs who had exhibited strong leadership abilities were Howeah (Gap in the Woods) and Iron Mountain, both of whom were Yamparikas, and Horse Back, a Noconi. All three had placed their "mark" on the Treaty of Medicine Lodge, which provided the legal structure for life on the reservation.

Quanah's influence among the Comanches was attributed to his courage and skill as a war leader. Polygamy was also a status symbol among the Indians, signifying wealth and importance, and as early as 1865, Quanah had at least two wives, according to Butterfield, who owed his escape to one of them. Certainly, Quanah's revelation to Mackenzie that he was the son of Cynthia Ann Parker created special interest in him, prompting his rivals to credit his white blood as the reason for his rise to preeminence among The People. Wallace, however, said of Quanah, "He co-operated intelligently as a free Comanche—not to be mistaken for a white man's Indian."[33]

When he learned of Quanah's identity, Mackenzie immediately sought to contact Cynthia Ann, only to learn that she was dead. According to Hagan, "Two years later Mackenzie wrote one of Cynthia Ann's brothers in Texas, conveying Quanah's desire to meet his Texas relatives and his request for a wagon to help him live like a white man. His letter apparently brought no response. It was not until Quanah became a celebrity that his white relatives were interested in acknowledging their relationship to a former Comanche raider."[34]

From the beginning, Quanah was cooperative with agency officials. His first few faltering steps on the "white man's road" were straight and true. The former war chief of the fierce Quahadas was now bent upon a path of peace, even though he was, as were all The People, "politically, economically, socially, and spiritually bankrupt. Traditional culture patterns were no longer applicable."[35] Showing the same leadership qualities he had exhibited in taking charge after the death of Bear's Ear in the battle with soldiers several years before, Quanah now sought to fill the leadership vacuum created by the loss of the tried and true cultural patterns of life in the Stone Age world in which the Comanches had recently lived. So one of the Eagle's first services to the agency, and to his people, was to use his influence in finding the few scattered bands who remained in the wild and inducing them to come to the reservation. Herman Lehmann gives this account of Quanah's visit to the band with whom he was living at that time:

> We went far up on the plains, and Quanah Parker and four other Indians came to us and urged us to go on the reservation, saying that the Indians' wild life was over. Quanah told us that it was useless for us to fight longer, for the white people would kill all of us if we kept on fighting, but that if we went on the reservation the Great White Father at Washington would feed us, and give us horses, and we would in time become like the white men, with lots of good horses and cattle, and pretty things to wear. He said the white men had us completely surrounded; that they would come in on us from every side, and we had better give up. Some of the braves wanted to go to the reservation at Fort Sill, and some did not want to go, so there was much disputing and arguing. Quanah remained with us about four days, promising us that if we would go to Fort Sill we would not be punished or hurt in any way, and that all would be well with us. Finally our band agreed to go in, and when Quanah started we went along with him.
>
> There were several of us who went reluctantly, myself, Hishortry, Cotopak, Esatema, and Watsacatova. We started on and Quanah sent scouts ahead to notify the soldiers at Fort Sill that we were coming in, and to give us all protection. In a few days we began to meet white people everywhere, but as Quanah could speak English we got along all right.
>
> We were within about fifteen miles of Fort Sill when I saw a cloud of dust and heard the soldiers coming to meet us. I was riding a black mare and a pretty swift animal, so I turned and rode for life back toward the Wichita Mountains.

Quanah took after me and ran me for three or four miles before he caught me. He told me there was no need to be afraid, that I would not be hurt. I would not agree to go with him; then he told me to go to his camp, and gave me directions how to get there. When he got back to the crowd the soldiers were there and had my comrades surrounded. All were disarmed and were taken on to Fort Sill, where they were placed in a stockade and kept prisoners for some time. I followed Quanah's instructions and found his camp without being seen by the soldiers. My comrades were made to work around the post and to do farm work, with which they were not familiar. I stayed with Quanah and herded his horses for him, hunted occasionally, and soon became somewhat reconciled to my situation.[36]

Lehmann lived with Quanah for some time. Although the authorities at the agency wanted the adopted Comanche to return to his family, he steadfastly refused. General Mackenzie later saw Lehmann's mother in Fredericksburg, Texas, and described the young man who was living with Quanah. Mrs. Lehmann did not think the description fit her long-lost son, but she wanted to be sure. So Mackenzie returned to Fort Sill and discussed the situation with Herman Lehmann and Quanah. Lehmann later wrote, "Quanah Parker told me how to find the way back to his camp, and promised to take care of my horses while I was gone. He said he would be a brother to me, and insisted that if I did not have any people that I should come back and live with him."[37]

But Herman Lehmann, after nine years with first the Apaches and then the Comanches, did find his white family and, after a lengthy readjustment to a language, culture, and religion he had long forgotten, lived once again as a white person.

Quanah, too, was beginning the second portion of his life. In his late twenties, the great war chief of the Quahadas was embarking on an uncharted course as a civil chief among a people he had, since his first raid thirteen or fourteen years before, constantly fought. Not only did Quanah pass within the span of a single lifetime from a Stone Age warrior to a statesman in the age of the Industrial Revolution, but he accepted the challenge and responsibility of leading the whole Comanche tribe on the difficult road toward their new existence.

In July of 1877, Quanah returned to his old haunts on the plains of Texas as an emissary from General Mackenzie to Old Nigger Horse and the 170 Comanche warriors who had slipped away from the reservation the previous December. Soon after leaving Indian Territory, Old Nigger Horse and his braves had attacked buffalo hunters who were camped below the caprock near present-day Post, Texas. A hotly contested battle between Comanches and hunters was later fought in Yellow House Canyon in what is now Lubbock County. Soon after that fight, Captain Phillip Ludwell Lee of Company G of the 10th Cavalry went onto the Staked Plains and killed Old Nigger Horse. After the chief was killed, his band scattered across the plains and continued their attacks against the buffalo hunters.

A band of hunters was organized under James Harvey, a hunter and veteran Indian fighter, and they vowed to chase the Comanches down and make "good" Indians of them. Throughout May, June, and half of July, the party of twenty-four hunters scouted the Llano Estacado in search of the Indians. John R. Cook, who was a scout for the expedition, wrote, "Three different times we arrived at places the Indians had recently left. But they were elusive, and were cunning enough to send us on two fool's errands."[38]

In mid-July, the hunters were camped on Bull Creek in present-day Borden County, where they were joined by forty black soldiers of Company A of the 10th Cavalry under the command of Captain Nicholas Nolan and Lieutenant Charles Cooper. The hunters scouted for the soldiers, who were supposed to do the fighting if the Indians could be found. A few days later, the scouts saw Indians near Lagunas Sabinas, or Cedar Lake, in present-day Gaines County. Word of the sighting was sent to Captain Nolan, but pursuit of the Indians was not required, for according to John R. Cook in *The Border and the Buffalo*, "five or six Indians were coming straight for camp from the south, bearing a white flag. When they arrived at our camp it proved to be Quinnie or Quana [Quanah], a half-breed Comanche, two oldish bucks and two squaws. Quana handed Nolan a large official envelope, which contained a commission from General McKenzie, post commander at Fort Sill, to Quana to hunt up the Indians and bring them in. . . . The document was on heavy crisp paper, and was addressed to whom it might concern. It stated that the Indians wanted to give themselves up to him at Fort Sill, but they did not want to fall into the hands of the Texas authorities. The document cautioned people against molesting Quana in his mission."[39]

Captain Nolan was not happy with Mackenzie's decision to involve Quanah in the chase, for bloodying Indians was still the best way for officers to distinguish themselves on the western frontier. Quanah's search for the renegade Comanches was, in effect, a threat to Nolan's success, for if Quanah found the Indians first, Nolan would be robbed of his own chance for glory. Quanah indicated to Nolan that the Indians had gone southeast toward Mustang Spring in what is now Martin County and that he was going there to urge them to return to the reservation. Cook later noted that Quanah's ruse had worked to perfection, for the Comanches escaped to the north while Nolan's command was scouting in the opposite direction.

While Quanah was completing his mission of finding the Comanches and leading them back to the reservation, Nolan and his men succumbed to the heat and lack of water on the treeless llano. Just after Quanah had left, some scouts rode into camp shouting that they had seen Indians leaving Laguna Rica, or Rich Lake, in present-day Terry County. In their excitement to get under way, many of the men either filled their canteens only partially or did not fill them at all. In the days ahead, they were to learn how precious water was on the Llano Estacado. At the end of the second day in search of Indians, the object of their pursuit changed to water. All thought of fighting Indians had passed from the men's minds. The trail led across present-day Hockley and Cochran Counties and into New Mexico to what is now southeastern Roosevelt County, where they stopped near Lingo at a mound rising some fifty feet above the plains, now known, because of the black troopers of the 10th Cavalry, as Nigger Hill. There the men drank their own urine and that of their horses, liberally sprinkled with sugar to make it more palatable. On at least two occasions, horses were killed and the men drank their blood. At last Nolan's command found water at Double Lake, northwest of present-day Tahoka in Lynn County.

Once he had succeeded in bringing in the renegade bands, keeping his fellow Comanches on the reservation was only one of Quanah's problems. The greatest challenge was, and would continue to be for some time, the specter of hunger; there was sometimes beef, and occasionally buffalo, to satisfy the Indians' hunger for food, but the aching of the heart required food of a spiritual nature—peyote.

7

PEYOTE

Between the songs Quanah tried to explain the meaning of this worship to me. It was the peyote worship . . . under the influence of the peyote, Quanah said they got their inspiration from the Great Father while the white man got his from the Book. He said, "All the same God, both ways good."
— Reverend J. J. Methvin, 1937[1]

The spiritual dimension of Native American life had for centuries sustained the red man. The quest for a vision that would show the emerging young warrior the power that would sustain him in his physical life and prepare him for the afterworld to come was the most important experience of an Indian's life. Peyote enhanced the quest, and a religious ritual involving its use combined psychic experiences with a physical feeling of well-being, easing the warriors' boiling anger and feeding their spiritual hunger for divine guidance, especially after they were confined within the boundaries of the reservation. Removed from what had once been their home, they were prevented from making the migrations that had once extended for hundreds and thousands of miles as they searched for game or went on the war trail; now The People sought journeys of a different kind through the use of peyote.

The word *peyote* is derived from the Aztec *peyotl,* which was one of the offerings made to the gods in Aztec temples, where the "buttons," or roots, of this small, hallucinogenic cactus plant were ritually consumed. Down through the ages, in other regions of Mexico and in South Texas, particularly in the deserts where peyote grows most profusely, men of less advanced civilizations also consumed this "medicine of the gods." And late in its history, according to Alice Marriott and Carol K. Rachlin in *Peyote,* "the story of peyote is inextricably entangled with the lives of two men: Quanah Parker, a half-blood Comanche Indian leader, and James Mooney, an ethnographer from the Smithsonian Institution, Washington, D.C."[2]

Mooney "discovered" the peyote religion in Indian Territory in 1891, but its use by the Indians was known well before that. Another white man, E. L. Clark, in a letter written at the request of Agent E. E. White in 1888, said, "The Indians of this reservation have used very little of this article prior to 4 years ago except a few of the Quahadas (Comanche of the band of Quanah Parker) who happened to be associated with the Lipan Apaches. . . . Ten years ago (1878) during the period of the subjugation of the Kiowa and Comanche and other Indians of this and [the] Cheyenne Reservations by General Mackenzie, there was but very little of this medicine in circulation and [it] became very difficult for the Indians to obtain. They paid one dollar a piece for it, but since that time it has been introduced more and more by Mexicans and renegade Apaches and Comanches. But now having been such a source of speculation the price is greatly reduced."[3] Clark's letter was included in Agent E. E. White's annual report for 1888. In his introduction, the agent described Clark as "a gentleman who has lived among the Comanche many years and knows their habits and language probably better than any person on the Reservation. He is a truthful man. . . ."[4]

Other evidence that Apaches, specifically the Lipans, introduced peyote to the Comanches in the late 1800s was recorded in 1949 by a man named McAllester, in an interview with two old Lipans living with the Comanches in Oklahoma. The two Apache elders said that they had taught Lipan Apache peyote songs to their Comanche friends. (Interestingly enough, one of the Lipan peyote singers was Billy Chiwat, or Billy Chevatts, who had been one of Herman Lehmann's captors.)

Another Lipan made a statement regarding peyotism that appeared in the *American Indian YMCA Bulletin* of November 1918. Below is an excerpt:

> My name is Pa-na-ro. I am a Lipan Apache; I live five miles northeast of Indiahoma, Oklahoma, on my allotment. I am about 57 years old.
>
> I knew about peyote before any of these Indians in the Oklahoma country knew about it. I first ate peyote in Mexico. My great-grandfather was the first [Lipan] to make use of it in Mexico, and it was brought among the Indians here years after. It was used as a medicine at first, and no women or young people ate it as they do now. It is called mescal-peyote in Mexico; here in Oklahoma it is called peyote. . . .[5]

While the agents and missionaries on the reservation did not know about the peyote religion until the late 1880s, once they did get wind of the Indians' use of "drugs," Quanah and the other peyote men were hard-pressed to prevent the disruption of their religion. In 1883, E. L. Clark, who obviously disdained the peyote ritual, told one of the officers at Fort Sill of a medicine man who "has in his possession some of those poison roots which Quanah and Black Beard used to be so crazy to get hold of. He calls several of the Indians together and has them eat those roots which acts directly upon the brain and throws them into a sort of dream, and after recovery they conclude that they have had a divine revelation, and the secret of their sickness is then imparted to each of them by him."[6] Five years later, Clark was again agitating against the peyote religion when he wrote to Agent E. E. White, "Having seen a copy of your order prohibiting Indians of this reservation from the use of mescal beans I write this for your information. . . . The Comanche name of this article is *Hoce* or *Wok wave*. . . . almost every boy 15 years of age has adapted [adopted] the practice and think of nothing else. . . . I understand it is kept by almost all of the little stores in Greer County . . . also in large quantities at Doans Store."[7]

The peyote ritual was (and still is) complicated and formal, as befits a religious ceremony. Mooney describes it as the Kiowas and Comanches practiced it:

It is usually performed as an invocation for the recovery of some sick person. It is held in a tipi specially erected for the purpose, and begins usually at night, continuing until the sun is well up in the morning. As many men as can sit comfortably within the tipi may participate, but, as a rule, women do not take part in the ceremony proper, but occupy themselves with the preparation of the sacred food and of the feast in which all join at the close of the performance. A fire is kept burning in the center of the tipi, enclosed within a crescent-shaped mound, on the top of which is placed a sacred peyote. Following an opening prayer by the chief priest, four peyotes are distributed to each participant, who chews and swallows them, after which the sacred songs begin to the accompaniment of the drum and rattle, each man singing four songs in turn, and are kept up all night, varied by the intervals of prayer and other distributions of peyote, with a peculiar baptismal ceremony at midnight. The number of "buttons" eaten by one individual during the night varies from 10 to 40, and even more, the drug producing a sort of spiritual exaltation differing entirely from that produced by any other known drug, and apparently without any reaction. The effect is heightened by the weird lullaby of the songs, the constant sound of the drum and rattle, and the fitful glare of the fire. At some point during the ceremony the sick person is usually brought in to be prayed for, and is allowed to eat one or more specially consecrated peyotes. At daylight the Morning Star song is sung, when the women pass in the sacred food, of which each worshiper partakes, and their ceremony concludes with the Meat song. The rest of the morning is given to friendly gossip, followed by a dinner under leafy arbors, after which the various families disperse to their homes.[8]

Mooney also mentioned the Christian elements of the ritual, which began to appear in the early 1890s. He wrote, "It may be proper to state that many of . . . [the peyote] eaters wear crucifixes, which they regard as sacred emblems of the rite, the cross representing the cross of scented leaves upon which the consecrated . . . [peyote button] rests during the ceremony, while the Christ is the [peyote] goddess."[9] Sun worship was also an influence, since the circular peyote, like the sun, was considered to be between the supplicant and the Creator.

Although Quanah utilized his leadership skills as a founder of the peyote religion among the Comanches, having practiced it before going to the reservation,* he, along with most of The People, did not find meaning in the Ghost Dance, which sought power to drive out the whites and bring back the dead Indians and the buffalo. In May 1890, Quanah dictated a letter to David

---

* Ernest Wallace, after interviewing Post Oak Jim, Breaks Something, White Wolf, and Frank Moeda for *The Comanches: Lords of the South Plains*, concluded that the Comanches used peyote before the middle of the nineteenth century. Since Quanah was born just before 1850, he must have been familiar with peyote throughout his lifetime. In the early days of its use, its purpose was to provide a war medicine to aid the warrior in foreseeing danger and in hunting animals or fighting enemies. The late Peyote Chief Red Codynah of Cyril, Oklahoma, concurred, saying, "There was peyote among the Comanches long before Quanah's time, but Quanah started it up again and made it a big religion throughout North America."[10]

Grantham, his business manager, who wrote it for him and addressed it to Agent Adams. The letter informed Adams of the advent of the Ghost Dance on the southern plains. Quanah said, "I hear that the Koway [Kiowa] and Shianis [Cheyennes] say that there are Indian come from heaven and want me to take My People and go see them. But I tell them that I want My People to work and pay no attention to that, that we depend on the Government to help us and no them."[11]

Quanah understood the potentially tragic consequences of the Ghost Dance, having followed the incantations of Esa-tai in the medicine lodge sixteen years before, when the Wolf Prophet had promised invincibility to the white man's bullets, just as Ute medicine man Wovoka, the Messiah of the Ghost Dance, was currently predicting a return to the old way of life and promising that ghost shirts and dresses would protect those who wore them against the enemies' guns. Quanah believed that Wovoka's claims of Indian invincibility were as empty as Esa-tai's erstwhile promises that his sacred paint would ward off the deadly slugs of the buffalo guns had been. Quanah had believed Esa-tai in 1874 to his sorrow; now he refused to believe Wovoka. It was clear that the old life and the buffalo would not return, no matter how desperately Wovoka's disciples among many tribes wanted to believe the vision of life as it had been before the invasion of the Europeans.

In the *Annual Report of the Bureau of Ethnology, 1892–93 Part II*, Mooney described the most important feature of the Ghost Dance as hypnotism. "It has been hastily assumed," he wrote, "that hypnotic knowledge and ability belong only to an overripe civilization, such as that of India and ancient Egypt, or to the most modern period of scientific investigation. The fact is, however, that practical knowledge, if not understanding, of such things belongs to people who live near to nature, and many of the stories told by reliable travelers of the strange performances of savage

shamans can be explained only on this theory . . . hypnotic ability
no less than sleight-of-hand dexterity formed part of the medicine
man's equipment from the Saint Lawrence to the Gulf. . . ."[12]

It is obvious that Quanah's action in counseling against the
Ghost Dance prevented the Comanches from experiencing a horror similar to what befell Big Foot and his band of Miniconjou
Sioux at Wounded Knee only seven months after Quanah had
sent his letter to Agent Adams. For in December 1890, the 7th
Cavalry under Colonel James W. Forsyth killed 84 men and boys
of Big Foot's band, along with 44 women and 18 children, as they
danced the Ghost Dance. None of the Indians' ghost shirts and
dresses protected them from the bullets and cannon shot of the
soldiers. The myth of Wovoka's vision of the Indians' return to
the old ways was forever shattered by the twisted bodies of the
dead, grotesquely frozen in the ice and snow as they fell along
the gullies and in the open meadows of the little valley of
Wounded Knee Creek, South Dakota. "As for the great messiah
himself," Mooney stated in the *Annual Report*, "when last heard
from [several months after the Massacre of Wounded Knee] Wovoka was on exhibition as an attraction at the Midwinter Fair in
San Francisco. By this time he has doubtless retired into his
original obscurity."[13]

While Quanah was leading The People on a spiritual path
over the white man's rocky road, his leadership skills continued
to impress the agents who headed the Kiowa–Comanche–Apache
Reservation in southwestern Indian Territory. To reward him,
Agent P. B. Hunt, who served from 1878 to 1885, hired a Texas
attorney in an attempt to establish Quanah's right to the tract of
land granted to his mother in Texas, but because Cynthia Ann
had failed to confirm her title, Quanah was denied ownership of
his mother's land.

In spite of his reputation as a warrior and the esteem in which
he was held by the agents, who had the ability to influence a

chief's rise to power, Quanah was not considered a true chief by some members of The People. There existed an anti-Quanah faction among the Comanches that believed that the agents favored him because he was related to the Parker family in Texas. But Quanah *was* a chief; perhaps his detractors had forgotten, for example, that in 1874 he had worn his eagle feather war bonnet in the attack against the buffalo hunters at Adobe Walls. According to Nye in *Bad Medicine and Good*, ". . . a man who is poor in spirit does not have an eagle feather war bonnet. They are worn only by men with strong hearts—chiefs! That has always been the custom, from earliest times."[14] Also, Quanah had been a polygamist at least as far back as 1865, and polygamy was practiced mainly by chiefs and leading warriors. An investigator from Washington, in an attempt to counter charges that agents were promoting Quanah, who was both a polygamist and a leader in the peyote religion, explained in a report to his superiors in 1904 that Quanah was chief of the Comanches, and was so because of his ability and his status among the Indians, not as a result of government favoritism. "If ever nature stamped a man with the seal of headship she did it in his case. Quanah would have been a leader and a governor in any circle where fate may have cast him—it is in his blood."[15]

So long as he could practice the peyote religion, Quanah's spiritual hunger was satisfied, but it was harder to quiet the physical hunger that gnawed at him and all of The People—hunger for the food that for centuries they had hunted and gathered for themselves. The Comanche leaders were faced with the problem that they were now dependent on the United States government for everything they ate. Beef, the white man's domestic "buffalo," was sometimes scarce. Unscrupulous contractors often delivered fewer cattle, in poorer condition, than the regulations required. Even more intolerable, perhaps, were the white rustlers who periodically went on horse stealing raids among Indian herds. With the Indians now restricted to the reservation, the white criminals had free access to trails leading to and from Indian country while the Indians were denied them. General Randolph B. Marcy, in his *Border Reminiscences*, published in 1872, said, "Nearly all the trouble we have encountered, in our dealings with the Indian tribes for the last fifty years, has resulted from the noncompliance on our part with treaty stipulations, together with the injustice and fraud practiced upon them by dishonest agents; and this is as well understood and appreciated by them as it would be by white men."[16]

In 1878, officials at the reservation at last decided to allow the Kiowas and Comanches to go on a buffalo hunt. What the Indians found, however, were not herds of living buffalo but plains strewn with decaying corpses of the once numerous animals, and buffalo skulls bleaching in the sun. In an effort to locate even a small herd of their staple food, Quanah led a band of men, women, and children to Prairie Dog, or Palo Duro as the whites knew it. Charles Goodnight was now the proprietor of Prairie Dog. The big canyon, with its sheltering walls, sacred cedar, and clear running water that had once been shared by the Indians and other creatures of the wilderness, was now *owned* by Charles Goodnight. He was not unaware of potential threats to "his" land, however. His account of Quanah's visit follows:

> In February or March of 1878, Indians made their appearance on the border of our ranch. We maintained outposts on all outer borders of our property whose responsibilities were two-fold, curtailing wanderings of stray cattle and watching for rustlers. At that time I had headquarters in the upper canyon at what is known as the "Old Home Ranch." The outposts sent me a runner stating that Indians were coming in considerable numbers. I at once mounted a good horse and started to meet them. In cases like this it was better to do so, as a fight was less likely to result.

The weather was bitter cold, with snow on the ground. Before I could meet the Indians, they had entered the canyon, where they split in three bands. This necessitated my following up three trails. There being no buffalo at this late year, the Indians were killing cattle at a fearful rate, having killed about forty before I got to them. The Kiowas seemed to be in one band with two bands of Comanches cooperating.

When I met the Kiowas, they were in an ugly mood. It looked like trouble. I thought my time had come. Fortunately, there was with them a renegade Mexican with a good knowledge of Spanish. I soon reached an understanding to the effect that the band was to proceed up the canyon to Headquarters for a parley. Quanah himself was with the last bunch I found. It was sundown and he was making camp. Designated as the Captain by a captive [a captured Mexican] whom I encountered, Quanah, upon my asking him his name, made this memorable reply, "Maybe so two names—Mr. Parker or Quanah." Quanah meant "odor" or perfume.[17]

After reaching "headquarters," a log house constructed two years previously, Goodnight took a diplomatic approach. The man who had led the Rangers and U.S. soldiers to Pease River where Quanah's mother had been captured now proposed a treaty, but first he had to submit to the questions of ten Comanche inquisitors standing in a circle around himself and the interpreter. Quanah, suspecting that the white man the Comanches called Leopard Coat Man (The Dangerous Man) was a Texan, asked, "Are you a Tejano?"[18] "Knowing their bitterness toward the Texans and knowing that they knew little of the United States as a whole," Goodnight said, "I told them I was from Colorado—which was in a sense true. They set out to prove or disprove my statement, asking me concerning every prominent point in Colorado. Luckily, my trail work had made me familiar with the country from the Rockies to the Texas line. I could and did answer every question correctly. . . . They were finally convinced that I was, as they

expressed it, 'no Tejanos,' and expressed themselves ready to
negotiate a treaty."[19] One of the questions Goodnight answered
was, "What are you doing here?"[20] The pioneer cattleman replied
that the great Captain of Texas also claimed the country that the
Comanches had always considered theirs, so the controversy was
really between The People and the State of Texas. He went on
to promise to settle with the Indians if they proved to be the
rightful owners. Quanah was impressed with this answer.

Goodnight and Quanah measured each other in an effort to
determine what the other man had to offer. "I've got plenty of
guns and plenty of bullets, good men, and good shots, but I don't
want to fight unless you force me," Goodnight said. He then
pointed to Quanah and said, "You keep order and behave yourself, protect my property and let it alone and I'll give you two
beeves every other day until you can find out where the buffaloes
are. . . ."[21] This was the treaty agreed upon, the famous treaty of
Chief Quanah Parker and the Leopard Coat Man.

On the second or third day of the Comanches' presence in
Prairie Dog, twenty-five black soldiers under the command of a
white lieutenant rode up to headquarters. Said Goodnight, "When
old Quanah saw them he turned white. I told the Lieutenant to
turn his horses loose and make camp—everything was all right.
The troops and the Indians remained at the ranch about three
weeks, until orders came from Fort Sill for the return of the
Indians to the reservation."[22]

For a reason Goodnight could not quite decipher, the Comanches and Kiowas hated black people. So strong was their
conviction that the buffalo soldiers (so called by the Indians because they thought the hair of blacks resembled that of the buffalo) were "heap bad medicine," the Indians had long refused to
scalp fallen blacks. "One morning," Goodnight related, "there was
a disturbance between the Indians and the Negro soldiers, and it
looked like Hell would be popping in a few minutes. I got the

Lieutenant, Quanah, and the interpreter together to find out what the trouble was. The Lieutenant told the interpreter in English to tell Quanah if he did not make the young braves behave themselves that he would take their guns away from them. The interpreter told Quanah in Spanish what the Lieutenant said. Quanah's reply in Spanish was, 'You can have the guns,' then pointing to some tepee poles, he said, 'We will use those on the negroes.' "[23] The implication was that he would not waste a bullet on a "buffalo soldier."

Accompanying this group of black soldiers from Fort Elliott in the eastern Texas Panhandle was Billy Dixon, who wrote in his autobiography, "I met Quanah at this time, having gone out with the troops. As we were riding along one day, he began talking about the fight at the Walls. When I told him that I was one of the men that had fought against him, he leaned over his horse and shook my hand. We became good friends."[24] It is doubtful that his response would have been the same had Dixon been black.

After spending three weeks in Prairie Dog, Quanah received the order from Fort Sill to return to the reservation. The buffalo hunt, if it could be called that, was over. The Eagle turned his back on the country he had considered his since childhood and went back to the little "island" of the reservation. Only in the spiritual realm could Quanah find release for his wandering soul.

While the peyote religion, later to be called the Native American Church, was spreading among the Comanches and Kiowas, white missionaries were seeking to bring Christianity to the "wild Indians." Thomas Battey, a young Quaker teacher working among the Kiowas, recorded his early efforts to influence them:

> I first went to the Kiowa camps on the first day of the 12th month, 1872, but did not attempt to open a school among them until the 23rd of the 1st month of the present year. Having erected a tent, and fitted it up, I commenced a school,

with twenty-two children in attendance, which continued for something over a week, during which time the children manifested their aptitude to learn by the progress they made. The elder people also manifested much interest in it by their frequent visits, their attention to the exercises, and their encouraging words to the children. About this time, much sickness prevailing among the children in the camp, some superstitious Caddoes, who happened there, attributed the sickness among them to me, telling them I was a bad medicine man, and had made some of their children sick when I was with them, two of whom died. . . . They usually listened attentively to my talk, but mostly consider their own mode of life far preferable for them.[25]

Reverend A. E. Butterfield was another missionary to the Indians, and he became friends with Quanah, who had captured his father in 1865. Although Quanah never accepted Christianity in a formal sense, like most other Comanches he believed that Jesus was the Brother of the Red Men as they sat in their peyote tepees and prayed to the Creator.

According to the late peyote medicine man Red Codynah, "The center of the Peyote Religion is the sacred button. We ask Him to talk good things to the Man, The Creator. We say, you put us here. You are supposed to help everyone. Come now and have pity on us poor Indians as we bow before you."[26] The ritual itself has been the same since Mooney's account in 1896. Throughout the night, participants smoke tobacco, eat the sacred buttons (or drink peyote tea), pray to the Man, drum, and sing. Every man seeks something good. If he is ill or is praying for the health of another, he is looking for what Christians call "a miracle." If the peyotist seeks an answer to a problem or direction in his future course of action, he seeks a vision to point the way. Every supplicant prays for his fellow worshipers, thus feeling an infusion of power from the communal experience. At midnight and again at daybreak, the peyote man sprinkles cedar on the fire burning behind the crescent-shaped altar. As the fragrance of the sacred cedar perfumes the lodge, the peyote chief spreads the smoke with an eagle-feather fan or a fan made from the sacred feathers of the cormorant or water turkey. Sometimes a fan made with feathers from the yellow hammer is used. The healing, fragrant smoke washes over every participant, leaving him (or her, in present times) purified and at peace.

Before a peyote ceremony can be held, someone must go to the peyote chief and ask for a service. Perhaps someone is sick or someone has a big problem that requires a lot of prayer. Those in need will be prayed for during intervals between the drumming and singing.

J. J. Methvin's account of his presence at a peyote ceremony in the summer of 1888 verifies other versions:

Early one morning when the Indians were camped near the Agency, I heard the noise of the tom-tom. I supposed that someone was sick and the Medicine Man was going through his performance to frighten the evil spirits away. I thought I would go and see if I could give them a more intelligent way of caring for the patient. I made my way through the camps following the sound of the tom-tom until I came to the tepee I sought. I saw instantly that it was a special medicine tepee and that some kind of worship was going on.

Lying in front of the tepee on the grass were two of Quanah Parker's wives. I asked what was going on in there and one of them motioned for me to go in and see for myself. I lifted the flap and went in; I quietly took my seat in the circle of worshippers. They all had their eyes shut, beating the tom-tom, rattling the rattle gourd and singing in a wild way. When the noise had stopped Quanah opened his eyes and discovered me; he smiled his recognition and welcome.

Between the songs Quanah tried to explain the meaning of this worship to me. It was the peyote worship. . . . Under the influence of the peyote, Quanah said, they got their inspiration from the Great Father while the white man got his from the Book. He said, "All the same God, both ways good."

Quanah was dressed in a costly buckskin suit, his face painted in fantastic colors. His hair was long and plaited, rolled in strips of beaver skin, hanging down his back. The Medicine Chief sat beside him on the west side of the tepee. . . . After the worship was over that morning, the women came about nine o'clock with an ample supply of food and placed it before the worshippers. Each one before partaking of the food, offered a portion to the sun and to . . . the peyote button lying on the furnace.[27]

Though he was a strong proponent of the peyote ritual, Quanah had immense respect for the missionaries who came to minister to his people. Reverend Butterfield, and Reverend and Mrs. A. J. Becker, who were Mennonite missionaries to the Comanches at Post Oak* near present-day Cache, Oklahoma, made a strong impression on all of the Indians. Dorothy Lorentino and the late Anona Birdsong Dean, granddaughters of Quanah, remembered the Beckers with deep affection. Nevertheless, when the Mennonite couple first arrived at Post Oak, they could get no response from the Indians. Reverend Becker managed to preach to them through an interpreter, but they did not quickly embrace Christianity. "I feel more comfortable in my Peyote Church," said Edward Mahseet in 1986. "You don't have to have all the restrictions of being a Christian. It's a one way approach to God."[28]

Contemporaries of Quanah felt much the same way. But Mrs. Becker gradually persuaded the Indians around Post Oak to become Christians, acting as a field matron and using her position as nurse/social worker to gain access to the homes and hearts of The People. Those who knew her described her face as if the light of God emanated from her sparkling eyes and bright smile.

---

* According to Quanah's granddaughter, Dorothy Lorentino, "Grandfather gave the land for the mission, and as there was a large oak tree there, the Beckers named it Post Oak Mission."

The Indians, humble and hungry as they were, saw God's love in Mrs. Becker's benign visage and in her selfless acts of generosity to others. Mrs. Lorentino said of the Beckers, "They did everything for the Indians, from delivering babies to making coffins. They taught us how to cook, can, and sew. The Beckers stayed with families when they lost loved ones. They were like parents to the Indians."[29] And according to Mrs. Dean, "The Becker boys would wail and carry on when an Indian died."[30] Both women said, "They lived and died with us. They're buried in our cemetery. They gave us something that can't be described. They gave us religion and taught us how to live. They were very gentle people. They gave us a foresight to education, morals, ideals. They are still an influence in our lives."[31]

One of the early influences of the missionaries was to teach the Indians to bury their dead in cemeteries and not to cut themselves as a way of mourning for lost loved ones. In 1897, Dick Banks, one of Quanah's adopted white sons, saw an Indian man die and witnessed the old ritual that the missionaries were trying to supplant. An elderly Indian called his family and friends together and told them, "At noon I go away."[32] Those he had called there early in the morning began to prepare for the burial of the dying man. Banks described the process:

> They gathered up his bedding, guns and all other personal belongings, caught two horses and hitched them to an almost new wagon, left them standing nearby and waited. About noon this man ceased to breathe. They immediately bent his feet back to his hips, securely tying them in this position. . . . Then he was placed on his bed of blankets, rolled up inside them and securely tied. Then placed in the waiting wagon with his squaws and his sister, they started their journey not far distant up into the mountains on the south side of the Wichita range. They carried in this wagon besides themselves and the corpse, all of his clothing that they could not get into the pack or bundle with him, an ax and a butcher knife. On

reaching the foot hills of the mountain there was a gradual slope up to, or near some ragged cliffs. They drove as near this point as they possibly could, using force on the team of horses. This being accomplished, they dismounted from the wagon, lifted the corpse out and laid it out to one side on the ground of rocks, took the butcher knife and cut the harness off the horses, cutting each piece of leather many times. In earlier days they would kill these two horses but the Government forbade their doing this so they would take the butcher knife and disfigure the horses by cutting the hair on the neck down to the hide as close as possible, also shaving the tail close to the hide. Then they would leave the horses to die, or hunt for food and water. Most always there was plenty of grass and water, and this treatment very seldom worked any hardships on these dumb animals. The immediate family did not want to see these animals anymore, so by the time the hair was grown out they were then usually sold or given to some of their friends in the tribe. Then the Indians took the ax and chopped each spoke of the wagon wheels into two pieces, cut the tongue, single-trees and double-trees in two, and busted up the body of the wagon as much as they could, broke the handle out of the axle and left it with the rest of the wreck. Then they proceeded with the corpse up into the cliffs, placing it in under the rocks and completely covering it. This accomplished they took the butcher knife and cut or haggled about one half the hair out of their heads, hacked their arms from the wrist to the shoulder in a manner of places, fully believing that by shedding some of their blood, that the wrath of the "Great Spirit" who had just taken their loved one from them, would be appeased. They then threw the knife away and bleeding profusely from their self-inflicted wounds, started afoot the homeward journey back to camp.

On reaching camp the entire village would break out anew into wailing and crying and beating their chests. The dead man's name was very seldom spoken again, in the presence of his loved ones.

I have counted as many as twenty hacks or wagons on top of the mountains which have been destroyed when some Indian man was buried in this same vicinity.

About this same year the Post Oak Mission was established, and as I recall the first grave was dug at this mission burial ground in the winter of 1898, and through the Christian teachings and preaching of the Reverend Kobfeldt, the Comanche Indians began accepting the Christian mode of burying the dead.[33]

The Indians learned many good things from the missionaries, most of whom Quanah respected. One day he was riding with Reverend Butterfield soon after the ice house at Fort Sill was completed. (It had been the roofless prison of the Quahadas in 1875.) Butterfield went inside and emerged with a block of ice, prompting Quanah to say, "White man heap smart. Pretty soon he make hot in winter."[34] Butterfield asked Quanah why he thought so, to which the Chief replied, "He make ice come in summer, so he make hot in winter."[35]

But while Quanah enjoyed the company of Butterfield and other missionaries like the Beckers, he believed in the peyote religion, and he had many followers, as this letter from a man he had helped indicates:

Cantonment, Okla.
March 8, 1909

Mr. Quanah Parker
Dear Friend,

Well Friend I will tell you how I feel. You know when I got to your place I was sick, and this time I got well now. I am now working for agent now. Every morning I feel better and better. I always think about you and thank you for it. I am glad I working for money. I been making $45.00 for two weeks now. My wife and daughter are very glad to see I am well and this is all. As you told me to write back and tell you how I feel. If you got any [thing] to tell me write soon. I also like to have one of your pictures. I am glad you are truly Friend.

Mr. Bob Finger
Cantonment, Okla.[36]

Quanah had become a man of peace, and the peyote religion had helped him in his transition from warrior to U.S. Government subject. In his worship of the Creator through the intercession of the sacred peyote, the Eagle of the Comanches would continue to seek a vision of the path his people were to follow.

8

CATTLE

Their [Comanche] government is essentially patriarchal, guided by wise and fraternal councils. They are insensible to the wants and luxuries of civilization, and know neither poverty nor riches, vice or virtue, and are alike exempt from the deplorable vicissitudes of fortune. Theirs is a happy state of social equality, which knows not the perplexities of political ambition or the crimes of avarice.

— Randolph B. Marcy, 1866[1]

That someone had to lead the Comanches as a single spokesman was decreed by the whites who governed the southern plains tribes after the close of the Buffalo War. American bureaucrats had "chains of command" that always ended at the top: One big chief held sway over a well-defined governmental hierarchy. The Comanches, who had always settled questions of an important nature in council, were being pressured by reservation agents and those over them to accept one chief, in spite of the fact that each band was loyal to its own. The longer The People were on the reservation, the more this pressure for a single chief was brought to bear. Obviously, the one they chose had to have earned their respect through good leadership qualities and integrity of character. Although he had his detractors, Quanah rated high in both areas, and he was also highly intelligent.

In 1875, when the Quahadas rode proudly in to surrender to General Mackenzie, Quanah was in his late twenties. He was one of two young charismatic leaders in the Quahada band who, after the defeat at Adobe Walls, became rivals for the post of head chief of the Comanches; Esa-tai was the other. The Quahadas' Wild Horse was also qualified, known to be brave and generous. Other bands offered good candidates as well, but the Quahadas were blessed with three great leaders, and so many Indians from other bands were eventually forced to follow a Quahada chief instead of one of their own.

Some of the Quahadas preferred Esa-tai or Wild Horse to Quanah, but a considerable number of The People looked to Quanah for leadership in that critical point in their lives, just as Mow-way and Tabananaka had designated him to lead the village away from General Mackenzie during the Battle of Cañon Blanco in 1871. Although Parra-o-coom was still alive, healthy, and in camp when Mackenzie and his troops appeared, the older chiefs chose Quanah to devise a plan of escape. And Mackenzie himself appointed Quanah as chief of the Comanches shortly after the Quahadas' surrender at Fort Sill in 1875, though he must have been aware that the older chiefs still resented Quanah's youth, and his white blood in particular.

Although the initial action in placing Quanah over the Comanches was made by General Mackenzie, Agent P. B. Hunt concurred with Mackenzie's choice. Certainly, Quanah's white ancestry on his mother's side had made the Eagle a celebrity among the soldiers and frontiersmen he had so vehemently fought only a few months before, though they were unaware that the fierce Quahada war chief was the son of Cynthia Ann Parker until Quanah surrendered. The color of his skin did not betray his white blood, but his eyes did. The late Tom Corridon, a pioneer banker in Iowa Park, Texas, reminisced about Quanah's blue-gray eyes in 1985: "Very wonderful eyes. They were penetrating. He looked through you."[2] Pioneer Olive King Dixon described Quanah as "the finest looking man in all the Comanche tribe; tall, straight and well-proportioned, darker than many warriors, and with the dignity in his features which marks the higher type of North American Indian. . . . He was a born leader and had great influence among his people."[3]

Nevertheless, many did think that Quanah's white blood was the principal reason for his rise to power, and no doubt it was a factor in that most racist of eras in American history. Anti-Indian sentiments were high among the uneducated masses crowding in around the reservation, while antiwhite feelings ran just as high among the Indians. So by virtue of his mixed blood, Quanah found himself in the middle of opposing cultures. Though admired by whites and many Indians, he was still the focus of considerable envy on the part of his fellow Comanches, some of whom continued to balk at the new restrictions being imposed upon them and thought that Quanah was being favored. William T. Hagan writes, in *United States–Comanche Relations,* that on the reservation, Indians "were pressured to break down into smaller groups and to open family farms. Hunt [the agent for the Kiowas and Comanches] deliberately whittled away at obstreperous chiefs by singling out members of their bands and making them responsible for receiving rations and annuities for subdivisions of the band. Several actions of this kind could reduce a chief's following from over a hundred to a mere twenty or thirty members."[4]

When Hunt became agent in 1878, he divided the Comanches into thirty-three bands for the issue of rations. These bands ranged in size from Cheever's 115 members to two bands having only 10 each. Esa-tai had 91 followers and Quanah had 93, placing him in third place numerically among the various leaders. According to Hagan, "Quanah's rise to prominence revealed the new elements at work in the Comanche hierarchy. He was about twenty years of age in 1875, the year he surrendered to Colonel [sic]

Mackenzie. Despite his growing reputation as a warrior it probably would have been many years before he could have hoped to become a band leader had the Indians remained free nomads. However, in the new order he became a band chief in 1875, singled out for preferment by the agent and Colonel Mackenzie."[5]

Though he was still a very traditional Comanche, Quanah soon drew criticism from Comanche conservatives, who thought he was catering to the whites. He did indeed have a good relationship with the cattlemen; many of them aging Indian fighters, they remembered him most as a warrior, and they enjoyed exchanging accounts of the battles of old. Also in his favor was the fact that Quanah had always been true to his word; he did not belong to that group of Indians who had abused the Quaker Peace Policy by buying guns and ammunition on the reservation and heading for Texas, New Mexico, Colorado, or Kansas to steal horses, plunder, and kill. In refusing to sign the Treaty of Medicine Lodge in 1867, Quanah had elected to fight to the end, but when he did surrender to General Mackenzie, he cooperated fully with white military and civilian authorities on the reservation. So his integrity, intelligence, and force of character, along with his willingness to work within the system, propelled him into the role of primary chief for a widely divergent group of people. This was a challenge he met with all his energy and thought, as the whites believed he would do; every agent for the Comanches chose him as Chief.

Owning individual property was, of course, a concept foreign to the Comanche culture, but it was one of the provisions of the treaty that led them to the reservation, and one that caused trouble and confusion. When The People entered into their new life, the only form of wealth they had was horses. Their lodges had always been constructed in the same way and were simply and similarly furnished. Members of the band had always shared the kill, regardless of who made it. To be generous, to give everything one had, was—and is today—a highly valued characteristic among all Native Americans. Life on the reservation was a severe contrast; The People had to depend on the government for beef and game, which, as Quanah learned when he led the buffalo hunt to Charles Goodnight's Palo Duro in 1878, was becoming scarce, not only on the reservation but off it. Hunger in those days was endemic, prompting General Mackenzie to write to his superiors that "in order to give these people an opportunity to work they must be fed. This is not now properly done. . . . It is due to the Indians if we intend to control them and keep them from their old life, to feed them properly; and it is our clear duty to our own people to so control them. . . . It is all very well to say you ought not to run away or behave badly to people who are driven to do so by the pangs of hunger, but it is not likely to be very efficacious. The case is so clear, the duty of the United States so plain, that a long discussion is not needed."[6]

In Quanah's vision of the future, cattle were to become the Indians' wealth, and education their hope. Keenly observant, Quanah studied his white friends and learned not only to speak their language, English (if somewhat brokenly), but also to follow their thought patterns, to analyze the reasons for their success. Early on, he learned about the cattle business from Charles Goodnight and General Mackenzie. The first time Quanah discussed cattle with Goodnight was after they had forged their treaty at Prairie Dog, as Goodnight mentioned in the following letter to Agent Hunt:

September 25, 1880

Dear Sir:

I have for two years past promised Quanah a good Durham Bull for cattle which General Mackenzie gave him. I will do this if he can come for him and I may give him one or two cows. . . . If he should get such stock, you will please assist him keeping them from Texas cattle not acclimated as the cattle taken from here will take the Texas fever . . . and he will lose them for that cause.

> Yours respectfully,
> Charles Goodnight[7]

So in 1878, Goodnight had given Quanah, an experienced horse breeder, advice on raising cattle, and according to the above letter, Mackenzie had given him some cattle himself before 1880. Quanah was becoming a pioneer cattleman along with his white counterparts, and he was to develop strong personal friendships with the cattle barons in the Red River country of the late nineteenth century. Through Goodnight, Burk Burnett, the Suggs, the Waggoners, and others, Quanah met leading political figures, and he always made a strong impression on the veteran Indian fighters. His former foes were now his colleagues in the cattle business, and the Comanche war chief and the white frontiersmen joined together in preserving the last remaining outpost of the open range.

Even if the buffalo were gone, Quanah and his people could still ride across open reaches of rolling prairie lands, lush with grass and carved with deep, narrow creeks and rivers that during the spring rains roared in pristine fury, while in the languid heat of August they gurgled along lazily. At chosen times, The People had powwows and peyote ceremonies under the towering cottonwood trees that rose majestically from the banks of the streams of the reservation.

Out on the prairie, where Quanah's horses and cattle grazed, the circle of his brand burned into their hides—a design in the shape of the sun, peyote, and the tepee—and up in the Wichita mountains, a man could pray and make medicine. In the mountains, visions came especially readily on the edge of a cliff called Medicine Bluff. So there remained a measure of freedom the Indians could treasure. Thus far, The People did not have to live close to whites unless they chose to.

For generations, the Quahadas and all northern Comanches had *not* chosen to, nor did they want "squaw men" in their camps. Numunu had a tradition of disliking any Europeans, beginning with the Spanish. During the period when the Indians maintained control over their own reservation land, they were able to avoid the whites except for trail drivers pushing cattle through, soldiers, and people at the agency headquarters and agency store.

Of course, there were still the white outlaws; once the City of Refuge for Indians returning from raids into Texas, the Kiowa–Comanche–Apache Reservation was now instead a refuge for rustlers, murderers, gamblers, and thieves, most of them from that same Texas. Mackenzie was so disturbed by the lawless element of the whites encroaching on Indian lands that he wrote to his superiors asking for more law-enforcement authority for the Army. Frequently, he sent out detachments of troops to pursue the horse thieves who were plundering the Indians' herds. For example, in January of 1876, Howea, a Comanche chief, sent word to Mackenzie that thieves had made off with sixty-six of his horses. Troops were dispatched to look for the outlaws, but even an hour's head start across the three-million-acre expanse of the reservation gave the thieves ample time to escape. As a last resort, Mackenzie placed three squads of men on permanent patrol and ordered them to arrest "any and all parties found on the reservation who have not proper authority for being within said limits."[8] Though thefts of horses continued, they did decrease in frequency.

In spite of the irritant of the lawless element, Quanah still saw the necessity of dealing with the whites. A man of two worlds, he realized that every Indian, regardless of his feelings in the matter, would have to adapt to the dictates of white civilization. His son Baldwin said of his father, "Recognizing the inevitable, Quanah set about making the best of the new conditions, and being still young . . . he quickly adapted himself so well to the white man's road as to become a most efficient factor in leading his people up to civilization."[9]

Not only did the Indians face many changes in their transition from their old life on the prairies to a semi-sedentary life on the reservation, but so also did the whites who wandered across Indian Territory in search of work. In 1891, a family by the name of Mayes came into the country around Cache looking for work splitting rails for fence posts. Several of the Mayes boys asked Quanah for jobs, and he readily agreed to hire them and their father. According to Lena R. Banks, Quanah's neighbor at that time, "There was no house in which the family could live, so the wagon bed was set on the ground and used as a sort of a store room and they improvised a little shack in which they slept and ate. They hewed out timber in a long thick piece which looked like a piece of lumber, walled up the sides to about five feet in height and about ten by fourteen, with the means of stakes and poles and a roof was shaped and over this the wagon sheets were drawn taut. . . . there was much fear among the white people who live in this part of Oklahoma, in the early days of wild animals; there were a great many panthers in the mountains, also great herds of cattle and horses in the country and in the evenings the panthers came down in the valley and would kill a great many calves and colts. On a balmy spring evening the mournful and constant lowing of the cattle interspersed with the screams of the panthers was enough to instill fear into the bravest heart."[10]

The unfortunate Mayes family had unwittingly chosen for their makeshift home an area frequented by the big cats. A wall had been built around the shack to ward off cattle and other animals, and two dogs guarded the family at all times. Nevertheless, one night after the family had retired, a panther struck. Both dogs began to bark, and "just outside the wall and on the side where the baby was sleeping there was heard a clawing and scratching noise. . . . The father and one of the boys grabbed their Winchesters, but were afraid to venture outside as the night was pitch dark and they had no lantern. The dogs continued barking; after the baby had been moved away from the wall the scratching sound ceased and the animal rushed at the dogs, catching one of them. The family, huddled together in stark terror, heard the dog being strangled and as the last struggling sounds were made, they could hear the animal dragging the dog toward the creek. The other dog rushed into the camp and in terror huddled up to the family, whimpering and crying. . . . As soon as daylight came the men searched outside the camp and found the tracks of a huge panther."[11]

The next day Mr. Mayes broke camp and went to Quanah to get the wages due him and his sons. Quanah liked the Mayes family and offered them better wages to get them to stay, but the father said he was "not going to live where there was so much danger from wild animals."[12]

Cowboys on both sides of Red River, however, were undaunted by the dangers of the Indian wilderness. Cattlemen loved the land in their way almost as much as the Indians did, and many of them were eager to learn more about Indian ways. Dick Banks left Vernon, Texas, when he was seventeen years old and rode alone across Red River onto the reservation with the specific intention of getting better acquainted with Chief Parker, whom he had previously met on the H-S Ranch. The year was 1897. In Banks's words, "[there] were no way-side inns nor human habitations along my pathway where I might obtain shelter or food. . . . When night overtook me, I was at the mouth of Coffee Creek where it empties into Deep Red Creek some ten miles due east of where the town of Frederick is today. My three horses were tired and I was weary myself after being in the saddle all day, so stopped under a big tree just at dusk. . . . Underneath the tree, I raked down deep to get dry leaves to kindle a fire and had a pleasant surprise. The ground was covered with well-seasoned pecans."[13] After roasting pecans in the embers of the fire, young Banks drank from Deep Red Creek and bedded down for the night. To make his bed he laid a tarpaulin on the ground and then spread his blankets over it, his boots and saddle serving as a pillow. After slipping under the blankets, he pulled the lower end of the tarpaulin up to make a warm, dry bed. "During the early morning hours," he wrote, "I was awakened by a pack of howling wolves and a little later the wild turkeys began their morning call, which meant that day was breaking. On pushing the tarpaulin off my bed, I found that I was snowed under some four inches of snow, which accounts for me being so warm."[14] Banks did succeed in reaching Quanah, with whom he lived as an adopted son for a period of one year.

The cattle business had really begun in earnest in 1867, thirty years before young Banks's entry into Indian Territory, with the advent of the railroad and the blazing of the Western Trail, the westernmost version of the Chisholm Trail, through land that was later to become the Kiowa–Comanche and Cheyenne–Arapaho reservations. The Chisholm Trail had first traversed the Indian country farther east in Chickasaw territory, but as farmers in Arkansas, Missouri, and eastern Kansas offered resistance to the cowboys and their droves of cattle, trail drivers moved west into Indian Territory just north of present-day Vernon, Texas, at Doan's Crossing. The destination for cattle heading north was now a new cow town called Abilene, on the westward-expanding Kansas Pacific Railroad; Joseph McCoy of Illinois had opened a cattle market at Abilene in 1867, when thirty-five thousand head of longhorns walked the long trail from South Texas to the plains of Kansas.

At that time, steers were selling for an average of fifteen dollars a head. "In the off-season," according to J. Marvin Hunter in *Trail Drivers of Texas,* "he [McCoy] sent several men into Texas to carry word of the opportunity for disposing of cattle that had opened at Abilene. This missionary work bore fruit, and in 1878 75,000 head were shipped out. . . . It was only the beginning. Abilene became an island in a sea of cattle. For fifty miles around, wherever there was living water, Texas cattle were held to fatten before being offered for sale."[15]

Just south of the reservation, Doan's Crossing was named for the proprietor of the general store. Built on the Texas side of Red River, Doan's Store served as a supply center and gathering place for cowboys and Indians alike. Hunter writes, "There was no town there; just the trading post established by Corwin Doan. It was at Doan's Store that the new Western Trail to Dodge City, which became the main traveled route when the Chisholm Trail began to fade, due in part to the granger agitation in Kansas against Texas cattle, reached Red River."[16]

Doan's Store was the "jumping-off place" for Texas cattle and the cowboys who drove them. Corwin Doan recalled meeting Quanah shortly after the young Comanche went to the reservation in 1875. "After moving to Doan's Store," Mr. Doan said, "I saw a great deal of Quanah, who at that time had become head chief. He told me that he had often been invited to return to his white relations near Weatherford but he had refused. 'Corwin,' he said, 'as far as you see here I am chief and the people look up to me. Down at Weatherford I would be a poor half breed Indian.' "[17]

In the spring and summer of 1879, Doan marveled at the first herds coming up the trail from Texas. "One hundred thousand cattle passed over the trail by the little store in 1879,"[18] he said. "In 1881 the trail reached the peak of production and three hundred and one thousand were driven by to the Kansas shipping point."[19] The store did a thriving business, and the Doans thought nothing of "selling bacon and flour in carload lots, though getting our supplies from Denison, Sherman, Gainesville, and later Wichita Falls."[20] After the post office was established at the store in 1879, "many a sweetheart down the trail received her letter bearing the postmark of Doan's and many a cowboy asked self-consciously if there was any mail for him while his face turned a beet red when a dainty missive was handed to him."[21] The first house at Doan's was made of pickets, and had a dirt roof and dirt floor, with a buffalo robe for a door. On cold winter days a huge fireplace warmed hunters, Indians, and the family, who sat together around it.

Quanah was beginning to enjoy the power of his position as Chief, and one of his moves was to join forces with the cattlemen to push through the complicated arrangements that had begun to be made in 1885 that would permit Indians to lease grazing lands to the Texas whites. According to Herbert Woesner of Cache, Oklahoma, "Quanah's friendship with Burk Burnett's son Tom helped to bind the relationship between the cattlemen and the Indians. Contact between Quanah and Tom Burnett was probably made before the leasing agreements were signed. Quanah's friendship with Tom probably came as a result of the negotiations. Quanah and Tom worked cattle together and hunted the wide reaches of prairie and meadows in the mountains."[22] Quanah was always reaching forward, and he profited from Tom's knowledge of the cattle business, while Tom himself learned patience, a heightened appreciation for the wild, and even the Comanche language from Quanah. Woesner, a longtime neighbor of Quanah's daughter, Neda Birdsong (now deceased), quoted her as saying, "Tom Burnett stayed at my father's part of the time. He would rather live in the wilds with my father than work with Burk Burnett."[23] A letter from Tom to Quanah, written several years after the reservation had been opened to settlement, reveals the close personal relationship between the two men:

Fort Worth, Texas
February 4, 1909

Quanah Parker
Cache, OK.

Yours received this morning and are glad to know that you
have a nice looking party for the show and you can count on
me being there early in March. I am feeling first rate now and
think will go to my ranch in a day or so, suppose you know
that I bought the Burk Station ranch in Wichita Co. You have
been there and know the place, am very proud of it and am
sure it will make me lots of money. Quanah my advice in
regard to your little boy, is to take him to Lawton with his
mother and get them in the hospital where there will be a
trained nurse to look after him, if you do, tell his mother not
to let him have any thing to eat other than what the doctor
may suggest and also to see that he takes it bitter or sweet
and not to expect the medicine to cure him in one day. I have
seen lots of Comanches die for the want of a little medicine
and proper food. Trusting you will be on hand for the show,
etc.

I am as ever your friend
T. L. Burnett

The forty people will be all O.K.
S.B.B.* has not returned from the north yet, but am looking
for him any minute.
Tell Too-ni-cy [one of Quanah's wives] not to for-get my hat
band.

Tom B.[24]

---

* S. B. ("Burk") Burnett, Tom Burnett's father.

The herding of hundreds of thousands of cattle across Indian lands alarmed Quanah and the other chiefs, as well as the officials of the United States Indian Service. In an attempt to secure some benefit to the Indians from their rich grazing lands, on August 18, 1879, Agent P. B. Hunt wrote the Commissioner of Indian Affairs as follows: "Sir: I have the honor to state that I have for some time been trying to arrive at some conclusion as to how the vast area of fine grazing land now unoccupied, belonging to this agency, could be utilized advantageously to the Indians. There are tens of thousands of acres that are not touched any year, out of which a nice income might be realized. . . . If the grass of the reserves can be converted into cattle, why not do it? To make these people self-supporting they must have herds of cattle, and I am anxious to press the matter forward as fast as I can. The sooner they are supplied with cattle that much sooner will they be in that condition and to that end I want to bring all the points to bear."[25]

This letter was succeeded by correspondence from H. A. Lewis on October 19, 1881, in which Lewis asked the Commissioner of Indian Affairs for permission to lease grazing land in Greer County, which was claimed by Texas, although it was north of Red River. (Texas's claim to Greer County in the southernmost portion of the Kiowa–Comanche–Apache Reservation was predicated on that area's being bounded on the north by the North Fork of Red River. The Supreme Court later ruled that the Prairie Dog Fork of Red River was the boundary between Texas and Oklahoma, not the north fork, thereby excluding any claims by Texas to the area.) Indian Commissioner Price replied to Lewis's request to lease lands by saying, "Upon similar applications, the honorable Secretary of the Interior held that he had no power to grant the desired permission."[26]

Meanwhile, the Indians were getting their share of beef to eat—Quanah being an exception—but they had not yet learned the necessity of breeding cattle and building up their own herds. Having been helped by Mackenzie and Goodnight, Quanah was already in the cattle business. Nonetheless, he was not averse to taking a few steers as payment from the cattlemen for crossing the reservation. After all, the trail drivers relaxed their pace and allowed their cattle to graze as they passed through Indian country, and besides, unofficially the cattlemen were already paying the Indians for the right to cross. Robert Lemond was only sixteen when he helped nineteen other men to trail a herd of Texas cattle from Jack County to Dodge City in 1878. The herd consisted of twenty-five hundred fat steers ranging in age from three to six years. The cowboys from Jack County forded Red River at Doan's Crossing and, according to Lemond's account, "The first night in the Indian Territory, the Indians frightened the herd and a grand stampede took place, but the cowboys were expecting the Indians to do this, as it was their usual way of getting a quantity of beef left on the range, so that they could have plenty of beef to eat without the trouble of hunting for it."[27] Most of the scattered cattle were soon rounded up, and trail boss George Atkison "ordered the boys not to do anything at all to the Indians, but to cut out of the herd and give to them the number of fat beef which they felt was right for pay for the grass and water which the herd was using."[28]

In 1883, T. J. Burkett rode up the trail under the guidance of trail boss Daniel P. Gipson. Burkett described his first meeting with Quanah as follows: "One day Quanah Parker, accompanied by another Indian, came to me and wanted 'wohaw,* plenty fat, heap slick.' I pointed to Gipson and told Quanah he was the wohaw chief, but the . . . Indian shook his head and said Gipson

---

* This expression came from the Indians' hearing wagon drivers give commands to their oxen, before horses and mules were widely used to pull wagons.

was 'no bueno.' Gipson told me to ride into the herd and cut them out a yearling, and they went off with it. There were about 500 Indians camped near the trail, and nearly every herd that passed gave them a beef. Hundreds of cowboys knew Quanah Parker, and he had scores of friends among the white people."[29]

On another occasion, Quanah and one of his Comanche friends intercepted a herd of longhorns near the Wichita Mountains. Quanah was dressed like a white man. In the words of the cowboy who recorded the story, "Quanah had on a hat and pants with a six-shooter in cowboy style. . . . I made friends with Quanah. . . . When the boss returned to the herd after dinner, he gave Quanah a yearling and by that time four or five other warriors had appeared. They drove the yearling to their camp."[30]

One of the more interesting incidents occurred on the Western Trail in 1884. "When we reached the Comanche reservation," related T. T. Hawkins of Charlotte, Texas, "the Indians demanded horses and provisions from us. As George Saunders could talk Spanish fluently our outfit and Carroll Mayfield's outfit, which had overtaken us, decided to appoint George to settle with the Indians as best he could. Accordingly he accompanied the chiefs and some of the bucks to a tepee and held a council with them."[31] When the chief learned that Saunders could speak Spanish, the Indian and the cowboy talked about the old days of battles on the frontier. The chief (identity unknown, but surely not Quanah, as he was easily recognized by hundreds of trail drivers) became quite friendly as he discussed the streams between Indian Territory and the ranches of northern Mexico. He told Saunders that he had killed "heap white man" but was now "heap good Indian, no kill no man."[32] Saunders offered one horse and some provisions, and the chief gladly accepted. After the council, "About twenty young bucks riding on beautiful horses, came and helped us swim the cattle across the Canadian River. A number of our horses bogged in the quicksand and had to be dug out, which sport the Indians enjoyed immensely. They fell right in with our boys and helped in every way they could to pull the horses out, and when this work was finished they gave us an exhibition of their riding."[33]

This manifestation of goodwill would have brought smiles to the faces of the old mountain men and artists like Catlin and Russell. But while Texas cattlemen trailing cattle through the reservation got along surprisingly well with the Indians, Indian leaders and officials in the Department of the Interior were alarmed at the utilization of Indian grasslands by cattlemen from the south side of Red River. Undaunted by the government's refusal to allow them to lease Indian lands for grazing, the big ranchers of northwest Texas pushed their cattle over the river, thereby trespassing on the reservation. As Texans had done from the beginning of their associations with the Comanches, they relentlessly pressed for the use of the land, possession of it for the moment being out of the question.

In June 1882, Major Guy V. Henry, Commander at Fort Sill, wrote to the Assistant Adjutant General at the Department of the Missouri, "Sir: I have the honor to report my return from detached service, in the field, having been with Troop G west of here to the North Fork of Red River. Across that stream large herds of cattle are kept, they and the cowboys crossing from time to time to this side by accidental 'drifting'. The country is well watered and fine grazing, and is a strong inducement for citizens to take for that purpose. The Indians are watching along the river for any such actions, which in my opinion, would lead to hostilities. . . . The Indians here—Kiowa, Comanche and Apaches—are apparently well satisfied, but are in a nervous state of *tensive*, fearing an occupation of their country."[34]

General Sheridan responded to Major Henry's letter by writing to his superiors in Washington, "I do not think the troops should be required to perform this duty [of patrolling Indians' lands]. It is costly, unsatisfactory, and disagreeable work, and I doubt if it is in their power to do it if it is required of them."[35] Clearly, the Army was not going to "play cowboy." Instead, General Sheridan supported General Pope's contention that the Cheyennes, Arapahos, Kiowas, and Comanches be allowed to accept payment for leasing of their grazing lands. In his letter dated July 21, 1882, Pope wrote, "It is done by the Cherokees and other Indian tribes, and this lease of grazing privilege is part of their proper support derived from their own lands. In this case it would cure a trouble which may soon be past dealing with except by war."[36]

While the Departments of War and Interior were arguing over the question of leasing, the cattlemen, according to William Hagan in *United States–Comanche Relations,* "were making themselves at home, building corrals and fences and establishing camps. Obviously this could not have been done on such a scale without the cooperation of the agent and the Indians. Hunt had convinced himself that cattle could not completely be kept off, and under the circumstances the Indians might as well be paid."[37]

If the cattlemen from Texas were bold in grazing the Indians' lands without permission from the government of the United States, their trump card was "wining and dining" the chiefs. Because the Comanche sector of the reservation was in the south, bordering Red River, Comanche chiefs were royally courted by the cattle barons. Hagan writes, "According to one rancher involved, Quanah was put on the payroll for $50 a month, with four other Comanches receiving $25 each. In addition, at one stage in the negotiations Quanah was promised 500 cattle."[38]

Nonetheless, most of the Kiowas, whose lands were on the northernmost portions of the reservation, along with Comanche Chiefs Tabananaka and White Wolf (both older chiefs of considerable influence), opposed leasing land to the cattlemen. In councils convened to discuss the question of leasing, the arguments

went back and forth. Finally, on December 23, 1884, the Comanches, Kiowas, and Apaches held a council near Red River and
agreed to lease part of their reservation to the Texas cattlemen.
Agent Hunt filed the following report to his superiors in Washington detailing the decision reached by the Indians:

> It is a lease agreement made with certain cattlemen to occupy
> a portion of their reservation for grazing purposes for a period
> of six years for which six (6) cents per acre per year, is to be
> paid the Indians, besides the cattlemen are to give employ-
> ment to fifty-four (54) Indians as parties with whom the agree-
> ment is made are known to me to be reliable and responsible.
> . . . The section embraced in the agreement is on the border
> of their reservation and has never in any way been used by the
> Indians, but to a great extent has been depredated upon by
> trespassers and the most of it is unsuitable for farming. . . .
>
> I believe it is a wise thing for the Indians to make this
> agreement, as it will be a source of considerable income—will
> give employment to many young men—and will not deprive
> them of any lands needed by them for grazing their own stock
> and for farming purposes—and in addition it will protect them
> from the inroads made by trespassers upon their grass and
> timber.
>
> It is clear the paper is signed by a majority of the adult
> male population, embracing chiefs, head men and others, and
> is their own act made in conformity with the concerted right
> given them under the provisions of . . . statutes.[39]

Three months later, Quanah, Permansu, and a delegation of
Kiowas composed of Big Bow, Howling Wolf, and Tohauson went
to Washington to lobby for the leasing agreement. As a result of
their efforts, the Commissioner of Indian Affairs sent Special
Agent Paris H. Folsom to investigate conditions on the Kiowa–
Comanche–Apache Reservation. After spending a month on the
site, Folsom came to the conclusion that most of the Indians
opposed leasing. He also suspected collusion among Agent Hunt,

his chief clerk, Quanah and his backers among the Indians, and the Texas cattlemen; therefore, Folsom strongly opposed a leasing agreement.

But the political climate shifted in favor of Quanah and Permansu when a new Secretary of the Interior was appointed. In order to seize the opportunity accompanying this new development, two cattlemen, George W. Fox and E. C. Sugg, traveled with Quanah and Permansu to Washington to see the new secretary, Lucius Q. Lamar, who promptly appealed to the attorney general for a ruling on the legality of leasing Indian lands. In the absence of a treaty or convention ratified by Congress, the attorney general concluded that those leasing the land might be ejected from reservations, but they could not be treated as trespassers. So the Secretary of the Interior tacitly condoned the six-cent-an-acre lease that the cattlemen had negotiated with the Kiowas, Comanches, and Apaches.

Later that summer, the cattlemen made the first "grass" payment of $9.50 to each member of the Kiowa, Comanche, and Apache tribes. Many of the Kiowas and a few of the Comanches refused the money in protest. The leasing issue, in fact, was just one in a series of disagreements that plagued the reservation's inhabitants throughout the expansion of the cattle industry. But Quanah's position during this period remained strong due to his association with the Texas cattlemen and his cooperation with Agent Hunt. From the time he laid down his lance and shield, Quanah, while retaining his Comanche culture, attempted to acquaint himself with and adjust to the realities of The People's new existence in an alien world. In the first issue of the *Chronicles of Oklahoma*, a son of Reverend A. J. Becker wrote, "Quanah Parker was a born politician and orator, could speak English, but not read. He took many papers and had them read to him."[40]

Not only was Quanah well informed, but he was intelligent enough to use what he learned from newspapers, Washington politicians, Indian agents, and Texas cattlemen to his benefit and, as events were to prove, for the good of his people. In regard to the leasing agreement, not everyone agreed that it *was* good; Hagan wrote, "It would have been far better for the Indians if the cattlemen had been barred from the reservation and the grass reserved for Indian herds."[41] But it is doubtful that the War Department would ever have agreed to the use of troops to keep Texas cattle off the reservation in the face of General Sheridan's strong objections. Even if the Army had been inclined to protect the Indians' grasslands, a skirmish line of hundreds, perhaps thousands, of soldiers would have had to be deployed around the clock to do so. Clearly, the Army was unwilling, if not unable, to expend the resources in money and manpower to protect land that the Indians were not using. Even former Quaker Agent Lawrie Tatum advocated leasing. In a letter to Commissioner Price dated January 1, 1883, Tatum wrote, "Now, I would be thankful to know if the Kiowa and Comanche Indians saw proper to rent some of their reservation for a certain annual sum for the benefit of the whole tribe, to be paid directly to them in the way that annuities are paid by the Government, would such a contract be likely to be nullified by the Department? I learn that the Cherokees receive an income that way. If these Indians could rent a portion of their land for a term of years to a party who would employ the Indians as herders they would receive a double benefit."[42]

In spite of accusations by both Indians and whites that he was in cahoots with the whites, Quanah foresaw gain not only for himself, but for his people in earning money from lands that were already occupied by scores of Texas cowboys and tens of thousands of cattle. (Only those cattle trailed across the reservation on their way to the Kansas cowtowns were on the reservation legally.) Surely Quanah remembered the fields he had burned, the stock he had stolen or killed, and the "nesters" he had scalped or set afoot in his raids into Texas. It is clear from remarks he made at a celebration in Hobart, Oklahoma, shortly after the reservation was broken up for settlement, that he had little respect for farmers. L. H. Colyer wrote, "Two very special guests were Chief Lone Wolf and Quanah Parker. They each made a talk and I shall never forget one statement Quanah Parker made. He said, 'We love you white men, but we have fear of your success because it is so dry. This is a pretty country but you white men take it away from us. The only thing this country is good for is red ants, coyotes, and cattle men.'"[43] Quanah's love for the land was an integral part of his effort to keep it for himself, his people, and his partners in the cattle business.* The cattlemen had been good not only for Quanah, but also for the Kiowa, Comanche, and Apache people as a whole. According to Hagan, "The cattlemen's grass payments to the Comanches and associated tribes had reached $232,000 by 1900. In addition, some of the Comanches had opened farms and most of them owned cattle, a few holding herds that ran into the hundreds. Hunger was no longer the problem it had been through most of the 1880s."[44]

Some of his detractors accused Quanah of accepting bribes from the cattlemen. What has been termed "bribery" or "putting on the payroll" might be characterized as doing business in the Gilded Age. To be sure, while Mark Twain was attacking the corruption at New York's Tammany Hall and defending the rights of the laboring masses, the capitalists of the late nineteenth century were making money by the carload. For most of them, ethics and morality had no place in the business world, an attitude that Twain and other writers deplored in print and many deplored in general. Some have charged that Quanah and the cattlemen fit

---

* To this day, after many attempts and the expenditure of untold thousands of tax dollars, the U.S. government has, with few exceptions, failed to make farmers of the Comanches.

into this category of amoral capitalists. Clearly, the Big Five cattlemen—Burk Burnett, Daniel W. Waggoner, E. C. Sugg, J. P.
Addington, and C. T. Herring*—whose influence was felt from
Austin, Texas, to Washington, D.C., needed an advocate among
the Comanches for leasing Indian grasslands, and the logical person for them to contact was the chief of the Comanches. There
are three factors, however, that tend to make Quanah's relationship with the cattlemen less dastardly than it has sometimes been
pictured: the Big Five, as well as Quanah himself, were all men
of their word and men of high standing in their respective com-
munities; all of their official business was done under the aegis
of the United States Government; and, finally, correspondence
between Quanah and the cattlemen reveals a genuine respect for
Quanah long after the lease agreements had expired. For example,
here is an excerpt from a letter from Burk Burnett dated July 21,
1910:

My Dear Friend Quanah:

I stopped off at Quanah the other night and met Mr.
Elder who was down to see you the other day. I think the
arrangement you have made with him is all 'OK' for your
people to go on up to Quanah and wait there until you return
from Dallas, as you should be out on the Matador ranch by
the first day of November as there are not a great many deer
out there and if you do not get there on the start you will not
be able to kill any.

Now I kept a copy of the McKenzie [manager of the
Matador ranch in Colorado] permit that I sent you thinking
you might lose the original, and I am enclosing you the copy
and have fastened it to the letter so that you will not throw

---

* Quanah was a good friend of C. T. Herring, and they often dined at each other's
houses. On one occasion, Quanah, who was very impressed with Mrs. Herring's
cooking, offered her husband twelve horses for her.[45]

it away or lose it, and you must take good care of it as we might not be able to get another one from McKenzie as he is hard to get hold of.

It is pretty dry on my ranch, while it has rained in some places, but cattle are fine and fat and I will let you smack your old mouth on a fat cow or two as you come by my ranch. Now this I know will sound good to you and good to your women.

Your friend,
S. B. Burnett
6666[46]

The question of leasing was really a continuation of the battle for land that had raged in the Americas from the first landing of Europeans in the New World until Manifest Destiny had been realized. Quanah's compact with the cattlemen was novel in the respect that the contest for the use of lands on the Kiowa-Comanche–Apache Reservation pitted Comanches and Texas cowboys, formerly the most bitter of foes, against the white flood of small farmers, wood and rock cutters, traders, horse thieves, and cattle rustlers who were invading the reservation. The strength of the bond between Quanah and his Texas allies was evidenced by a confrontation between Quanah and Kiowa Chief Lone Wolf over the question of continuing the leases; the potentially deadly showdown took place sometime between 1885 and 1890 at a remote place on the reservation. The *Hobart Democrat-Chief* (of Oklahoma) gave this account of the fight in its August 4, 1925 edition:

Quanah Parker started the fight by slapping Lone Wolf, but the latter did not move. Then Quanah hit Lone Wolf over the head with a sixshooter, but still the Kiowa chief refused to offer resistance or strike back at his assailant. Nothing Quanah would do would provoke Lone Wolf to fight. Consequently, the Comanches won their argument.[47]

In return for Quanah's loyalty, and out of friendship for him, the ranchers made every effort to make the Comanche Chief comfortable. In the mid-1880s, Burk Burnett built him a house,* since the Eagle preferred a dwelling commensurate with his standing as Chief of the Comanches to money payments in return for his efforts to secure the lease. Also, Quanah traveled extensively, sometimes at his own expense, or, if the trip involved cattle, at that of the ranchers. One of his trips nearly killed him. George W. Briggs, who worked for Dan Waggoner, accompanied Quanah and Yellow Bear to Fort Worth in 1885. Briggs's job was to entertain the two Comanches and see that they had a good time. Instead, tragedy struck. No one had thought to warn the Indians about the gaslights in their rooms. According to Eunice M. Mayer, who interviewed Briggs in 1937, this is what happened:

> The Comanche leaders were sleeping in the same room; Quanah Parker returned early, while Yellow Bear was out seeing the sights. When Yellow Bear went to the hotel, he undressed and prepared to retire. He turned out the gas lights, then turned the gas on again immediately and was asphyxiated.
>
> Mr. Briggs was sleeping in a nearby room but did not learn of the tragedy until the next day; he arose early the next morning and went to visit an artesian well, returning to the hotel about eleven A.M.
>
> When he returned to the hotel some of the hotel officials asked if he had seen Chief Yellow Bear and Quanah Parker. Learning that they had not appeared that morning, Mr. Briggs went to their room and broke down the door.
>
> Chief Yellow Bear was dead. Quanah Parker had rolled off the bed and fallen in such a way that his nose was immediately in front of the crack under the door only six inches away. He had breathed enough pure air to escape death.

---

* Previously, Quanah and his family had lived in tepees.

Quanah Parker was unconscious for two days and little hope was held for his recovery, but he did recover to become the great leader of his tribe and the friend of Theodore Roosevelt. Mr. Briggs remained constantly at Quanah Parker's bedside until he began to show marked improvement.[48]

Thus was saved the life of a man whose remarkable rise to prominence inspired a generation of Americans, both red and white. The Eagle of the Comanches, by virtue of this narrow escape from death, was to serve his people for another twenty-six years.

9

STATESMANSHIP

What is the Indian Title? It is mere occupancy for the purpose of hunting. It is not like our tenures; they have no idea of a title to the soil itself. It is overrun by them, rather than inhabited. It is not a true and legal possession.
> — John Quincy Adams, to the Justices of the
> Supreme Court of the United States, 1822[1]

Every day when Chief Quanah Parker was home at his ranch near the Wichita Mountains, "Dummy," his deaf and dumb Comanche driver, drove the chief in his stagecoach or buggy the four miles into the little hamlet of Cache and stopped at the post office for Quanah to get his mail. In addition to correspondence relating to his duties as chief of the Comanches, Quanah also received the several newspapers that he had someone read aloud to him so that, as a fellow Comanche described it, "He writes on his tongue and we learn from him."[2]

Communications of all kinds were unusually good at Quanah's rural home in comparison with those of his neighbors, many of whom lived in dugouts, log cabins, or clapboard shacks. Burk Burnett had provided Quanah with an imposing twelve-room house, and as early as 1908 it had a telephone. In a letter dated March 17, 1908, W. R. Mattoon wrote, "I was sorry not to get to see you while at the Wichita Park for a few days recently. If your phone had been working, I would have liked to have you and your family come up to the buffalo yards last Sunday."[3]

Such communications were necessary not only for the sake of friendship, but also for business and political reasons. From 1884, when Quanah made the first of his many trips to the nation's capital, until his death in 1911, he was very active in politics, and, through the influence of the cattlemen and his own magnetic personality, he was invited to many social functions in southern Oklahoma and north Texas. He reciprocated with invitations to his spacious two-story house, called Star House because of the pattern of stars on its roof, where he entertained such notables as Theodore Roosevelt, whose picture hung on the wall in the dining room (just behind Quanah's place at the head of the table) from the time of the president's first visit in 1905. Others who enjoyed Quanah's hospitality at Star House were Commissioner of Indian Affairs R. G. Valentine; British Ambassador Lord Brice; Texas cattlemen Charles Goodnight, Burk Burnett, Tom Burnett, and Dan Waggoner; Army officers General Hugh Scott, General Nelson Miles, and General Frank Baldwin; Sioux Chief American Horse; and Comanche Chiefs Wild Horse, Esa-tai, and Powhay. For some reason, Charles Goodnight always slept on the porch when he visited.

Because the railroad had not yet reached the heart of the reservation by the mid-1880s, when construction was started on the house, double teams of mules were used to pull wagons loaded with lumber across Red River from the railroad terminal at Harrold, Texas, to Quanah's ranch north of Cache. Though Burk Burnett is credited with building the house, it is likely that other members of the Big Five shared in the expense of buying and transporting lumber and in hiring carpenters to erect the imposing structure. Each of Quanah's wives (some six or seven) had a bedroom to herself, while Quanah had his own private quarters. Next to his bed hung a photograph of his mother and his little sister Prairie Flower, a copy of which had been sent to him by Governor Sul Ross of Texas, who was Naudah's former captor.

Etta Martin recalled visiting in the Parker home in the early 1900s. She came to Oklahoma with her family in 1901, and described Quanah's household as it was then:

> A white man and his wife were the house keepers and, of course, they had white ways of serving their food. They told me that the squaws liked plain food best, meat and vegetables mostly, caring little for sweets of any kind. Pies and cakes were never served unless Quanah was at home. I met several of the wives and remember some of the names, but do not know how to spell the names, except TooNicy, who was his favorite. . . . He always took TooNicy everywhere with him and had her dressed like an American woman when he took her to Washington, D.C. with him. Also all the silverware was kept in her room and other nice things that were used only when they had special company. I visited in several of the wives' rooms and always found everything neat and clean and lots of fancy bead work, for that was the way the squaws spent their time, having nothing to do except keep their own rooms. . . . TooNicy took me to her room once and showed me a hunting jacket she was beading for Quanah that was very beautiful. No one shared Quanah's room except by special invitation from him.[4]

Quanah's hospitality and generosity carried over to those who worked for him, eliciting strong loyalty from them for reasons their stories make clear. Among them were Dick Banks, Knox Beal, Rudolph Fisher, Dave Grantham, and Charlie Hart. Banks—who at seventeen had spent a night in the wilderness under four inches of snow on his quest to meet Quanah—experienced his idol's hospitality and generosity from the moment he met him in 1897. Moving toward Fort Sill, Banks saw a company of Indian soldiers around the post. "Continuing my journey down to the Trading Post," he said, "I met, face to face, Chief Quanah Parker, whom I had met on the H-S Ranch. He greeted me with a hearty handshake and asked me what I was doing in his country. I replied, 'I am on my way to make you a visit, get acquainted with your people, find out what they were doing and how they were living.' Quanah said, 'Fine, come on out to my home and be my boy.' This act was the turning point in my life, opening up opportunities that rarely come but once in a lifetime to a wayward, wandering and homeless boy. On reaching Quanah's home, I had a hearty welcome and was made to feel at home because of the heart-felt interest taken in me by Quanah and all of his family. I was given a room upstairs in his beautiful mountain home and a certain chair at the table on his left. . . . In a short time I was able to speak and understand their language."[5] Banks lived with Quanah almost a year and remained a life-long friend of the chief.

Knox Beal was born in Texas. His mother was a first cousin of Cynthia Ann Parker, making Quanah and Beal blood relatives. While he was still a child, Beal's mother died. His father remarried soon after his mother's death, and young Beal did not get along with his new stepmother. Infected with wanderlust and still in his teens, Beal attended a one-ring circus in Fort Worth, his home town, and hired on as a water boy for the elephants. After the last performance of the circus he stowed away in one of the wagons and bade farewell to Fort Worth. After that, he recounted:

> One day we were showing in a little town near San Antonio and there were quite a few Indians present. After the show was over the Indians were standing around looking at the animals. When I came by leading one of the Shetland ponies one of the Indians stopped and asked to buy the pony, but the owner refused to sell. Then the Indian asked me my name, and said he would like to take me to his home in the Indian country in Oklahoma. . . . I lived in Quanah's home until I was grown. When the Spanish American War broke out, Quanah said to me, "Me fought for my people, now you go

fight for your people." With his blessing, I enlisted and served through the conflict.[6]

Rudolph Fisher told his story to pioneer H. M. Lindsay, in an interview with him in the 1930s. Lindsay had known Fisher before; he said, "One summer while we were at Fort Sill putting up the hay for the fort, I met Quanah Parker's right hand man, Rudolph Fisher. He was a captive. Quanah Parker was the Comanche war chief, and Fisher was his chief warrior. When I first knew Fisher, he had three wives, but I believe that one ran away from him."[7] Fisher had been born in Texas and had been carried away by a band of Comanches (not by Quanah's band; the Eagle was only a few years older than Fisher) when he was a small boy. When his natural parents learned of his whereabouts after the Indian wars had ceased, they wanted him to live with them, but by then Fisher could not adapt. He repeatedly ran away, and finally his white family gave up. Quanah became a father/brother figure for Fisher, and Fisher was content with that relationship.

Dave Grantham moved to Indian Territory from Texas in 1882. He secured a job working for Quanah, and as time passed he grew more and more influential in matters relating to Quanah's business affairs. According to *The Hobart Democrat-Chief* of August 4, 1925, Grantham was the one who hauled the first lumber to the reservation and supervised the building of Quanah's house.

Charlie Hart was perhaps the most colorful of the white boys Quanah either employed or adopted as his own. Hart was born in 1876 in Comanche County, Texas, to Zack Hart, a frontiersman from Alabama, and Ziffie Parker, whose father was a first cousin to Cynthia Ann Parker. When Charlie was ten years old, his father died, prompting Charlie's mother to move her six children to Quanah's ranch in Indian Territory. At that point, Charlie went to work for Quanah. He earned ten dollars a month doing odd jobs around the recently completed Star House. Quanah was soon rewarded for helping the widow Hart and her family, for Charlie proved to be honest, hardworking, reliable, and courageous.

Probably the most daring exploit Charlie ever performed for Quanah was riding to Arkansas to purchase cattle for the chief's son-in-law, Emmett Cox. Quanah "ordered his women to sew $1,000 in currency into the tail of Charlie's shirt. This now 14-year-old boy was sent all the way across the Indian Territory and part of Arkansas with this large sum of money. He rode for eight days through the lawless country knowing that his only protection was, as Mr. Hart himself put it, that 'no one would expect such a kid of a boy to have more than a quarter on him.' He rode alone in the day and camped alone at night, eating the jerky prepared by Quanah's wives and staking his horse nearby where he could get grass and water. He safely delivered the forfeit and helped trail 1,100 head of cattle back to his famous employer."[8]

When Charlie was nineteen, Burk Burnett, who was grazing cattle near Quanah's house, offered him a job. Tom Burnett was his father's wagon boss on the Indian lands that, at that time, were leased to the cattlemen, and Charlie worked with Tom from 1895 to 1905. Both men spoke Comanche and were very close to Quanah, and their knowledge of Indian customs and high regard for the chief provided a stabilizing influence on what was still a semiwilderness inhabited by high-spirited men, both red and white. It was due to this influence that a pastoral atmosphere generally prevailed on Quanah's range.

In 1892, however, Texans led by J. S. Works, commonly known as Buckskin Joe, had begun martialing forces to have the Kiowa–Comanche–Apache reservation opened to settlement. As General Manager and Editor of the *Iowa Park Texan*, Buckskin Joe used his newspaper to stir up land-hungry whites living to the south across Red River from the domain of the Indians and the cattlemen. In March of 1892, Works printed an unsigned letter in his paper under the headline "The Struggle Is On!"

Dear Sir:

By this morning's train Judge Flood left for Washington in charge of Quanah Parker, chief of the Comanches, and three other chiefs representing different tribes in the Nation. Their mission is in the interest and to protest against the opening of the Fort Sill country. They were met by cattlemen who arranged with Flood to accompany them. It would be advisable for you to wire our representatives to protest against them and state that they only represent, and are there in the interest of a few cowmen and do not represent the people of Northwest Texas or the Nation.[9]

At the conclusion of the letter, which may very well have been written by Buckskin Joe himself, was the following: "The above letter shows that people are 'on guard' and the following telegram was sent to Secretary Noble forthwith: 'Gen. J. W. Noble, Secretary Interior, Washington, D.C. Indian chiefs and cattlemen's attorneys en route to Washington to frustrate the opening of the Comanche reservation. Please favor settlers and expel cattlemen.' "[10]

On the same page as the preceding, Buckskin Joe urged all settlers from counties adjacent to and including Wichita County, Texas, to meet at Iowa Park on April 2. Those who wanted to travel directly to Fort Sill were urged to meet the Iowa Park delegation there. "To the settlers on the borders: Keep your eyes open. The cattlemen are in the last ditch," wrote Buckskin Joe, who added, "The common Indians want to rent their land to the settlers in order that each Indian may have the benefit of what is his own. The chiefs want to prevent it and stand in with the cattle kings. The common Indians and the settlers will combine and win the day."[11]

The "common" Indians, however, had less regard for the thousands of farmers who had broken out much of the virgin prairie of northwest Texas than they had for the cattlemen, who not only provided them with lease money, but were also generous with beeves when Indians held powwows. By the time of Buckskin Joe's initial efforts to force the opening of the reservation, hunger had been virtually eliminated. And although Buckskin Joe averred that the cattlemen were "in the last ditch," their influence, though indeed on the decline, was to prevail in Congress and with the Interior Department for almost another decade. Six months after the telegram to the Secretary of the Interior, Mr. Chandler, Acting Secretary, wrote to the Commissioner of Indian Affairs authorizing grazing leases on the reservation: to D. Waggoner and Son for 502,490 acres in return for an annual payment to the Indians of $30,149.40; to E. C. Sugg and Brother for 342,638 acres at $20,558.28; to S. B. Burnett for 287,867 acres at $17,272.02; and to C. T. Herring for 90,000 acres at $5,400.00.

Nevertheless, the year 1892 was to signal the beginning of the end of the open range for cattle king and Indian alike, for pressure from settlers in northwest Texas, Kansas, and the new Oklahoma Territory began to bear fruit for Buckskin Joe and his cohorts. The cattlemen, while still influential with Congressmen from their own districts, were greatly outnumbered by small farmers and ranchers who lusted after Indian lands. With each passing year, the settlers' numbers increased, as did their political clout. The result of this agitation was the convening of the Cherokee Commission on the Kiowa–Comanche–Apache Reservation. The commission was so named because it had originally been instituted to open Cherokee lands to white settlers. By the time the three judges who comprised the commission arrived at Fort Sill, they had already closed nine contracts with different tribes in Indian Territory to do just that.

From the outset, the proceedings were charged with suspicion, since the Indians were all too well aware of the fate that had already befallen the Cheyennes and Arapahos to the north.

Big Tree, a Kiowa, said to Commissioners David H. Jerome, War-
ren G. Sayre, and Alfred M. Wilson, the three men appointed by
the president of the United States to serve on the Cherokee Commission, "I want you to look at the three tribes that are before
you; they give a very good picture of what they have been, what
they are, and what they will be in the future; they do not know
how to take care of themselves. Take pity on them, because they
are ignorant. . . . A year ago [1891] this commission came to the
Cheyenne and Arapaho Indians; they talked to those Indians very
good. These Indians came to the Kiowa and Comanche Reservation; we saw tears in their eyes; we saw that they had nothing to
their name. They are poor; they will be poor in the future; they
had made a mistake in selling their country; that money was given
them but it was all gone. . . . If I were to come to your house and
your place and attempt to buy something that you prize very
highly, you would probably laugh at me and tell me you were not
anxious to sell it."[12]

Quanah's introductory statement on the subject of taking
individual allotments and breaking up the tribal character of the
reservation was to be his theme throughout the battle to save the
land for the Indians. He said to the commissioners, "To say to
the people that the country should be opened now is too quick,
but now I want to know how much will be paid for one acre, what
the terms will be and when it will be paid."[13] Although Quanah
knew as well as Big Tree the awful fate that had befallen the
Cheyennes and Arapahos, he also knew the reality of the situation:
Congress was determined to open the reservation to white settlers,
and the most eloquent speeches expressing the Indians' deepest
desire to keep their lands would be to no avail. So in the same
breath in which he asked for a delay, Quanah asked how much
the government was prepared to give for the land.

His analysis of the grim situation proved to be accurate when
on the second day of the proceedings Commissioner Jerome stated

to the representatives of the three tribes, "The real friend of the Indian will tell him all the facts, whether they are for or against him. The Government of the United States, including the Congress and the President, decided some time ago—three years ago—that all the land in the Indian Territory west of the ninety-sixth degree of longitude should be opened to settlement, except such as was needed for the Indians' homes."[14] After dropping this bombshell, Jerome added, "This commission also hopes that when you go by yourselves tonight that you will understand that Congress is pushed from the outside to have this work go on, and sooner or later it will go on. And this commission comes here to put you in condition, if possible, that you may be benefitted by it when it comes."[15]

The outside pressures referred to by Jerome were being exerted by people who understood the power of numbers in a representative democracy. Buckskin Joe, along with the editors of other newspapers in the Southwest, continually pressed for the opening of the reservation. The *Minco Minstrel,* published in the Chickasaw Nation, Indian Territory, featured the following article datelined Vernon, Texas, October 13, 1893:

> A mass meeting of citizens was held last night to take action looking to the opening of the Comanche, Apache, and Kiowa country. J. R. Talbert was elected chairman and W. J. Potter, Secretary. Speeches were made by ex-Senator Stephens, D. A. Timer, Dr. Dodson and others, after which a committee ... was appointed to draft resolutions memorializing Congress to open the country and calling upon senators and congressmen to work for the measure. The meeting was large and enthusiastic.[16]

One week later, the October 20, 1893, edition of the *Minco Minstrel* reported on a meeting in Charlie (Clay County), Texas, which had been held on the same date as the meeting in Vernon. The object was the opening of what the "boomers" called the

"Fort Sill Country." Boomers were settlers in Indian Territory and Texas who had allied themselves with farmers and shopkeepers in Kansas for the settlement of Indian lands in what was to become the state of Oklahoma. The boomers who met in Charlie passed a resolution calling for Texas congressmen to "lay the matter before Congress at the earliest day possible, to the end that the barriers to the occupation of that fertile domain by the white man be speedily removed, and that fair land made to produce figs instead of thistles, grapes instead of thorns."[17]

The alliance of former Senator Stephens with the farmers and merchants pouring into northwest Texas in ever-increasing numbers is ample proof of the declining influence of the cattle barons. Ten years before, the country south of Red River had been much more sparsely populated, and the big ranchers were still kings of the range. By 1893, however, the era of the open range was coming to a close on the southern plains, hastened by the steady flow of immigrants, many of them from Western Europe, into the country.

Quanah, therefore, could no more have prevented the opening of the reservation than he could have stopped a speeding locomotive. Knowing this, he hoped to get the best deal possible from the Cherokee Commission, and he intended to forestall the final doom as long as possible. Other chiefs, most notably Tabananaka, who was one of the elders of the Comanches, also realized the reality of the situation. He spoke to the commission as follows: "I think we are putting off and standing in the way of our kin folks and taking up time that we might utilize. I have listened to this good talk you have been making us. Any plan that the Government puts before us I am ready to take hold of. The Government is strong and the plans of the Government we can not break; we can ask for a little more money, that does not make any difference; but I am ready to enter into this agreement now. I depend altogether upon our Father at Washington, and not upon any outside persons. I give my talk to a great many of my friends, and the talk of different individuals is only putting the matter off. The Government is doing this and not the Indians; there is no Comanche chief or Kiowa chief doing this for us; it is the Government."[18]

Another Comanche who spoke for cooperating with the Cherokee Commission was Howear (or Howeah), who wanted independence because he did not like the cattlemen. He was so much in favor of opening the reservation that he said, "I feel like shouting for joy at the chance to make this trade."[19] Cheevers, a Comanche, also advocated signing the agreement. "And now," he said, "what is the use of holding back—why not go ahead and make this trade? The three commissioners are undoubtedly representing the Government and come here to talk what the Government has for the Indians, and while the road is soft, and before it gets too hard, we had better travel it."[20]

Lone Wolf of the Kiowas said to the commissioners, "The representatives of the Government have been with us a few days, and have told us of the good intentions of the Government so plain to us that each Indian present this afternoon understands every word of it."[21] Lone Wolf, however, would later say he signed the document to be known as the Jerome Agreement *without* understanding it. Even during the proceedings he had seemed to waver. In the same speech in which he said he understood the proposed agreement, he stated, "Very few of our young men and women are educated or partially educated. Here is Joshua Givens [a Kiowa], myself, Quanah Parker, and a few others, you can talk to them and they will answer you in English. Look at them; the rest are not dressed as well as they are. When the worst comes, they will be the only ones that will be able to cope with the white man when he comes to this country. The rest will not know what to do."[22]

Quanah concurred with Lone Wolf on what was going to happen to his people. "There has [sic] been several statements as to the amount of money that we receive. It is a great deal of money to be paid each person, and if the Indian makes good use of it he can live like Tabananaka and myself," he said. "You look around you and see so many good faces, but they will take their money and buy whisky."[23] In another comment to the commissioners, Quanah echoed the sentiments of all Indians present when he said, "We think that we understand what the commission has said to us, but do not think the commission has understood what we have said. . . . This land is ours, just like your farm is yours; but for one reason we can not hold on to ours, because on the right hand is what you are trying to do and on the left hand is the Dawes bill."[24]

The Dawes Act provided Congress with the right to take any Indian lands remaining after each Indian had been allotted a farm. Allowing Indians 160-acre allotments per person would leave thousands of homesteads for land-hungry whites poised on the southern and western borders of the reservation. Quanah accurately saw the choices available to his people: making a deal with the Cherokee Commission for what he could get, or having the Dawes Act forced on him at a price the government would dictate. As Tabananaka said, "My people, a great many of them are inclined to do as I do, because we know that Washington controls everything in the country; I expect all my people are willing to do this and expect to do this. . . . Whenever the Government sees fit, I am ready."[25] Clearly, Tabananaka saw the inevitability of selling the land, although he, like Quanah, did not wish to do so. White Eagle said of the Eagle, "Quanah stands just as I do in loving and wanting to keep the country."[26]

The laws of the white men would prevail. Quanah's only choice was to delay the signing of the document, as well as its

ratification, as long as possible. In light of this he said to the
commissioners, "I know that the commissioners are in favor of
making this trade; that they want to push ahead so much that we
have almost forgotten about dinner time."[27] His veiled sarcasm
was surely not lost on Jerome and his associates, for they had
realized from the outset of their talks with the Kiowas, Comanches, and Apaches that these Indians knew what the Cherokee Commission was all about.

But the commissioners, in their haste to get the signatures
of the necessary three-fourths of the adult males on the reservation, continued to speak as if the Indians did not recognize the
grim realities of the impending doom. On October 3, 1892, Commissioner Wilson said, "It may be that you will find someone in
your midst that will say wait, wait. Tell him it is dangerous to go
into the waiting business. I said to you a bit ago that what we
agreed to pay you would make you rich."[28] So outrageous was this
lie that when pressed by Quanah to specify how much each Indian
would receive from the government, the commissioners hedged,
indicating that the decision on the amount would be up to Congress. Quanah replied:

> Now the commission says that we will sign this contract today
> and then we can not tell any definite time when it will take
> effect; but say we will take this contract and give it to the
> President; he will give it to Congress, and whenever Congress
> says it is all right, then in four moons from that the Indians
> will be paid $65. . . . Now, I do not think that it would be
> enough, and for that reason I think this [additional] half
> million dollars would be in good play, so we want this com-
> mission to help us get it from Congress. And when the dele-
> gation [of Indians] gets there we will sing the same tune and
> try to get it. This $165 that the half million dollars would
> make for each man would help us out considerable. That is
> the main thing I have to talk about—how to get this extra
> money.[29]

Quanah's plea for an extra half-million dollars was in response to the commission's offer of $2,000,000 for "surplus"
lands, the lands remaining after each Indian had been allotted
160 acres; Quanah wanted $2,500,000. In the same speech, he
let the commission know that he would wait until the Jerome
Agreement was ratified by Congress before he told the cattlemen
they must move their cattle south of Red River. "I know that the
law is a very particular thing. Then when we get through discuss-
ing it I am ready for you to sign my name."[30] So on October 6,
1892, Quanah Parker made his mark beside his name and forever
split his people into two factions: those who realized—as did
Cheevers, Howear, and Tabananaka—that all that could be done
had been done for the Indians; and those who blamed Chief
Parker for selling their country.

Seven years later, the House of Representatives passed a bill
providing for the allotment of the lands of the reservation, but
the bill still had to be passed in the Senate. At this juncture the
Indian Rights Association at Philadelphia took up the fight in
favor of the Indians. In their publication of 1899, the Association
stated, "The Indians claim that the treaty did not represent their
wishes in the matter, and the pending legislation not being in
accordance either with the treaty or their desires, strong opposi-
tion is made to its passage in the Senate. They desire that an
allotment of 640 acres be made to each member of the tribe, in
case the lands are allotted at all, to which many of them are
opposed."[31]

In an attempt to secure as large an allotment for the Indians
as they possibly could, assuming that the Senate passed the
Jerome Agreement, the Indian Rights Association secured the
services of F. H. Newell, hydrographer of the Geological Survey,
whose job it was to ascertain the average amount of annual rainfall
on the reservation. Newell concluded that if allotments were made
to the Indians, they should be much larger than the 160 acres

recommended by the commission. "A fair allowance, therefore," the Indian Rights Association reported, "would be twenty acres for each animal for pasturage."[32] The Association recommended 480 acres per member of the tribe.

Efforts to forestall the Jerome Agreement's implementation into law had begun as early as 1893, when Reverend J. J. Methvin opened his church to a gathering of Indians who collected four hundred signatures against ratification. Also in 1893, Methvin hosted a meeting of Indians to recommend a delay of allotment of reservation lands until the annuities promised in the Treaty of Medicine Lodge expired in 1898. During these meetings, a large number of Kiowas declared that they wanted their names removed from the Jerome Agreement, claiming that their interpreter had tricked them into signing by saying the Agreement would not be ratified until 1898. But the Cherokee Commission refused to let any names be withdrawn.

Lone Wolf and Quanah traveled to Washington in January and March of 1893 to lobby for a postponement of ratification. Before a subcommittee of the House, they testified to the overbearing manner of the commissioners and their threat of invoking the Dawes Act to accomplish their goals. While the Indian Rights Association was working to block ratification through their lobbyist, C. C. Painter, Quanah, Lone Wolf, and 321 other Indians signed a petition protesting the Agreement; at the same time Congressman Joseph W. Bailey of Texas was also fighting against ratification on behalf of the cattlemen.

During the next three years the Jerome Agreement was voted down, but the boomers were still determined to get the Indians' "surplus" lands. Quanah and Esa-tai, who was making his first trip to Washington, met with Commissioner of Indian Affairs Browning in January of 1896 in yet another effort to postpone the flood of white settlers into their country. Browning made no predictions as to what Congress would do, but he promised to fight ratification. However, with more and more boomers clamoring for land, many of them in Oklahoma Territory north and east of the reservation, the Indians were surrounded by hostile whites whose increasing numbers were exerting more and more pressure on their representatives in Congress.

In the spring of 1897, Quanah again led a delegation of Indians to Washington, where they were joined by Captain Hugh Scott, a longtime friend, who made an impassioned speech to Commissioner Jones. "To plunge them at this time into the midst of the hostile population of Oklahoma would as surely work their destruction as the abandonment of a baby to a pack of hungry wolves," he said.[33] He also asserted that the signatures on the Jerome Agreement had been secured by means of fraud and coercion, a statement supported by Quanah and Apiatan of the Kiowas.

In July of 1897, the headmen of the three tribes proposed the idea of selling part of their land to the homeless Wyandots and to Geronimo and his tribe of the western Apaches, who had been displaced. Agent Baldwin endorsed this idea, strongly urged by Quanah, but it was squelched by congressmen whose constituents were in the opposite camp.

The Indian Rights Association, meanwhile, continued to work for the benefit of the Indians, but the group was too unsophisticated politically to hope that the reservation could be kept intact and that the cattlemen could continue to lease Indian lands indefinitely. The principal thrust of the association, then, was to secure as many acres as possible for each Comanche, Kiowa, and Apache when allotment was finally forced upon them.

A new and powerful ally now lined up on the side of the boomers, the Rock Island Railroad, which had influential friends in Congress: Representative Charles Curtis of Kansas and Senator James K. Jones of Arkansas. Democratic senators in general favored ratification because it would lead to statehood for Oklahoma, an area likely to send Democrats to Washington. By 1899, it had become politically viable to vote in favor of ratification, and the Senate Committee on Indian Affairs reported in favor of the bill in that year.

Again the Indian Rights Association lobbied the congressmen, repeating their demand for allotments no smaller than 480 acres. Alarmed by the imperial tone of the nation's foreign policy, the association said, "It seems especially important that Congress should refuse to sanction so gross an act of injustice . . . at the very moment when we are assuming responsibility for the elevation and protection of millions of island wards [the Filipinos]. The enactment of this measure will create an additional bad precedent in the treatment of our dependent races."[34]

The majority ruled, however, and a version of the Jerome Agreement passed. It had taken eight years from the time the Cherokee Commission secured the signatures of three-quarters of the adult male Indians on the reservation until the bill became law. During that time, income from the lease money had greatly profited the Indians. The new arrangement allowed them to keep 480,000 acres of land and secured $500,000 for the land the United States was taking from them. According to William Hagan, in *United States–Comanche Relations,* "A clause in the bill as it finally was passed was a clue as to who could get justice. It granted preference in filing land claims on the reservation to the white squatters who had occupied illegally the strip in the bend of the Washita River since the early 1890s, notwithstanding Agent Baldwin's best efforts to remove them. They now had been rewarded for their persistence by legislation that otherwise clearly violated the United States' pledge to the Comanches and associated tribes in the Treaty of Medicine Lodge."[35]

So eager were land-hungry whites to possess the Indian lands that they poured into the "Fort Sill country" before legal procedures had been established for the registration of homesteaders.

The *Daily Oklahoman* reported on June 28, 1900, "Colonel Rand-lett said today that these trespassers number about 3,000 and exceed the Indian population. Orders will be issued at once to compel the intruders to leave the ceded lands. If they fail to do this within ten days, the military forces at Fort Sill, O.T. [Oklahoma Territory], will be called upon for aid."[36] The article went on to say, "No lands would be available for mining or settlement until part of the lands had been allotted to the Indians in severalty, and others had been set aside to be used for grazing purposes for the benefit of the Indians in common."[37]

The Army, however, was only partially successful in driving out trespassers. Over a year later, Agent Randlett wrote to the Commissioner of Indian Affairs complaining of two deputy United States marshals who had taken land illegally and defied Randlett's efforts to have them removed. "While these two deputies remained on the allotments they claimed to locate upon, each erected a small lumber shack to be called a house, and were defiant of Agency authority. I am not able to state how far their example influenced others, but scores of persons have located upon other allotments and some declare they will remain upon the lands, and if ejected, will return as often as ejected."[38]

In July 1901, 21,000 homesteaders registered at Fort Sill. On August 6, 1901, five miles south of that frontier post, the city of Lawton sprang to life. The day of the Indian and the trooper was over. All that remained of the vast reaches of Comanchería were little 160-acre tracts, doled out to every Indian. The Big Pasture was held in reserve for the younger generation.

If the Indians were angry about the opening of the reservation, so were the cattlemen and those who worked for them. Polk Fry, Sr., a settler, moved to Frederick, near the Big Pasture, at the time of the first wave of homesteaders. The immigrants, he said, "had arrived from Maine to Mexico, and this was truly the melting pot of the American people looking for homes."[39] Cowboys who had considered the area their home for years bitterly resented the "nesters" coming in and breaking out the sod. Mr. Fry recalled the army of cowboys who drove the thousands of cattle out of the country. "The pioneers will never forget when they started moving their saddle horses through the streets of our little town and believe me, we stayed inside our places of business to get out of the way of that some three or four hundred head of horses and cowboys. The cow punchers made us a number of visits and on one occasion they put on quite a show and like to have caused some serious trouble. I have never seen as many guns at one time drawn for action as at that time but through the cool headedness of our grand old city marshal and a few of the leading citizens a tragedy was averted."[40]

The Big Pasture remained open for grazing and hunting, however, and served as the setting for President Theodore Roosevelt's wolf hunt in April 1905. Only a few months before, Quanah had ridden in Roosevelt's second inaugural parade. Among those who stood along the parade route was Captain Carter, whom the Eagle of the Comanches had lured into an ambush in the Battle of Cañon Blanco in 1871. Of Quanah, Carter wrote in *Tragedies of Cañon Blanco,* "He came to Washington many times, and at Theodore Roosevelt's second inauguration in 1905, the writer saw him ride up Pennsylvania Avenue in the inaugural column with other 'good Indians,' most of whom had dipped their hands in many white settlers' blood on the once far off borderland of the West."[41]

If Captain Carter could not realize that Quanah had fought for what he considered to be rightfully his, President Roosevelt had no problem in understanding the warriors of the recent Indian wars. His own love for the outdoors had led to the establishment of America's national parks system, thereby forestalling the private ownership of all the nation's natural wonders. Roosevelt hosted

Quanah and the other Indians who rode in his inaugural parade, and it was during this time that Quanah Parker invited the president to the Big Pasture for a wolf hunt. Official hosts for the president, in addition to Quanah, were the Burnetts and the Waggoners. According to pioneer banker Tom Corridon of Iowa Park, Texas, "Burk Burnett and Waggoner got the wolf hunt up. The cattlemen, along with Quanah, were trying to save pasturage. Teddy Roosevelt came to Wichita Falls on a special train. I saw him get off the train. He was escorted off and taken to a speaker's stand about fifty feet from his private car. He talked about Texas. I remember in one part of his speech he said when he wanted good men for his Rough Riders, he came to Texas and found them."[42]

From Wichita Falls, Roosevelt went to Frederick, Oklahoma, where Quanah met him at the train. Roosevelt gave a brief speech and then invited Quanah to talk. The chief of the Comanches later told his friend R. B. Thomas that he got more applause than Teddy.*

In *Outdoor Pastimes of the American Hunter*, Roosevelt recalled the wolf hunt in the Big Pasture. It was in April of 1905, only a month or so prior to the oppressive heat of the region's long summers. He wrote, "We were the guests of two old-style Texas cattlemen, Messrs. Burnet [Burnett] and Wagner [Waggoner], who had leased great stretches of the wire-fenced pasture from the Comanches and Kiowas. . . . Burnet's brand, the Four Sixes, has been owned by him for forty years. Both of them had

---

* Roosevelt's hunt in the Big Pasture served to familiarize the President with the Indians' problem. Accordingly, Roosevelt, after receiving a telegram from Quanah, vetoed the bill authorizing the opening of the Big Pasture for settlement because there were no provisions made for allotting land to Indian children. Congress amended the bill, and the President signed it. Quanah also succeeded in getting the extra $500,000 he had bargained for with the Cherokee Commission.

come to this country thirty years before, in the days of the buffalo, when all game was plentiful and the Indians were still on the war-path."[43] After mentioning the other cattlemen and one law-enforcement officer, Captain McDonald of the Texas Rangers, who were his companions, Roosevelt wrote, ". . . and finally there was Quanah Parker, the Comanche chief, in his youth a bitter foe of the whites, now painfully teaching his people to travel the white man's stony road."[44] As the men thundered across the rolling grassland of the Big Pasture, Burk Burnett drove General Young in a buggy, and ". . . as Burnet invariably followed the hounds at full speed in his buggy, and usually succeeded in seeing most of the chase, I felt that the buggy men really encountered greater hazards than anyone else. It was a thoroughly congenial company all through."[45]

The high-spirited group caught seventeen coyotes and wolves, and the president killed a five-foot rattlesnake with his quirt. After eating supper on a creek bank, the hunters rode into Frederick. Roosevelt wrote, "We entered the town after dark, some twenty of us on horseback. Wagner [sic] was riding with us, and he had set his heart upon coming into and through the town in true cowboy style; and it was he who set the pace. We broke into a lope a mile outside the limits, and by the time we struck the main street the horses were on a run and we tore down like a whirlwind until we reached the train."[46]

While in Indian country the president dined at Quanah's Star House. According to the late Anona Birdsong Dean, "President Roosevelt came to see Grandfather more than once. Mother was hostess for one occasion. She was home from school. Grandfather wanted to entertain Roosevelt just so-so. He had a table that sat thirty people. Each woman had a job. Mother went to see if the table was set properly. She found goblets filled with wine setting next to each plate. Grandfather, who never drank, had gotten wine somewhere and had told one of the women to fill big glasses

with the wine. Mother said, 'Why did you do that?' Grandfather
explained that when he went to Washington, Roosevelt served
wine in small glasses and he wanted to be more generous than
Roosevelt."[47]

While the president understood Quanah's journey on "the
white man's stony road" better than most, there were pitfalls along
the way that Quanah in his pride almost surely did not share with
Roosevelt. Because he knew the wilderness and the men who
drew their sustenance from it, the old Rough Rider accepted
Quanah's Indian character and ways, but there were those who
did not. Pressures that resulted in the breaking up of the reservation had root not only in the white man's lust for the land, but
also in a desire to force the Indians to accept the values of the
dominant society. Officials in the Indian Service had been critical
of Quanah from the beginning of the peyote ritual on the reservation. Others criticized the Comanche tradition of polygamy and
the way the Eagle wore his hair. In response to a letter from the
Commissioner of Indian Affairs voicing these objections, Agent
Randlett wrote in 1902, "I have the honor to report that the
majority of the elder males among the Indians of the Agency wear
their hair long, plaited in two braids extending down in front of
their shoulders. This is an inherited custom to which they appear
determined to adhere. At the time this letter was received I talked
with Quanah Parker, who is in all other respects obedient to the
will of the Department. He asked if there was any law he was
disobeying in his fashion of wearing his hair, and if white people
did not wear their hair as they pleased. . . . He referred to the
fact that the Chinaman I employ wore his hair long and he could
not understand why he should not have as much privilege as the
Chinaman. He further said that he was glad that his own children
have their hair cut short and that he would never encourage them
or any other school boys to return to the customs of the old
Indians, but that he wanted them as well as the children of all

his people to be raised in the way of the civilized white people." Randlett concluded the letter by informing the commissioner that "the new conditions thrust upon these Indians through the opening of their reservation and making them citizens has lessened their respect for the authority of their Agent . . . for me to attempt forcibly to control them as you suggested would only tend to separate them from me and induce insubordination."[48]

Pressure exerted on Agent Randlett to make whites of the Indians was not an isolated act; rather, it was an integral part of Washington's strategy of dealing with them, as the following letter from the Office of Indian Affairs, dated thirteen years previous to Randlett's above letter, amply demonstrates:

Dec. 10, 1889

To Indian Agents and Superintendents of Indian Schools:

The great purpose which the Government has in view in providing an ample system of common school education for all Indian youth of school age, is the preparation for them for American citizenship. The Indians are destined to become absorbed into the national life, not as Indians, but as Americans. . . . Patriotic songs should be taught to the pupils, and they should sing them frequently until they acquire complete familiarity with them. . . . In all proper ways, teachers in Indian schools should endeavor to appeal to the highest elements of manhood and womanhood in their pupils, exciting in them an ambition after excellence in character and dignity of surroundings, and they should carefully avoid any unnecessary reference to the fact that they are Indians.[49]

As to the practice of polygamy, Charles Goodnight, who also admired and respected Quanah, thought it was a natural way of living for the Indians. In "Indians in the Panhandle," Goodnight wrote, "Quanah, at one point in his life, had seven wives. At one time Harrison told him he should be more like the white men and have just one, and made him promise to get him no new squaws. I met him on the train at one time, with all his wives, and noticed he had a new wife. Quanah never broke his word, and I wondered about it so asked him how he happened to have a new squaw. He said, 'But I let one of the others go when I got this one, so I still have just six with me.' "⁵⁰

Once while he was in Washington, Quanah was approached by an official who lectured him on the evils of polygamy. When told to choose just one wife and tell the others to leave, Quanah thought for a moment and then told the official that he could pick the one to stay and tell the others they must leave. This reply ended the conversation.

Aside from the rocks strewn in his path by the whites who disliked his adherence to Comanche traditions, Quanah had problems with some of the Comanches because of his white blood. After the death of his influential father, war chief Peta Nocona, in about 1863, Quanah suffered the taunts of the pure-blooded Indians. He had not even known about his mixed blood until Peta Nocona told him about Naudah after her recapture in 1860. But he was to hear a lot about it in the years to come. Even after he had become chief of the Comanches, there were those who resented his position in the tribe largely because of his ancestry. In one of their efforts to discredit him, his detractors spread rumors that he was dishonest. Eventually, Francis E. Leupp was appointed by the secretary of the Department of the Interior to investigate this charge and others made against Quanah and Agent Randlett. Leupp arrived in Anadarko in July 1903. In his report to the Senate Committee on Indian Affairs, he wrote, "I received one day a warning that I had better put Quanah Parker, the chief of the Comanches, through a very rigid examination, as it was understood that he had caused 'allotments to be given to 10 Indians who never surrendered and are yet in Mexico.' I accepted the warning in the spirit in which I assume it was offered; but with all my searching, including inquiry of Quanah and everyone else who presumptively would or could know of such a transaction, I have been unable to find any trace of it."[51]

Another rumor that Leupp tracked down was that Quanah had allowed a Mrs. John Le Barre and her ten children to receive allotments. Leupp reported on this one as follows: "Three or four years ago she appeared on the reservation and applied for admission into the Comanche tribe, of whom Quanah is chief, claiming to be the daughter of two full-blooded Comanches, who had been captured by Mexicans and carried across the border many years before. A committee of the tribe went over to Mexico to investigate her story, and on their return reported that it was true; though some later events have, in their opinion, cast doubt upon the subject. The upshot was that at the council at which Quanah, Eschiti, and other prominent Comanches were present, she was admitted."[52] As in the case of the Jerome Agreement, several Comanche leaders had agreed on a course of action, but a few members of the tribe chose to blame Quanah for the results of the joint decision. When closely questioned by Leupp, Mrs. Le Barre admitted that Congressman Stephens of Texas, to whom her husband had appealed for help, had been responsible for placing the names of the Le Barre family on the tribal roll.

Not only was Quanah found innocent of any charges, but Mr. Leupp diagnosed the rumors as being based on jealousy and resentment of Quanah and other leaders among the Comanches. "These cases and dozens of like tenor," he wrote, "had nothing whatever behind them except falsehood."[53] The investigation actually proved to be a blessing for Quanah, because Leupp's report to the Senate was so favorable:

> The choice by the Comanches of Quanah Parker as their chief dates back to the memory of any but the oldest members of the tribe, and if ever Nature stamped a man with the seal of headship she did it in his case. Quanah would have been a leader and a governor in any circle where fate may have cast

him—it is in his blood. His acceptability to all except an in-
considerable minority of his people is plain to any observer,
and even those who are restless under his rule recognize his
supremacy. He has his followers under wonderful control, but,
on the other hand, he looks out for them like a father. His
word is law, and in all essentials it is uttered in behalf of
civilization and progress. He sends his children to school and
helps the Government by exerting his influence with the
whole tribe in the same direction, with the result that the
Comanche have already filled their reservation school to over-
flowing and are knocking at the door for larger accommoda-
tions. . . . Quanah, though he grew up at a time when these
advantages were not to be had, has tried to educate himself,
and to-day speaks English better than many who have been
taught in a more formal fashion; and old man as he is, he is
not shamefaced about asking for more information from anyone who will give it to him. . . . so far from the Comanche
desiring to pull Quanah down, the only interference with his
chiefship of which I could learn was made by the authorities
in Washington, who were once moved by the false repre-
sentations of an interested party to raise Eschiti to a place of
equal if not greater power. The mistake was promptly discovered, however, and the old conditions restored.[54]

One of Chief Parker's major duties was serving as judge on
the three-man Court of Indian Offenses. Founded in 1886, the
court convened twice a month until it was dissolved when the
reservation opened up in 1901. According to Ernest Wallace,
"Quanah's verdicts were rather strict even by Indian standards,
and a few of them really baffled white observers. In one particularly tough case, he found it impossible to choose between two
Indian litigants who were contesting rights to a plot of land. Unable to find a satisfactory precedent in the white man's law,
Quanah reverted to Comanche standards. With the aid of Indian
police, who had been organized to keep order on the reservation,
the chief dug into the litigants' pasts to find which man had won

the greatest war honors. It turned out that one litigant had rescued an unhorsed comrade during a fight long ago. On the ground that he was more courageous than his rival, Quanah decided in his favor."[55]

Although the duties of statesmanship took much of his time and energy, Quanah also enjoyed the privileges of his station. One of his greatest pleasures was visiting among his people at the powwows held on the reservation or in the parades to which the Indians were frequently invited. Pioneer R. B. Thomas, a neighbor of Quanah's, recalled their love of horses and said that their proudest moments came when they rode in a parade on their pretty horses. The men would paint themselves with yellow, red, and green paint and put feathers of different birds in their hair. Their feet jingled with bells and the light caught flashes of ornaments on their moccasins. The women dressed in their finest buckskin dresses.[56] Altogether, the Comanches formed a colorful and imposing group when parading down the streets of Lawton, Frederick, Anadarko, and Fort Worth.

Every spring, Burk and Tom Burnett invited Quanah and a delegation of Indians to attend the Fort Worth Fat Stock Show. In a letter dated October 24, 1908, Burk Burnett wrote to Quanah:

> I note what you say about bringing the Kiowa Chief and Geronimo with you and your Indians to the Fat Stock Show. This you must be sure to do. I shall come up to see you after I return from the ranch, if I do not see you on the ranch, and spend two or three days with you, so as to let you know all about what we expect to do here during the Fat Stock Show, and why I want you and your people here, and there is one thing you can say to all Indians, that they will have a bully good time and not be out a cent of their own money, as all expenses are to be paid coming and going and while they are here. I will move my yellow and spotted horses from King County down to Burk Station about the 10th of next month

where I am going to winter them and have them in fine shape for you and your people to ride at the show, and as previously stated I want your people to bring their saddles with them.[57]

The Indians' love of parades was one indication of their sociable nature. Another was the powwow. Artist George Catlin in 1857 wrote about the Indians' love of conversation and their sense of humor: ". . . the wild, and rude and red—the graceful (though uncivil), conversational, garrulous, story-telling and happy, though ignorant and untutored groups that are smoking their pipes—wooing their sweethearts and embracing their little ones about their peaceful and endeared fire-sides; together with their pots and kettles, spoons, and other culinary articles of their own manufacture, around them; present altogether, one of the most picturesque scenes to the eye of a stranger, that can possibly be seen; and far more wild and vivid than could ever be imagined."[58] R. B. Thomas, who clerked in the old Red Store near Lawton, recalled "one payment in 1907 where every man, woman, and child received $100.00 each. If a man had seven children his family got nine checks for $900.00. This was money received from the rental of their lands and accrued interest. . . . I sold $286.00 worth of goods that day myself but I worked from six in the morning to two the following morning; and then I attended a dance the remainder of the night where all the tribes were dancing in front of the three stores. I smoked the Pipe of Peace with them that night and danced about twenty minutes. They had four Tom Toms and made a great deal of dance music. Some of the Indians were nearly nude, wearing only a breech clout and being painted with vermillion, yellow, red, and orange all over face and body. They would dance until exhausted but there was plenty to take their place."[59]

There were other festivities in which Quanah participated as well. His relatives in Texas invited him to their town and county celebrations. Just as gratifying as his acceptance by his mother's people, however, was the new town named in his honor. Quanah, Texas, across Red River from the southwestern portion of the reservation, was established in Hardeman County in 1884, less than a decade after the Eagle's final battle against the whites. So pleased was Quanah Parker that a few years after its founding he gave the town his blessing. On May 23, 1890, the *Quanah Tribune-Chief* quoted him as follows: "It is well, you have done a good thing in honor of a man who has tried to do right both to the people of his tribe and to his pale faced friends. May the God of the white man bless the town of Quanah. May the sun shine and the rain fall upon the fields and the granaries be filled. May the lightning and the tempest shun the homes of her people, and may they increase and dwell forever. God bless Quanah. I have spoken."[60]

Quanah's blessing on the little town on the edge of northwest Texas was remarkable in the sense that only sixteen years before, he had acquired lasting fame for his courage in leading the attack on the buffalo hunters at Adobe Walls. But perhaps even more amazing was the fact that the former war chief invested $40,000 in the Quanah, Acme and Pacific Railway Co., a small railroad that ran from Quanah to Floydada, Texas, north of Cañon Blanco, scene of Quanah's greatest military coup, where he threw Mackenzie off the Quahadas' trail until, with the aid of darkness and a howling blizzard, his band was able to escape. Original plans were to extend the railroad to the Pacific Ocean, but Floydada was to be the end of the line. In 1889, only a few years prior to his investment in the "Quanah Line," as it was known, Quanah had seen the Frisco Railroad Company go through the reservation and had foreseen the possibilities. Hugh Hannah, a member of the construction crew, said Quanah Parker "used to come and watch us. He would sit and ask questions about the 'great fire wagon.' In the hot summer months he always wore a white sheet around him and in the winter a bright colored blanket. On his feet he wore beaded moccasins and his hair was always twisted in two long rolls down his back. He was very friendly."[61]

Quanah frequently visited the town named for him. At times, he dressed in his traditional Indian costume, and just as often, he wore a business suit with a stylish hat and diamond breastpin. On one occasion, the chief and his entourage traveled on the "Quanah Line" to Dallas to take part in the State Fair of Texas. On October 24, 1910, the *Dallas Morning News* offered this report of his visit:

> Quanah Parker, a Comanche chief and one of the last of the historic figures of Indian life and frontier history of the Southwest, and the members of his family arrived yesterday, to be prominent figures in the features arranged at the State Fair today for Quanah Route Day.
>
> Today he will wear his war bonnet at the Fair Grounds, and in the afternoon in Convention Hall he will deliver an address at the Quanah Route meeting.... Yesterday afternoon he and his family, in an automobile, visited the State Fair, and attracted much attention as they rode about the grounds. ... The chief is a striking figure. He was attired in ordinary street costume and a soft black hat, his braided locks, tied in two plaits down his back, his erect bearing, his seamed and wrinkled countenance immediately disclosed to most observers his identity.[62]

According to Charles H. Sommer, president of the Quanah, Acme and Pacific Railway, "People journeyed from all sections of west Texas by special train to join in the occasion and pay homage to Chief Quanah, who appeared with his family, clad in their full war regalia, feathered headdresses, buckskin clothes, moccasins, beads, etc. The entire train of the Quanah, Acme and Pacific Railway, aboard which were Chief Quanah, his family and his braves, was parked within the exposition grounds of the Dallas State Fair through the entire period of the Fair. Quanah Parker was scheduled for an address. He delivered his speech with dignity (standing erect he was more than six feet tall), and almost every utterance, as was his custom, was accompanied by a gesture or a shrug. In his address he frequently referred to his 'knife,' which we would term a spear. His speech, as actually delivered before that vast assembly, was as follows:

> Ladies and gentlemen. I say a few words to you. You look at me. I put on this war bonnet. This is my war trinket. Ladies and gentlemen, I used to be a bad man. Now I am a citizen of the United States. I pay taxes the same way as you people do. We are the same people now. This is what I tell you, ladies and gentlemen. My friend, Colonel Elbert . . . spoke to you people and told you about my mother. She was Cynthia Ann Parker. That was my mother. A good long time ago, after the Indian people had been on the war path—about 700 were on war path—my father and an old Indian told me—He said that on the war path they had killed a lot of white people and burned their little houses. They got my mother. . . . Well, ladies and gentlemen, that is one matter I want to make straight up. My friend, Colonel Elbert, a little while ago told you that Governor Ross did not capture my mother but Colonel Goodnight did. The Texas history says General Ross killed my father. The old Indian tell me that no so. He no kill my father. I want to get that in Texas history straight up. My friend, Colonel Elbert, Colonel Goodnight and Mr. Daniels find out and make it straight up. No kill my father; he not there. I want to get it straight here in Texas history. After that—two year, maybe three year maybe—my father sick. I see him die. I want to get that in Texas history straight up.
>
> Now, ladies and gentlemen, you read the papers. We move from Texas over to Oklahoma, my country. Two year ago I been to Washington, I see John Stephens, Congressman from Texas. I tell him would like to get bill $1,000 to move my mother's remains. Two year ago bill passed and after that somebody, New York men, start that bill and last June I been

to Washington. I come again and see about it. Made bill $800. I use $200.00 to buy new coffin. Now, ladies and gentlemen, Texas objects me do that. I have over at my home my older son dead some seven or eight year ago. Nobody know when me die, maybe tomorrow or ten year. But me have family graveyard and me want bury my mother there.

Now here is another thing I want to tell you. Here is all my acquaintances come from Quanah. They come from my town, the Quanah country. All that used to be my hunting ground. Snakes up there. My town up there wanted to put railroad west of Quanah Line. I want to run it over to New Mexico and El Paso.

Well, now, I want to tell you one matter something else, ladies and gentlemen. See my two hands. Here is one Indian way and one white way. Here is Republican party and here is Democratic party. I watch the two parties close. Which is the best? The Democratic party are trying to work for good of all of us. It looks at rich man and poor man same. Republican party looks at rich man, but not for good of poor man. This is why times are hard. . . .

I hear somebody say something about Quanah—that not good country, all prairie dogs—all snakes. That not so. Quanah town good town. You can raise anything there, all nice houses in there. You see now? Good long time ago, maybe forty years ago, all pretty nearly bad man. Nothing but log houses. Keep building up and build railroads.

Well, now, you see here this knife [lance]. What I want tell you now—I got one good friend, Burk Burnett. He big heart, rich man, cow man. Help my people good deal. You see some big men hold tight to money. Afraid to die. Burnett help anybody.

I came from Fort Sill. No ride me in like horse or cow. Had big war. I fought General Mackenzie. He had 2,000 men. I had 450 men. I use this knife. I see little further, perhaps eight miles, lots soldiers coming. I say hold on—no go over there. Maybe we go at night. Maybe stampede soldier's horses first. I got my men around in circle and tell them holler. I gathered maybe 350 United States horses that night. You see how bad* me was at that time? Next morning they come up my trail. I ready to fight. I use this knife. Come up my trail lot men. Way ahead of it, maybe fifty or sixty men. I tell my men stand up behind hill, holler, shoot and run. I run to one side and use this knife. I came up right side and killed man sergeant and scalp. You see how bad man I was at that time?

Well, ladies and gentlemen, now I working for Government. I work for my Indians. Every year me want to go to Washington and I work for my Indians. Government say to me, "You work for Indians. Put your Indians in school and make Indians do like white men." They have houses like white men, but some my Indians no good. Some white people same. I tell you reason why some no good. You see many buy bottle whiskey and play cards. That reason some men no good. Some white people do that, too.

Well, over four year ago come President Roosevelt to Big Pasture. I see over at the White House President Theodore Roosevelt. He writes me a letter: "Mr. Parker, you meet me and go hunting with me over in the Big Pasture." I write: "All right—I be there." I wait for him to come. Tell me be there four o'clock. I see train coming up. I got twelve men and Sheriff. I put six-shooter on—afraid somebody might try to kill President. I keep away from the people. President get off on platform. He look at me and says, "Quanah Parker." I get off my horse. People hollered, "Two chiefs—chief red men and chief white men." President make speech. He said, "Ladies and gentlemen, I met Quanah Parker at my White House couple months ago. He made good speech for me at that time."

I go back home to Quanah tonight. Me want to go right over to Mr. Burnett's ranch.[63]

---

* From the white man's point of view.

At that point Quanah's speech seemed to be over, but someone on the stage asked the chief to introduce his family. After the introductions were completed, the audience began to rise. "Just one more minute," Quanah said. "Here is one more say. My ways call for money every time they send me to the Fair. Two men came to me about year ago to go to New York City. 'We give you $5,000 for tour six months, to take your family over there,' they say. I say, 'No—you put me in little pen. I no monkey.' That is all, gentlemen."[64]

Indeed, the Eagle of the Comanches had never been and never would be a curiosity for speculators to exploit. He had always been a man of pride, dignity, and intelligence. And it is certainly fitting that he should make his last major speech before a large assembly of Tejanos, his former foes. Having corrected the error perpetuated by historians that his father, Peta Nocona, was killed at Pease River, Quanah took advantage of the opportunity of speaking before the crowd to appeal for the return of his mother's remains from East Texas to her former home along Red River. In alluding to his coming death, he repeated what he had said four years before in Quanah, referred to in the October 10, 1907, issue of the *Quanah Tribune-Chief:* "Quanah looks well and does not talk so much about getting old and dying as he did last year."[65]

On December 4, 1910, less than two months after his speech at the Dallas State Fair, Quanah reburied his mother's remains at Post Oak Cemetery next to the mission. At her funeral, he said, "Forty years ago my mother died. She captured by Comanches, nine years old. Love Indian and wild life so well no want to go back to white folks. All same people anyway, God say. I love my mother. I like my white people. Got great heart. I want my people follow after white way, get educated, know work, make living when payments stop. I tell 'em they got to know [how to] pick cotton, plow corn. I want them know white man's God. Comanche may die today, tomorrow, ten years. When end comes then they all be together again. I want see my mother again then."[66]

Less than three months later, Quanah lay beside his mother. Separated in life, they were united in death. On February 23, 1911, the headline in *The Lawton Daily News* proclaimed, "Chief Parker Is Dead."

> Quanah Parker, chief of the Comanches, man among men and chieftain among chieftains, has gone to the Great Father. He died at his ranch near here at five minutes past noon today, twenty minutes after his return from a visit with Cheyennes near Harmon, Oklahoma.
>
> The immediate cause of death was heart failure caused by rheumatism, according to the physician called, Dr. J. A. Perisho of Cache. The Chief was dying on the train coming from Snyder but with primitive stoicism he determined to live until he reached home. His favorite wife, To-nicy, by his side, the dying chief sat quietly, his head bowed and his limbs trembling. When the train reached Cache he arose and walked from the train unaided and sat in the waiting room. Dr. Perisho was called and gave him a heart stimulant and the chief was then rushed to his home in the automobile of his son-in-law Emmit Cox.
>
> He was helped into the house and laid on a couch. He arose unaided while Knox Beal, a white man raised from childhood by the Comanche chief, took off his outer garments.
>
> "Have you any objections to the doctor of the white man treating you?" asked To-pay, one of his wives, in Comanche. "No—it is good—I'm ready," said Quanah.
>
> The Indian women seemed to know the end was near. They motioned to the physician, Beal, and a friend to leave the room while the "Cotes-E-Wyne," the Indians' last resort, was administered by Quas-E-I, a medicine man.
>
> "Father in heaven this our brother is coming," prayed the medicine man. Placing an arm about the dying chief, he

flapped his hands and imitated the call of the Great Eagle, the messenger of the Great Father.

Then an eagle bone was thrust in Quanah's throat to open it and To-nicy, his favorite, squirted a mouthful of water down his throat. He coughed, gasped, moved his lips feebly, and died, just twenty minutes after his arrival.[67]

It had been the Eagle's last wish to live until the marble monument was placed over his mother's grave. Only two weeks before he died, he had seen it in place, and now he lay beside his mother, united with her at last in the bosom of Mother Earth. A spear-shaped cedar, pointing toward heaven, was planted at the head of his grave. A red granite headstone, authorized by Congress, was quarried from the nearby Wichita Mountains. On it was inscribed the following:

Resting Here Until Day Breaks
And Shadows Fall and Darkness
Disappears is
Quanah Parker
Last Chief* of the Comanches
Born — 1852
Died Feb. 23, 1911

Of all the eulogies in honor of the departed chief, there is none more fitting than what Knox Beal, his adopted son, said of him: "Quanah Parker, my father, fed a great many Comanche Indians. He had a great herd of cattle and horses in 1890 and when he died in 1911, he did not have many left because he was so generous."[68] Chief in two worlds, he was Comanche to the last.

---

* Since Quanah's death, the Comanches have called their elected leader chairman.[69]

NOTES

CHAPTER 1
The Birth of a Native American: The Attack on Parker's Fort

1. Col. Edward Stiff, *The Texan Emigrant* (Cincinnati, Ohio: George Conclin, 1840), p. 17.

2. Donald F. Tingley, "Illinois Days of Daniel Parker, Texas Colonizer," *Journal of the Illinois State Historical Society*, No. 51 (Winter 1958), p. 401.

3. George P. Garrison (Editor), "The Records of an Early Texas Baptist Church," *The Quarterly of the Texas State Historical Association*, Vol. XI, No. 2 (October 1907), p. 88.

4. Tingley, "Illinois Days," p. 402.

5. *Notes*, Vol. X, No. 1 (Fall 1985), Star of the Republic Museum, Washington-on-the-Brazos, Texas, p. 3.

6. T. R. Fehrenbach, *Comanches: Destruction of a People* (New York: Alfred A. Knopf, 1974), p. 295.

7. Rachel Plummer, *The Rachel Plummer Narrative* (Copyrighted 1926 by Rachel Loftin, Susie Hendrix, and Jane Kennedy), p. 92.

8. *Ibid.*, pp. 93–94.

9. *Ibid.*, p. 95.

10. *Ibid.*

11. *Ibid.*, p. 96.

12. T. A. Babb, *In the Bosom of the Comanches* (Dallas: Hargreaves Printing, 1912), p. 58.

13. James T. DeShields, *Cynthia Ann Parker: The Story of Her Capture* (St. Louis, Missouri: Woodward, 1886), p. 30.

14. P. M. Butler and M. G. Lewis to Commissioner of Indian Affairs, 8 August 1846, House Doc. No. 76, 29th Congress, 2nd Sess., Library of Congress, Washington, D.C., p. 8.

15. *Ibid.*

CHAPTER 2
Comanchería

1. Isidro Vizcaya Canales (Editor), *La Invasión de los Indios Bárbaros al Noreste de México en los Años de 1840 y 1841* (Monterrey, Nuevo León, México: Instituto Tecnológico y de Estudios Superiores de Monterrey, 1968), p. 80.

2. Marvin K. Opler, "The Origins of Comanche and Ute," *American Anthropologist*, Vol XLV (1943), p. 156.

3. Captain William F. Drannan, *Thirty-one Years on the Plains and in the Mountains* (Chicago: Jackson Publishing, date not given), pp. 134–136.

4. Lewis J. Wortham, *A History of Texas: From Wilderness to Commonwealth*, Vol. I (Fort Worth, Texas: Wortham-Molyneaux, 1924), pp. 224–225.

5. Nelson Lee, *Three Years Among the Comanches* (Norman: University of Oklahoma Press, 1957), p. 14.

6. *Ibid.*, p. 21.

7. Canales, *La Invasión de los Indios Bárbaros*, pp. 67–68.

8. *Ibid.*, pp. 71–74.

9. "Memoirs of Mary Maverick," Mary Maverick Collection, Archives Division, Texas State Library, Austin, pp. 53–54.

10. T. R. Fehrenbach, *Comanches: The Destruction of a People* (New York: Alfred A. Knopf, 1974), p. 330.

11. John Henry Brown, *The Indian Wars and Pioneers of Texas* (Houston: Union National Bank, 1933), p. 6.

12. *Ibid.*, p. 7.

13. *Ibid.*, p. 8.

14. *Ibid.*, p. 9.

15. *Ibid.*

CHAPTER 3
The Capture of Naudah

1. Quanah Parker to Captain Hugh Scott, interview, 1897, Ledger-book, Hugh Scott Collection, Fort Sill Archives, Lawton, Oklahoma, p. 19.

2. Quanah Parker to Charles Goodnight, undated, Charles Goodnight Papers, Research Center, Panhandle–Plains Historical Museum, Canyon, Texas.

3. James T. DeShields, *Cynthia Ann Parker: The Story of Her Capture* (St. Louis, Missouri: Woodward, 1886), p. 32.

4. Captain Randolph B. Marcy, *Exploration of the Red River of Louisiana in the Year of 1852,* House Executive Document, 33rd Congress, 1st Sess. (Washington, D.C.: Nicholson Public Printer, 1854), p. 103.

5. Colonel W. S. Nye, *Carbine and Lance* (Norman: University of Oklahoma Press, 1937), p. 17.

6. DeShields, *Cynthia Ann Parker,* pp. 58–60.

7. Nye, *Carbine and Lance,* p. 193.

8. *Ibid.,* pp. 192–200.

9. Fannie McAlpine Clarke, "A Chapter in the History of Young Territory," *The Quarterly of the Texas State Historical Association,* Vol. IX (July 1905 to April 1906), p. 58.

10. *The White Man* (Weatherford, Texas), 13 September 1860, The Barker Texas History Center, University of Texas, Austin.

11. Judith Ann Benner, *Sul Ross: Soldier, Statesman, Educator* (College Station: Texas A & M University Press, 1983), p. 36.

12. *The White Man.*

13. J. Evetts Haley, *Charles Goodnight's Indian Recollections* (Amarillo, Texas: Russell and Cockrell, 1928; Reprinted from *Panhandle–Plains Historical Review,* 1928), p. 15.

14. Benner, *Sul Ross,* p. 35.

15. Haley, *Charles Goodnight's Indian Recollections,* pp. 16–17.

16. *Ibid.,* p. 20.

17. Charles Goodnight, "My Recollections and Memories of the Capture of Cynthia Ann Parker," MS, Charles Goodnight Papers, Research Center, Panhandle–Plains Historical Museum, Canyon, Texas.

18. Haley, *Charles Goodnight's Indian Recollections,* pp. 25–26.

19. *Ibid.,* pp. 27–29.

20. Benner, *Sul Ross*, p. 56.

21. Haley, *Charles Goodnight's Indian Recollections*, p. 25.

22. Benner, *Sul Ross*, p. 57.

23. Pauline Durrett Robertson and R. L. Robertson, *Panhandle Pilgrimage* (Amarillo, Texas: Paramount Publications, 1978), p. 72.

24. Coho Smith, *Cohographs* (Fort Worth, Texas: Branch-Smith, 1976), pp. 69–71.

25. *Ibid.*, p. 72.

26. Parker to Goodnight.

CHAPTER 4
The Comanche War Trail

1. Virginia Irving Armstrong (Editor), *I Have Spoken* (New York: Pocket Books, 1972), p. 99.

2. Herman Lehmann, *Nine Years Among the Indians, 1870–1879* (Austin, Texas: Von Boeckmann-Jones, 1927), p. 159.

3. Red Codynah to the author, interview, 23 January 1986, at Cyril, Oklahoma.

4. Elliott Canonge, *Comanche Texts* (Norman: University of Oklahoma Institute of Linguistics, 1958), pp. 3–4.

5. *Ibid.*, pp. 9–11.

6. Clinton L. Smith and Jefferson D. Smith, *The Boy Captives* (Bandera, Texas: *Frontier Times*, 1927), p. 68.

7. Nelson Lee, *Three Years Among the Comanches* (Norman: University of Oklahoma Press, 1957), pp. 135–136.

8. *Ibid.*, pp. 154–155.

9. Ernest Wallace, "David G. Burnet's Letters Describing the Comanche Indians," *West Texas Historical Association Yearbook*, Vol. XXX (1954), p. 119.

10. Colonel Edward Stiff, *The Texan Emigrant* (Cincinnati, Ohio: George Conclin, 1840), p. 41.

11. *Ibid.*, p. 42.

12. *Ibid.*

13. Rachel Plummer, *The Rachel Plummer Narrative* (Copyrighted 1926 by Rachel Loftin, Susie Hendrix, and Jane Kennedy), pp. 107–108.

14. Arthur K. Moore, *The Frontier Mind* (New York: McGraw-Hill, 1963), p. 238.

15. Ernest Wallace, "The Comanche Eagle Dance," *Texas Archaeological and Paleontological Society Bulletin,* Vol. 18 (1947), p. 83.

16. *Ibid.,* p. 84.

17. *Ibid.,* pp. 84–85.

18. Quanah Parker to Captain Hugh Scott, interview, 1897, Ledgerbook, Hugh Scott Collection, Fort Sill Archives, Lawton, Oklahoma, p. 18.

19. Carl Coke Rister, *Border Captives* (Norman: University of Oklahoma Press, 1940), p. 42.

20. "Record Copy of the Proceedings of the Indian Peace Commission appointed Under the Act of Congress approved July 20, 1867," MS, Records of Secretary of Interior, National Archives.

21. *Ibid.*

22. *Ibid.*

23. *Ibid.*

24. *Ibid.*

25. Parker to Scott.

26. *Ibid.*

27. *Ibid.*

28. Zoe A. Tilghman, *Quanah, The Eagle of the Comanches* (Oklahoma City, Oklahoma: Harlow Publishing, 1938), p. 68.

29. *Ibid.*

30. *Ibid.,* pp. 68–69.

31. *Ibid.*

32. Floyd J. Holmes, *Indian Fights on the Texas Frontier* (Fort Worth, Texas: Pioneer Publishing, 1927), p. 60.

33. *Ibid.,* pp. 60–62.

34. Rister, *Border Captives,* p. 24.

35. *Ibid.*

36. Lee, *Three Years Among the Comanches,* pp. 86–88.

37. *Ibid.,* pp. 104–107.

38. Ben Moore, Sr., *7 Years with the Wild Indians* (O'Donnell, Texas: Ben Moore, Sr., 1945), p. 8.

39. Olive King Dixon, "Fearless and Effective Foe, He Spared Women and Children Always," MS, Olive King Dixon Papers, Research Center, Panhandle–Plains Historical Museum, Canyon, Texas.

40. *Ibid.*

41. *Ibid.*

42. *Ibid.*

43. Wayne Gard, *The Great Buffalo Hunt* (New York: Alfred A. Knopf, 1959), 155.

44. Thomas C. Battey, *The Life and Adventures of a Quaker Among the Indians* (Norman: University of Oklahoma Press, 1968), pp. 302–303.

45. *Ibid.,* pp. 303–304.

46. Billy Dixon, *Life and Adventures of "Billy" Dixon,* compiled by Frederick S. Barde (Guthrie, Oklahoma: Co-operative Publishing, 1914), pp. 211–231.

47. Parker to Scott.

48. Tilghman, *Eagle of the Comanches,* p. 81.

49. *Ibid.,* pp. 82–84.

50. *Ibid.*

51. *Ibid.*

52. G. Derek West, "The Battle of Adobe Walls (1874)," *The Battles of Adobe Walls and Lyman's Wagon Train, 1874* (Canyon, Texas: Panhandle–Plains Historical Society, 1964), p. 8.

53. J. Wright Mooar to J. Evetts Haley, interview, 11 April, 1936, Amarillo, Texas, Walter S. Campbell Collection, Western History Collections, University of Oklahoma, p. 36.

54. T. Lindsey Baker and Billy R. Harrison, *Adobe Walls: The History and Archaeology of the 1874 Trading Post* (College Station: Texas A & M University Press, 1986), pp. 58–59.

55. Dixon, *Life and Adventures,* p. 199.

56. *Ibid.,* pp. 201–203.

57. *Ibid.*

58. Baker and Harrison, *Adobe Walls,* p. 59.

59. Dixon, *Life and Adventures,* pp. 203–204.

60. Parker to Scott.

61. Dixon, *Life and Adventures,* pp. 205.

62. Tilghman, *Eagle of the Comanches,* p. 89.

63. Baker and Harrison, *Adobe Walls,* p. 63.

64. Dixon, *Life and Adventures,* p. 210.

65. *Ibid.,* pp. 210–212.

66. *Ibid.,* p. 215.

67. *Ibid.*, pp. 216–217.

68. *Ibid.*

69. *Ibid.*, pp. 219–220.

70. *Ibid.*, pp. 225–226.

71. *Ibid.*, pp. 230–231.

72. Tilghman, *Eagle of the Comanches*, pp. 91–92.

73. Parker to Scott.

74. Dixon, Life and Adventures, p. 233.

75. Wilbur S. Nye, *Carbine and Lance* (Norman: University of Oklahoma Press, 1937), p. 191.

76. Parker to Scott.

CHAPTER 5

The Battle of Cañon Blanco

1. Captain R. G. Carter, *On the Border with Mackenzie* (Washington, D.C.: Eynon Printing, 1935), p. 176.

2. Herman Lehmann, *Nine Years Among the Indians, 1870–1879* (Austin, Texas: Von Boeckmann-Jones, 1927), p. 154.

3. *Ibid.*, pp. 155–156.

4. Ten Bears, Comanche Chief, "Speech at Medicine Lodge Peace Council, October 20, 1867," Record Copy of the Proceedings of the Indian Peace Commission Appointed Under the Act of Congress Approved July 20, 1867, Records of Secretary of Interior, National Archives, Vol. I, pp. 104–106.

5. Ernest Wallace, *Ranald S. Mackenzie on the Texas Frontier* (Minneapolis: Lund Press, 1965), p. 5.

6. *Ibid.*, p. 29.

7. *Ibid.*

8. Ranald S. Mackenzie to William T. Sherman, 15 June, 1871, W. T. Sherman Papers, Library of Congress, Washington, D.C.

9. Wallace, *Ranald S. Mackenzie on the Texas Frontier*, p. 46.

10. Rupert Norval Richardson, *The Comanche Barrier to South Plains Settlement* (Glendale, California: Arthur H. Clark, 1933), p. 346.

11. Carter, *On the Border with Mackenzie*, p. 165.

12. *Ibid.*, p. 166.

13. *Ibid.*, p. 167.

14. Zoe A. Tilghman, *Quanah, the Eagle of the Comanches* (Oklahoma City: Harlow Publishing, 1938), pp. 68–72.

15. Carter, *On the Border with Mackenzie*, p. 168.

16. *Ibid.*, p. 170.

17. *Ibid.*, pp. 172, 173.

18. *Ibid.*, p. 173.

19. *Ibid.*, p. 176.

20. *Ibid.*, pp. 186, 187.

21. *Ibid.*, p. 187.

22. *Ibid.*, pp. 187, 188.

23. *Ibid.*, pp. 188, 189.

24. *Ibid.*, pp. 189, 190.

25. *Ibid.*, p. 191.

26. *Ibid.*, p. 195.

27. *Ibid.*, p. 198.

28. *Ibid.*, pp. 205–207.

29. Wilbur S. Nye, *Carbine and Lance* (Norman: University of Oklahoma Press, 1937), p. 156.

30. Lehmann, *Nine Years Among the Indians*, p. 167.

31. Wallace, *Ranald S. Mackenzie on the Texas Frontier*, pp. 82–83.

32. Lehmann, *Nine Years Among the Indians*, pp. 185–186.

33. Clinton L. Smith and Jefferson D. Smith, *Boy Captives* (Bandera, Texas: *Frontier Times*, 1927), pp. 133–134.

34. Lehmann, *Nine Years Among the Indians*, p. 159.

CHAPTER 6
Fort Sill

1. Iseeo to Captain Hugh Scott, interview, 1897, Ledgerbook, Hugh Scott Collection, Fort Sill Archives, Lawton, Oklahoma, pp. 58–60.

2. Lonnie J. White, "Indian Battles in the Texas Panhandle, 1874," *Journal of the West*, Vol. VI (April 1967), p. 283.

3. *Ibid.*, pp. 284–287.

4. Captain R. G. Carter, *On the Border with Mackenzie* (Washington, D.C.: Eynon Printing, 1935), p. 486.

5. *Ibid.*, p. 487

6. *Ibid.*, pp. 488, 489.

7. *Ibid.*, p. 489.

8. *Ibid.*, p. 491.

9. *Ibid.*, p. 493.

10. Colonel Ranald S. Mackenzie to Asst. Adjutant General, Department of Texas, 26 October 1874, Record Group 393, Special File–Indian Pony Fund, 1874–1878, No. 4310, National Archives.

11. Carter, *On the Border with Mackenzie*, p. 495.

12. Lonnie J. White, "Kansas Newspaper Items Relating to the Red River War of 1874–1875," *The Battles of Adobe Walls and Lyman's Wagon Train, 1874* (Canyon, Texas: Panhandle–Plains Historical Society, 1964), pp. 77–78.

13. Adrian N. Anderson, "The Last Phase of Colonel Ranald S. Mackenzie's 1874 Campaign Against the Comanches," *West Texas Historical Association Yearbook*, Vol. XXXX (1964), pp. 74–76.

14. *Ibid.*, pp. 77–81.

15. Quanah Parker to Captain Hugh Scott, interview, 1897, Ledgerbook, Hugh Scott Collection, Fort Sill Archives, Lawton, Oklahoma, pp. 14–17.

16. Ernest Wallace, "The Journal of Ranald S. Mackenzie's Messenger to the Kwahadi Comanches," *Red River Historical Review*, Vol. III, No. 2 (Spring 1978), pp. 230–233.

17. *Ibid.*, p. 234.

18. Charles Goodnight, "My Recollections of the Buffalo Days," *The Southwest Plainsman* (Amarillo, Texas), 14 November 1925.

19. Wallace, "Journal of Mackenzie's Messenger to Kwahadi Comanches," p. 234.

20. *Ibid.*, pp. 235–241.

21. *Ibid.*

22. *Ibid.*

23. *Ibid.*

24. *Ibid.*

25. *Ibid.*

26. *Ibid.*, p. 243.

27. *Ibid.*

28. *Ibid.*, p. 246.

29. Ernest Wallace, "Final Champion of Comanche Glory," in *The Great Chiefs* (Alexandria, Virginia: Time-Life Books, 1975), p. 118.

30. Wilbur S. Nye, *Carbine and Lance* (Norman: University of Oklahoma Press, 1943), p. 229.

31. *Ibid.*

32. William T. Hagan, "Quanah Parker," in *American Indian Leaders* (Lincoln: University of Nebraska Press, 1980), p. 177.

33. Wallace, "Final Champion of Comanche Glory," p. 119.

34. Hagan, "Quanah Parker," p. 179.

35. Ernest Wallace, "The Comanches on the White Man's Road," *The West Texas Historical Association Yearbook*, Vol. XXIX (October 1953), p. 5.

36. Herman Lehmann, *Nine Years Among the Indians, 1870–1879* (Austin, Texas: Von Boeckmann-Jones, 1927), pp. 186–188.

37. *Ibid.*, p. 192.

38. John R. Cook, *The Border and the Buffalo* (Topeka, Kansas: Crane, 1907), p. 249.

39. *Ibid.*, p. 265.

CHAPTER 7
Peyote

1. J. J. Methvin to Lillian Gassaway, interview, 17 December 1937, at Anadarko, Oklahoma, Indian–Pioneer Papers, Western History Collections, University of Oklahoma, Vol. 62, pp. 337–340.

2. Alice Marriott and Carol K. Rachlin, *Peyote* (New York: Thomas Y. Crowell, 1971), p. 5.

3. Omer C. Stewart, "Origin of the Peyote Religion in the United States," *Plains Anthropologist* (1974), pp. 212–213.

4. *Ibid.*

5. *Ibid.*, p. 218.

6. William T. Hagan, *United States–Comanche Relations: The Reservation Years* (New Haven: Yale University Press, 1976), p. 192.

7. E. L. Clark to E. E. White, 10 June 1888, Record Group 75, Bureau of Indian Affairs, Letters Received, File No. 17455, National Archives, pp. 55–58.

8. Stewart, "Origin of Peyote Religion in United States," p. 220.

9. *Ibid.*

10. Red Codynah to the author, interview, 23 January 1986, at Cyril, Oklahoma.

11. Hagan, *United States–Comanche Relations,* p. 189.

12. James Mooney, "The Ghost-Dance Religion and the Sioux Outbreak of 1890," *Annual Report of the Bureau of Ethnology, 1892–93,* Part II (Washington, D.C.: Government Printing Office, 1896), p. 922.

13. *Ibid.,* p. 927.

14. Wilbur S. Nye, *Bad Medicine and Good* (Norman: University of Oklahoma Press, 1962), p. 93.

15. Senate Document No. 26, 58th Congress, 2nd Sess., 1903, National Archives, Washington, D.C., p. 468.

16. Randolph B. Marcy, *Border Reminiscences* (New York: Harper and Brothers, 1872), p. 334.

17. Harley True Burton, "A History of the JA Ranch," *The Southwestern Historical Quarterly,* Vol. XXXI, No. 2 (October 1927), pp. 105–106.

18. *Ibid.,* pp. 105–108.

19. *Ibid.*

20. *Ibid.*

21. *Ibid.*

22. *Ibid.*

23. *Ibid.*

24. Billy Dixon, *Life and Adventures of "Billy" Dixon,* compiled by Frederick S. Barde (Guthrie, Oklahoma: Co-operative Publishing, 1914), p. 239.

25. Thomas C. Battey, *The Life and Adventures of a Quaker Among the Indians* (Norman: University of Oklahoma Press, 1968), pp. 191–192.

26. Codynah to Neeley.

27. Methvin to Gassaway.

28. Edward Mahseet to the author, interview, 22 January 1986 at Comanche Tribal Complex near Lawton, Oklahoma.

29. Dorothy Lorentino and Anona Birdsong Dean to the author, interview, 27 March 1985, at Cache, Oklahoma.

30. *Ibid.*

31. *Ibid.*

32. Dick Banks to Bessie L. Thomas, interview, 18 March 1938, at Marlow, Oklahoma, Indian–Pioneer Papers, Western History Collections, University of Oklahoma, Vol. 5, pp. 11–15.

33. *Ibid.*

34. Rev. A. E. Butterfield, *Comanche, Kiowa, and Apache Missions Forty-two Years Ago and Now* (Childress, Texas: A. E. Butterfield, 1934), p. 13.

35. *Ibid.*

36. Bob Finger to Quanah Parker, 8 March 1909, Fort Sill Archives, Lawton, Oklahoma.

CHAPTER 8
Cattle

1. Colonel Randolph B. Marcy, *Thirty Years of Army Life on the Border* (New York: Harper and Brothers, 1866), p. 20.

2. Tom Corridon to the author, interview, 22 May 1985, at Iowa Park, Texas.

3. Olive King Dixon, "Fearless and Effective Foe, He Spared Women and Children Always," MS, Olive King Dixon Papers, Research Center, Panhandle–Plains Historical Museum, Canyon, Texas.

4. William T. Hagan, *United States–Comanche Relations* (New Haven: Yale University Press, 1976), p. 154.

5. *Ibid.*, p. 155.

6. Jean Louise Zimmermann, "Ranald Slidell Mackenzie," M.A. thesis, 1965, Western History Collections, University of Oklahoma, p. 65.

7. Charles Goodnight to P. B. Hunt, 25 September, 1880, Ella Cox Lutz Collection, Museum of the Great Plains, Lawton, Oklahoma.

8. First Lt. Wentz C. Miller to Second Lt. Stanton A. Mason, 10 May 1876, Fort Sill Archives, Lawton, Oklahoma.

9. Baldwin Parker, "The Life of Quanah Parker, Comanche Chief," MS, The University of Texas Archives, Austin, p. 15.

10. Lena R. Banks to Bessie L. Thomas, interview, 18 April 1938, at Cache, Oklahoma, Indian–Pioneer Papers, Western History Collections, University of Oklahoma, Vol. 5, pp. 85–86.

11. *Ibid.*, pp. 87–88.

12. *Ibid.*

13. Dick Banks to Bessie L. Thomas, interview, 10 March 1938, at Marlow, Oklahoma, Indian–Pioneer Papers, Western History Collections, University of Oklahoma, Vol. 5, pp. 17–19.

14. *Ibid.*, p. 20.

15. J. Marvin Hunter (Editor), *Trail Drivers of Texas* (New York: Argosy-Antiquarian, 1963), Vol. 1, pp. x–xi.

16. *Ibid.*, pp. xii–xv.

17. *Ibid.*, Vol. 2, p. 775.

18. *Ibid.*, pp. 776–778.

19. *Ibid.*

20. *Ibid.*

21. *Ibid.*

22. Herbert Woesner to the author, interview, 1 February 1986, at Cache, Oklahoma.

23. *Ibid.*

24. Tom Burnett to Quanah Parker, 4 February 1909, Fort Sill Archives, Lawton, Oklahoma.

25. Senate Document No. 54, 48th Congress, 1st Sess., 1884, Library of Congress, pp. 53–54.

26. *Ibid.*

27. Robert Lemond to Ethel B. Tackitt, 11 November 1937, at Lone Wolf, Oklahoma, Indian–Pioneer Papers, Western History Collections, University of Oklahoma, Vol. 53, p. 212.

28. *Ibid.*

29. Hunter, *Trail Drivers of Texas*, Vol. 2, p. 927.

30. *Ibid.*, Vol. 1, p. 165.

31. *Ibid.*, pp. 391–392.

32. *Ibid.*

33. *Ibid.*

34. Senate Document No. 54, p. 69.

35. *Ibid.*

36. *Ibid.*, p. 74.

37. Hagan, *United States–Comanche Relations*, p. 151.

38. *Ibid.*

39. P. B. Hunt to Commissioner of Indian Affairs, 21 January 1885, *Letterpress*, Vol. 17, Kiowa Agency Records, Oklahoma Historical Society, Oklahoma City, pp. 55–57.

40. Daniel A. Becker, "Comanche Civilization with History of Quanah Parker," *Chronicles of Oklahoma*, Vol. I (1921–23), p. 247.

41. Hagan, *United States–Comanche Relations*, p. 153.

42. Senate Document No 54, pp. 81–82.

43. L. H. Colyer to Ruth Lee Gamblin, interview, 22 April 1937, at Frederick, Oklahoma, Indian-Pioneer Papers, Western History Collections, University of Oklahoma, Vol. 19, pp. 414–415.

44. Hagan, *United States–Comanche Relations,* p. 219.

45. *Texas Panhandle Forefathers,* compiled by Barbara C. Spray, Amarillo (Texas) Genealogical Society, 1983.

46. Burk Burnett to Quanah Parker, 21 July 1910, Fort Sill Archives, Lawton, Oklahoma.

47. *Hobart Democrat-Chief,* 4 August 1925, Western History Collections, University of Oklahoma, p. 10.

48. George W. Briggs to Eunice M. Mayer, interview, 17 June 1937, at Granite, Oklahoma, Indian-Pioneer Papers, Western History Collections, University of Oklahoma, Vol. 11, p. 173.

CHAPTER 9
Statesmanship

1. Rev. Jedidiah Morse, *A Report to the Secretary of War of the United States on Indian Affairs* (Washington, D.C.: Davis and Force, 1822), p. 283.

2. Senate Document No. 77, 55th Congress, 3rd Sess., Library of Congress, p. 15.

3. W. R. Mattoon to Quanah Parker, 17 March 1908, Fort Sill Archives, Lawton, Oklahoma.

4. Etta Martin to Zaidee Bland, interview, 12 July 1937, at Blair, Oklahoma, Indian-Pioneer Papers, Western History Collections, University of Oklahoma, Vol. 60, pp. 451–453.

5. Dick Banks to Bessie L. Thomas, interview, 10 March 1938, at Marlow, Oklahoma, Indian-Pioneer Papers, Western History Collections, University of Oklahoma, Vol. 5, p. 17.

6. Knox Beal to Bessie L. Thomas, interview, 15 April 1938, at Cache, Oklahoma, Indian-Pioneer Papers, Western History Collections, University of Oklahoma, Vol. 6, pp. 123–125.

7. H. M. Lindsay to Lillian Gassaway, interview, 14 October 1937, at Anadarko, Oklahoma, Indian-Pioneer Papers, Western History Collections, University of Oklahoma, Vol. 54, p. 157.

8. Ernest Lee, Jr., "Charlie Hart: A Cowboy Story," *Wichita Falls Times,* 27 January 1985 (reprinted from the *Junior Historian,* 1948).

9. Newspaper clipping filed as enclosure in letter from J. S. Works to Secretary of the Interior, Letters Received 1881–1907, Record Group 75, File No. 11488-1892, National Archives, Washington, D.C.

10. *Ibid.*

11. *Ibid.*

12. Senate Document No. 77, p. 14.

13. *Ibid.*, p. 11.

14. *Ibid.*, pp. 21–22.

15. *Ibid.*

16. *Minco Minstrel,* 13 October 1893, Newspaper files, Oklahoma Historical Society, Oklahoma City.

17. *Minco Minstrel,* 20 October 1893, Newspaper files, Oklahoma Historical Society, Oklahoma City.

18. Senate Document No. 77, p. 40.

19. *Ibid.*, p. 35.

20. *Ibid.*

21. *Ibid.*, p. 19.

22. *Ibid.*

23. *Ibid.*, p. 34.

24. *Ibid.*

25. *Ibid.*

26. *Ibid.*, pp. 28–29.

27. *Ibid.*, p. 34.

28. *Ibid.*, p. 27.

29. *Ibid.*, p. 39.

30. *Ibid.*, p. 40.

31. *Sixteenth Annual Report of the Executive Committee of Indian Rights Association* (Philadelphia: Office of Indian Rights Assoc., 1899), p. 43.

32. *Ibid.*

33. William T. Hagan, *United States–Comanche Relations* (New Haven: Yale University Press, 1976), p. 254.

34. *Ibid.* pp. 256–257.

35. *Ibid.*, p. 261.

36. *Daily Oklahoman,* 28 June 1900, Newspaper Files, Oklahoma Historical Society, Oklahoma City.

37. *Ibid.*

38. Agent James Randlett to Commissioner of Indian Affairs, 7 October 1901, Kiowa Agency Letterpress, Archives and Manuscript Division, Oklahoma Historical Society, Oklahoma City, Vol. 92, p. 160.

39. Polk Fry, Sr., to Ruth Lee Gamblin, interview, 22 April 1937, at Frederick, Oklahoma, Indian–Pioneer Papers, Western History Collections, University of Oklahoma, Vol. 32, p. 340.

40. *Ibid.*, p. 344.

41. Captain Robert G. Carter, *Tragedies of Blanco Canyon* (Washington, D.C.: Gibson Bros., 1919), pp. 79–80.

42. Tom Corridon to the author, interview, 28 March 1985, at Iowa Park, Texas.

43. Theodore Roosevelt, *Outdoor Pastimes of an American Hunter* (New York: Charles Scribner's Sons, 1905), p. 100.

44. *Ibid.*, p. 101.

45. *Ibid.*, p. 102.

46. *Ibid.*, p. 120.

47. Anona Birdsong Dean to the author, interview, 27 March 1985, at Cache, Oklahoma.

48. Agent James Randlett to Commissioner of Indian Affairs, 30 July 1902, Kiowa Agency Files, Archives and Manuscript Division, Oklahoma Historical Society, Oklahoma City, Vol. 101, pp. 96–97.

49. Office of Indian Affairs to Indian Agents and Superintendents of Indian Schools, Report of the Secretary of the Interior, House Executive Documents, 51st Congress, 2nd Sess., Vol. 2, 1890, National Archives, p. CLXVII.

50. Charles Goodnight, "Indians in the Panhandle," MS, Charles Goodnight Papers, Research Center, Panhandle–Plains Historical Museum, Canyon, Texas.

51. Senate Document No. 26, 58th Congress, 2nd Session, Library of Congress, p. 9.

52. *Ibid.*

53. *Ibid.*, p. 11.

54. *Ibid.*, pp. 20–21.

55. Ernest Wallace, "Final Champion of Comanche Glory," in *The Great Chiefs* (Alexandria, Virginia: Time-Life Books, 1975), p. 124.

56. Robert B. Thomas, MS, Indian–Pioneer Papers, Western History Collections, University of Oklahoma, Vol. 110, pp. 154–155.

57. Burk Burnett to Quanah Parker, 24 October 1908, Fort Sill Archives, Lawton, Oklahoma.

58. George Catlin, *Illustrations of the Manners, Customs, and Condition of the North American Indians,* Vol. I (London: Henry G. Bohn, 1857), p. 83.

59. Thomas, pp. 172–173.

60. *Quanah Tribune-Chief,* 23 May 1890.

61. Hugh Hannah to Mildred McFarland, interview, 19 August 1937, at Edmond, Oklahoma, Indian–Pioneer Papers, Western History Collections, University of Oklahoma, Vol. 38, p. 219.

62. *Dallas Morning News,* 24 October 1910.

63. Charles H. Sommer, *Quanah Parker: Last Chief of the Comanches* (Printed in the United States: Charles H. Sommer, 1945), pp. 39–45.

64. *Ibid.,* p. 45.

65. *Quanah Tribune-Chief,* 10 October 1907.

66. *The Lawton Daily News,* 23 February 1911, Ella Cox Lutz Collection, Museum of the Great Plains, Lawton, Oklahoma.

67. *Ibid.*

68. Knox Beal to R. B. Thomas, interview, 5 November 1937, at Cache, Oklahoma, Indian–Pioneer Papers, Western History Collections, University of Oklahoma, Vol. 6, p. 118.

69. James M. Cox to the author, interview, 18 July 1989, at Midwest City, Oklahoma.

BIBLIOGRAPHY

MANUSCRIPTS, LETTERS, AND THESES

Archivo General de Indias, Audiencia de México, 92-6-22. Cunningham Transcripts, 1763, pt. 1, "Testimonio de los autos sobre el asalto y attaque que los Yndios Comanches hicieron en el presidio de San Luis de las Amarillas, 1758." The Barker Texas History Center, University of Texas, Austin.

Birdsong, Aubrey. "Reminiscences of Quanah Parker." MS. Fort Sill Archives, Lawton, Oklahoma.

Blake, R. B. Collection. "Captain Antonio Gil Ybarro of Nacogdoches." MS. Nacogdoches Archives (Copy), Panhandle–Plains Historical Museum, Canyon, Texas.

Burnett, Burk. Letter to Quanah Parker, 24 October 1908, Fort Sill Archives, Lawton, Oklahoma.

Burnett, Burk. Letter to Quanah Parker, 21 July 1910, Fort Sill Archives, Lawton, Oklahoma.

Burnett, Tom. Letter to Quanah Parker, 4 February 1909, Fort Sill Archives, Lawton, Oklahoma.

Clark, E. L. Letter to E. E. White, 10 June 1888, Record Group 75, Bureau of Indian Affairs, Letters Received, File No. 17455, National Archives, Washington, D.C.

Dixon, Olive King. Papers. "Fearless and Effective Foe, He Spared Women and Children Always." MS. Panhandle–Plains Historical Museum, Canyon, Texas.

Finger, Bob. Letter to Quanah Parker, 8 March 1909, Fort Sill Archives, Lawton, Oklahoma.

Goodnight, Charles. Letter to P. B. Hunt, 25 September 1880, Ella Cox Lutz Collection, Museum of the Great Plains, Lawton, Oklahoma.

Goodnight, Charles. Papers. "Explorations Into the Plains Country." MS. Panhandle–Plains Historical Museum, Canyon, Texas.

Goodnight, Charles. Papers. "First Entrance to Palo Duro Canyon." MS. Panhandle–Plains Historical Museum, Canyon, Texas.

Goodnight, Charles. Papers. "Indians in the Panhandle." MS. Panhandle–Plains Historical Museum, Canyon, Texas.

Goodnight, Charles. Papers. "My Recollections and Memories of the Capture of Cynthia Ann Parker." MS. Panhandle–Plains Historical Museum, Canyon, Texas.

Goodnight, Charles. Papers. "The Making of a Scout." MS. Panhandle–Plains Historical Museum, Canyon, Texas.

Hill, J. A. "The Indian Policy of the United States on the Southwestern Frontier, 1830–1845." M.A. thesis. University of California, Berkeley, 1916. Panhandle–Plains Historical Museum, Canyon, Texas.

Hunt, P. B. Letter to Commissioner of Indian Affairs, 21 January 1885, *Letterpress*, Volume 17, Kiowa Agency Records, Oklahoma Historical Society, Oklahoma City.

Kinard, Knox. "A History of the Waggoner Ranch." M.A. thesis. University of Texas, Austin, 1941. Perry-Castañeda Library, University of Texas.

Mackenzie, Colonel Ranald S. Letter to General W. T. Sherman, 15 June 1871, W. T. Sherman Papers, Library of Congress, Washington, D.C.

Mackenzie, Colonel Ranald S. Letter to Assistant Adjutant General, Department of Texas, 26 October 1874, Record Group 393, Special File–Indian Pony Fund, 1874–1878, No. 4310, National Archives, Washington, D.C.

Mattoon, W. R. Letter to Quanah Parker, 17 March 1908, Fort Sill Archives, Lawton, Oklahoma.

Maverick, Mary. Papers. "Memoirs of Mary Maverick." MS. Archives Division, Texas State Library, Austin.

Miller, Lt. Wentz C. Letter to Second Lt. Stanton A. Mason, 10 May 1876, Fort Sill Archives, Lawton, Oklahoma.

Parker, Baldwin. "The Life of Quanah Parker, Comanche Chief." MS. The University of Texas Archives, Austin.

Parker, Quanah. Letter to Charles Goodnight, undated, Charles Goodnight Papers, Panhandle–Plains Historical Museum, Canyon, Texas.

Randlett, James. Letter to Commissioner of Indian Affairs, 7 October 1901, Kiowa Agency Records, Vol. 92, Oklahoma Historical Society, Oklahoma City.

Randlett, James. Letter to Commissioner of Indian Affairs, 30 July 1902, Kiowa Agency Records, Vol. 101, Oklahoma Historical Society, Oklahoma City.

Secretary of the Interior. Letter to Commissioner of Indian Affairs, 18 October 1892, Special Cases, Record Group 191, File No. 38066, National Archives, Washington, D.C.

Thomas, Robert B. MS. Indian–Pioneer Papers, Western History Collections, University of Oklahoma, Vol. 110.

Wallace, Ernest. Papers. "The Habitat and Range of the Comanche, Kiowa, and Kiowa-Apache Indians." MS. Southwest Collection, Texas Tech University, Lubbock.

Zimmerman, Jean Louise. "Ranald Slidell Mackenzie." M.A. thesis. University of Oklahoma, 1965. Western History Collections, University of Oklahoma.

INTERVIEWS

Banks, Dick. Interview with Bessie L. Thomas. Marlow, Oklahoma, 10 March 1938. Indian–Pioneer Papers, Western History Collections, University of Oklahoma, Norman, Vol. 5.

Banks, Dick. Interview with Bessie L. Thomas. Marlow, Oklahoma, 18 March 1938. Indian–Pioneer Papers, Western History Collections, University of Oklahoma, Norman, Vol. 5.

Banks, Lena R. Interview with Bessie L. Thomas. Cache, Oklahoma, 18 April 1938. Indian–Pioneer Papers, Western History Collections, University of Oklahoma, Norman, Vol. 5.

Beal, Knox. Interview with R. B. Thomas. Cache, Oklahoma, 5 November 1937. Indian–Pioneer Papers, Western History Collections, University of Oklahoma, Norman, Vol. 6.

Beal, Knox. Interview with Bessie L. Thomas. Cache, Oklahoma, 15 April 1938. Indian–Pioneer Papers, Western History Collections, University of Oklahoma, Norman, Vol. 6.

Briggs, George W. Interview with Eunice M. Mayer. Granite, Oklahoma, 17 June 1937. Indian–Pioneer Papers, Western History Collections, University of Oklahoma, Norman, Vol. 11.

Clark, Edward Louis. Interview with author. Comanche Tribal Headquarters, Lawton, Oklahoma, 11 March 1985.

Codynah, Red. Interview with author. Cyril, Oklahoma, 23 January 1986.

Colyer, L. H. Interview with Ruth Lee Gamblin. Frederick, Oklahoma, 22 April 1937. Indian–Pioneer Papers, Western History Collections, University of Oklahoma, Norman, Vol. 19.

Corridon, Tom. Interview with author. Iowa Park, Texas, 22 May 1985.

Dean, Anona Birdsong. Interview with author. Cache, Oklahoma, 27 March 1985.

Fisher, Rudolph. Interview with Lillian Gassaway. Anadarko, Oklahoma, 28 September 1937. Indian–Pioneer Papers, Western History Collections, University of Oklahoma, Norman, Vol. 62.

Fry, Polk, Sr. Interview with Ruth Lee Gamblin. Frederick, Oklahoma, 22 April 1937. Indian–Pioneer Papers, Western History Collections, University of Oklahoma, Norman, Vol. 32.

Hannah, Hugh. Interview with Mildred McFarland. Edmond, Oklahoma, 19 August 1937. Indian–Pioneer Papers, Western History Collections, University of Oklahoma, Norman, Vol. 38.

Iseeo. Interview with Captain Hugh Scott. Fort Sill, 1897. Ledgerbook, Hugh Scott Collection, Fort Sill Archives.

Lemond, Robert. Interview with Ethel B. Tackitt. Lone Wolf, Oklahoma, 11 November 1937. Indian–Pioneer Papers, Western History Collections, University of Oklahoma, Norman, Vol. 53.

Lindsay, H. M. Interview with Lillian Gassaway. Anadarko, Oklahoma, 14 October 1937. Indian–Pioneer Papers, Western History Collections, University of Oklahoma, Norman, Vol. 54.

Lorentino, Dorothy. Interview with author. Cache, Oklahoma, 27 March 1985.

Mahseet, Edward. Interview with author. Comanche Tribal Headquarters, Lawton, Oklahoma, 22 January 1986.

Martin, Etta. Interview with Zaidee Bland. Blair, Oklahoma, 12 July 1937. Indian–Pioneer Papers, Western History Collections, University of Oklahoma, Norman, Vol. 60.

Methvin, J. J. Interview with Lillian Gassaway. Anadarko, Oklahoma, 17 December 1937. Indian–Pioneer Papers, Western History Collections, University of Oklahoma, Norman, Vol. 62.

Mooar, J. Wright. Interview with J. Evetts Haley. Amarillo, Texas, 11 April 1936. Walter S. Campbell Collection, Western History Collections, University of Oklahoma, Norman.

Parker, Joe Bailey. Interview with author. By telephone, 13 December 1985.

Parker, Quanah. Interview with Captain Hugh Scott. Fort Sill, 1897. Ledger-book, Hugh Scott Collection, Fort Sill Archives, Lawton, Oklahoma.

Woesner, Herbert. Interview with author. Cache, Oklahoma, 1 February 1986.

Woesner, Herbert. Interview with author. Cache, Oklahoma, 15 March 1986.

GOVERNMENT DOCUMENTS

National Archives. "Record Copy of the Proceedings of the Indian Peace Commission Under the Act of Congress Approved July 20, 1867." Records of Secretary of Interior.

National Archives. "Speech at Medicine Lodge Peace Council, October 20, 1867." Record Copy of the Proceedings of the Indian Peace Commission Appointed Under the Act of Congress, Approved July 20, 1867. Records of Secretary of Interior.

U.S. Congress. House. 29th Congress, 2nd Sess., 1846, Doc. No. 76.

U.S. Congress. Senate. 48th Congress, 1st Sess., 1884, Doc. No. 54.

U.S. Congress. House. 51st Congress, 2nd Sess., 1890, Executive Document—"Report of the Secretary of the Interior."

U.S. Congress. Senate. 55th Congress, 3rd Sess., 1899, Doc. No. 77.

U.S. Congress. Senate. 58th Congress, 2nd Sess., 1903, Doc. No. 26.

JOURNAL AND NEWSPAPER ARTICLES

Anderson, Adrian N. "The Last Phase of Colonel Ranald S. Mackenzie's 1874 Campaign Against the Comanches." *West Texas Historical Association Yearbook*, Vol. XXXX (1964): 74–81.

Becker, Daniel A. "Comanche Civilization with History of Quanah Parker." *Chronicles of Oklahoma.* Vol. I (1921–1923): 247.

Burton, Harley True. "A History of the JA Ranch." *The Southwestern Historical Quarterly*, Vol. XXXI, No. 2 (October 1927): 105–108.

Carroll, H. Bailey. "Nolan's 'Lost Nigger' Expedition of 1877." *Southwestern Historical Quarterly*, Vol. XLIV (July 1940): 64–75.

Clark, Fannie McAlpine. "A Chapter in the History of Young Territory." *The Quarterly of the Texas State Historical Association*, Vol. IX (July 1905 to April 1906): 58.

Daily Oklahoman, 28 June 1990. Newspaper Files, Oklahoma Historical Society, Oklahoma City.

Dallas Morning News, 24 October 1910. Microfilm, Amarillo Public Library, Amarillo, Texas.

Garrison, George P. (Editor). "The Records of an Early Texas Baptist Church." *The Quarterly of the Texas State Historical Association*, Vol. XI, No. 2 (October 1907): 88.

Goodnight, Charles. "My Recollections of the Buffalo Days." *The Southwest Plainsman*, 14 November 1925, Panhandle–Plains Historical Museum, Canyon, Texas.

Hobart Democrat-Chief, 4 August 1925. Western History Collections, University of Oklahoma, Norman.

Jeter, Jerry B. "Pioneer Preacher." *Chronicles of Oklahoma*, Vol. XXIII (Winter 1945–46): 358–368.

Koch, Lena Clara. "The Federal Indian Policy in Texas, 1845–1846." *The Southwestern Historical Quarterly*, Vol. XXVIII, No. 4 (April 1925): 263.

Lee, Ernest, Jr. "Charlie Hart: A Cowboy Story." *Wichita Falls Times*, 27 January 1985 (reprinted from the *Junior Historian*, 1948), Archives of Wichita Falls Times and Record News, Wichita Falls, Texas.

Minco Minstrel, 13 October 1893. Newspaper Files, Oklahoma Historical Society, Oklahoma City.

Minco Minstrel, 20 October 1893. Newspaper Files, Oklahoma Historical Society, Oklahoma City.

Mooney, James. "The Ghost-Dance Religion and the Sioux Outbreak of 1890." *Annual Report of the Bureau of Ethnology, 1892–93*, Part II. Washington, D.C.: Government Printing Office, 1896: 922–927.

New York Times, 2 August 1885: 7.

Notes, Fall 1985. Star of the Republic Museum, Washington-on-the-Brazos, Texas. Vol. X, No. 1.

Office of Indian Rights Association. *Sixteenth Annual Report of the Executive Committee of Indian Rights Association*. Philadelphia: Office of Indian Rights Assoc., 1899.

Opler, Marvin K. "The Origins of Comanche and Ute." *American Anthropologist*, Vol. XLV (1943): 156.

Quanah Tribune-Chief, 23 May 1890. Microfilm, Archives of Quanah Tribune-Chief, Quanah, Texas.

Quanah Tribune-Chief, 10 October 1907. Microfilm, Archives of Quanah Tribune-Chief, Quanah, Texas.

Steele, Aubrey L. "Lawrie Tatum's Indian Policy." *Chronicles of Oklahoma*, Vol. XXII (Spring 1944): 93.

Stewart, Omer C. "Origin of the Peyote Religion in the United States." *Plains Anthropologist* (1974): 212–220.

Telegraph and Texas Register, 17 April 1844. Texas State Archives, Austin.

The Lawton Daily News, 23 February 1911. Ella Cox Lutz Collection, Museum of the Great Plains, Lawton, Oklahoma.

The White Man, 13 September 1860. The Barker Texas History Center, University of Texas, Austin.

Tingley, Donald F. "Illinois Days of Daniel Parker, Texas Colonizer." *Journal of the Illinois State Historical Society*, No. 51 (Winter 1958): 401.

Wallace, Ernest. "David G. Burnet's Letters Describing the Comanche Indians." *West Texas Historical Association Yearbook*, Vol. XXX (1954): 115.

Wallace, Ernest. "Prompt in the Saddle: The Military Career of Ranald S. Mackenzie." *Military History of Texas and the Southwest*, Vol. IX, No. 3 (1971): 161–177.

Wallace, Ernest. "The Comanche Eagle Dance." *Texas Archaeological and Paleontological Society Bulletin*, Vol. 18 (1947): 83.

Wallace, Ernest. "The Comanches on the White Man's Road." *The West Texas Historical Association Yearbook*, Vol. XXIX (October 1953): 5.

Wallace, Ernest. "The Journal of Ranald S. Mackenzie's Messenger to the Kwahadi Comanches." *Red River Valley Historical Review*, Vol. III, No. 2 (Spring 1978): 229–246.

Whisenhunt, Donald W. "Fort Richardson." *West Texas Historical Association Yearbook*, Vol. XXXIX (1963): 23–24.

White, Lonnie. "Indian Battles in the Texas Panhandle, 1874." *Journal of the West*, Vol. VI (April 1967): 283–287.

White, Lonnie. "Kansas Newspaper Items Relating to the Red River War of 1874–1875." In *The Battles of Adobe Walls and Lyman's Wagon Train 1874.* Canyon, Texas: Panhandle–Plains Historical Society, 1964: 77–78.

Works, J. S. "The Struggle Is On!" Newspaper clipping from *Iowa Park Texan* enclosed with letter from Works to Secretary of Interior. Letters Received 1881–1907, Record Group 75, File No. 11488-1892, National Archives, Washington, D.C.

Books

Abbott, E. C., and Helena H. Smith. *We Pointed Them North.* New York: Farrar and Rinehart, 1939.

Andrist, Ralph K. *The Long Death.* New York: Macmillan, 1964.

Armstrong, Virginia Irving. *I Have Spoken.* New York: Pocket Books, 1972.

Babb, T. A. *In the Bosom of the Comanches.* Dallas: Hargreaves Printing, 1912.

Baker, T. Lindsey, and Billy R. Harrison. *Adobe Walls: The History and Archaeology of the 1874 Trading Post.* College Station, Texas: Texas A & M University Press, 1986.

Bancroft, Hubert H. *The Native Races*, Vol. I. San Francisco: The History Co., 1886.

Barker, Eugene C. *The Life of Stephen F. Austin: Founder of Texas.* Chicago: The Lakeside Press, 1925.

Battey, Thomas C. *The Life and Adventures of a Quaker Among the Indians.* Norman: University of Oklahoma Press, 1968.

Benner, Judith Ann. *Sul Ross: Soldier, Statesman, Educator.* College Station, Texas: Texas A & M University Press, 1983.

Brown, John Henry. *The Indian Wars and Pioneers of Texas.* Houston: Union National Bank, 1933.

Butterfield, Rev. A. E. *Comanche, Kiowa, and Apache Missions Forty-two Years Ago and Now.* Childress, Texas: A. E. Butterfield, 1934.

Canales, Isidro Vizcaya (Editor). *La Invasión de los Indios Bárbaros al Noreste de México en los Años de 1840–1841.* Monterrey, Nuevo León, México: Instituto Tecnológico y de Estudios Superiores de Monterrey, 1968.

Canonge, Elliott. *Comanche Texts.* Norman: University of Oklahoma Press, 1958.

Carter, Captain R. G. *On the Border with Mackenzie.* Washington, D.C.: Eynon Printing, 1935.

Carter, Captain R. G. *Tragedies of Blanco Canyon.* Washington, D.C.: Gibson Bros., 1919.

Castañeda, Carlos E. *Our Catholic Heritage in Texas,* Vol. VI. Austin, Texas: Von Boeckmann-Jones, 1950.

Catlin, George. *Illustrations of the Manners, Customs, and Condition of the North American Indians.* 2 vols. London: Henry G. Bohn, 1857.

Cook, John R. *The Border and the Buffalo.* Topeka, Kansas: Crane and Co., 1907.

Deloria, Vine, Jr., *God is Red.* New York: Dell Publishing, 1973.

DeShields, James T. *Cynthia Ann Parker: The Story of Her Capture.* St. Louis, Missouri: Woodward, 1886.

Dixon, Billy. *Life and Adventures of "Billy" Dixon.* Compiled by Frederick S. Barde. Guthrie, Oklahoma: Co-operative Publishing, 1914.

Drannan, Captain William F. *Thirty-one Years on the Plains and in the Mountains.* Chicago: Jackson Publishing, date not given.

Fehrenbach, T. R. *Comanches: Destruction of a People.* New York: Alfred A. Knopf, 1974.

Fehrenbach, T. R. *Texas: A Salute from Above.* San Antonio, Texas: World Publishing Services, 1985.

Gard, Wayne. *The Great Buffalo Hunt.* New York: Alfred A. Knopf, 1959.

Hagan, William T. "Quanah Parker." *The American Indian Leaders.* Lincoln: University of Nebraska Press, 1980: 177.

Hagan, William T. *United States–Comanche Relations: The Reservation Years.* New Haven: Yale University Press, 1976.

Haley, J. Evetts. *Charles Goodnight's Indian Recollections.* Amarillo, Texas: Russell and Cockrell, 1928. Reprinted from *Panhandle–Plains Historical Review,* 1928.

Holmes, Floyd J. *Indian Fights on the Texas Frontier.* Fort Worth, Texas: Pioneer Publishing, 1927.

Hunter, J. Marvin (Editor). *Trail Drivers of Texas.* 2 vols. New York: Argosy-Antiquarian, 1963.

Lee, Nelson. *Three Years Among the Comanches.* Norman: University of Oklahoma Press, 1957.

Lehmann, Herman. *Nine Years Among the Indians, 1870–1879.* Austin, Texas: Von Boeckmann-Jones, 1927.

Marcy, Randolph B. *Border Reminiscences.* New York: Harper and Brothers, 1872.

Marcy, Randolph B. *Exploration of the Red River of Louisiana in the Year of 1852.* Washington, D.C.: Nicholson Public Printer, 1854.

Marcy, Randolph B. *Thirty Years of Army Life on the Border.* New York: Harper and Brothers, 1866.

Marriott, Alice, and Carol K. Rachlin. *Peyote.* New York: Thomas Y. Crowell, 1971.

Merk, Frederick. *History of the Westward Movement.* New York: Alfred A. Knopf, 1978.

Moore, Arthur K. *The Frontier Mind.* New York: McGraw-Hill, 1963.

Moore, Ben, Sr. *7 Years with the Wild Indians.* O'Donnell, Texas: Ben Moore Sr., 1945.

Morse, Rev. Jedidiah. *A Report to the Secretary of the War of the United States on the Indian Affairs.* Washington, D.C.: Davis and Force, 1822.

Neighbours, Kenneth F. *Robert Simpson Neighbors and the Texas Frontier 1836–1859.* Waco, Texas: Texian Press, 1975.

Nye, Colonel W. S. *Bad Medicine and Good.* Norman: University of Oklahoma Press, 1962.

Nye, Colonel W. S. *Carbine and Lance.* Norman: University of Oklahoma Press, 1937.

Pike, Albert. *Prose Sketches and Poems Written in the Western Country.* Albuquerque: Calvin Horn Publisher, 1967.

Plummer, Rachel. *The Rachel Plummer Narrative.* Copyrighted 1926 by Rachel Loftin, Susie Hendrix, and Jane Kennedy.

Richardson, Rupert Norval. *The Comanche Barrier to South Plains Settlement.* Glendale, California: Arthur H. Clark, 1933.

Ridings, Sam P. *The Chisholm Trail.* Guthrie, Oklahoma: Co-operative Publishing, 1936.

Rister, Carl Coke. *Border Captives.* Norman: University of Oklahoma Press, 1940.

Robertson, Pauline D., and R. L. Robertson. *Panhandle Pilgrimage.* Amarillo, Texas: Paramount Publications, 1978.

Roff, Joe T. *A Brief History of Early Days in North Texas and Indian Territory.* Roff, Oklahoma: Johnston County Capital-Democrat, 1940.

Roosevelt, Theodore. *Outdoor Pastimes of an American Hunter.* New York: Charles Scribner's Sons, 1905.

Smith, Clinton, and Jeff D. Smith. *The Boy Captives*. Bandera, Texas: Frontier Times, 1927.

Smith, Coho. *Cohographs*. Fort Worth: Branch-Smith, 1976.

Smith, Jane F., and Robert M. Kvasnicha. *Indian-White Relations: A Persistent Paradox*. Washington, D.C.: Howard University Press, 1976.

Sommer, Charles H. *Quanah Parker: Last Chief of the Comanches*. Printed in United States: Charles H. Sommer, 1945.

Spray, Barbara C. *Texas Panhandle Forefathers*. Amarillo, Texas: Amarillo Genealogical Society, 1983.

Stiff, Colonel Edward. *The Texan Emigrant*. Cincinnati, Ohio: George Conclin, 1840.

Thomas, Alfred Barnaby. *Forgotten Frontiers: From the Original Documents in the Archives of Spain, Mexico and New Mexico*. Norman: University of Oklahoma Press, 1932.

Tilghman, Zoe A. *Quanah, The Eagle of the Comanches*. Oklahoma City: Harlow Publishing, 1938.

Utley, Robert M. *The Last Days of the Sioux Nation*. New Haven: Yale University Press, 1963.

Wallace, Ernest. "Final Champion of Comanche Glory." In *The Great Chiefs*. Alexandria, Virginia: Time-Life Books, 1975.

Wallace, Ernest. *Ranald S. Mackenzie on the Texas Frontier*. Publication of the West Texas Museum Association. Minneapolis: Lund Press, 1965.

Wallace, Ernest, and E. Adamson Hoebel. *The Comanches: Lords of the South Plains*. Norman: University of Oklahoma Press, 1952.

Webb, Walter Prescott. *The Great Plains*. New York: Ginn, 1931.

Webb, Walter Prescott. *The Texas Rangers*. New York: Houghton Mifflin, 1935.

West, G. Derek. *The Battles of Adobe Walls and Lyman's Wagon Train, 1874*. Canyon, Texas: Panhandle-Plains Historical Society, 1964.

Wilbarger, J. W. *Indian Depredations in Texas*. Austin, Texas: Hutchings Printing House, 1889.

Wortham, Louis J. *A History of Texas: From Wilderness to Commonwealth*. Vol I. Fort Worth, Texas: Wortham-Molyneaux, 1924.

INDEX